Varieties of
JUVENILE DELINQUENCY

Varieties of
JUVENILE DELINQUENCY

CARL FRANKENSTEIN

Professor of Special Education
The Hebrew University
Jerusalem,   Israel

GORDON AND BREACH SCIENCE PUBLISHERS

London   New York   Paris

Copyright © 1970 by

Gordon and Breach, Science Publishers Ltd.
12 Bloomsbury Way
London W.C.1

Editorial office for the United States of America

Gordon and Breach, Science Publishers, Inc.
150 Fifth Avenue
New York, N.Y. 10011

Editorial office for France

Gordon & Breach
7–9 rue Emile Dubois
Paris 14ᵉ

Foreword

THIS IS A book on the *varieties* of juvenile delinquency. Delinquency is not considered to be a unit of deviant behavior with a number of sub-units, according to different causes. The contention is that each "variety" is in fact a unit in its own rights, each being the outcome of a different set of essential causes and each manifesting itself in specific symptoms or variations of symptoms.

One variety may be represented by a large number of cases, at least in a certain society or in a certain historical situation or under certain social or cultural conditions, another may be very rare. And yet, both are of equal importance within a study of social pathologies.

Moreover: one variety may, indeed, be "rare", but certain of its essential elements may be present in other forms of behavior as well, normal or abnormal. An analysis of the syndrome in its pure form, as an "ideal type", to use Max Weber's term, therefore fulfils an additional function: it contributes to our understanding of human behavior even beyond the limits of an analysis of circumscribed and defineable clinical pictures.

Another point in which the present study differs from certain principles of interpretation, as they are today accepted in most analyses of juvenile delinquency, concerns the evaluation of the relative weight of structural as against environmental causes. The present author does not share the view of those who adhere to theories of "pure" psychogenesis and therefore tend to emphasize experience more than constitutional factors. Intelligence, congenital type factors, preference of structural tendencies (toward staticness or expansion) determine the behavioral outcome no less than factors of environmental experience.

In certain instances, structural determinants account for a certain behavioral outcome almost by themselves (such as aggressive delinquency of the psychopathic or of the feebleminded variety, or asocial behavior of the passive psychopath or feebleminded, the "drifter"). In other cases, structural determinants act as modifiers or as reinforcers only, in con-figuration with environmental or developmental factors. But even in these, much more frequent, cases, the role of structural determinants is one of essential factors.

Another emphasis in the present study is on the relative place of social and cultural conditions as differential determinants. Sociologists often choose such conditions either to prove the connection between social maladjustment in general and negative environmental influences, or to support a "sub-culture" theory. In the present study, the emphasis is different: It is claimed that certain varieties of juvenile delinquency are essentially linked with certain environmental conditions. Thus, the variety defined and analyzed as "waywardness" is shown to be linked with poverty, just as neurotic delinquency emerges more frequently under social conditions conducive to intimate family relationships, which a life in poverty does not always allow for. Class differences are also shown to account for different patterns of adolescent delinquency. The cultural situation of our time with its emphasis on technology and bureaucracy, with its values and attitudes of insecurity, accounts for a certain type of adolescent delinquency that will be analyzed and described.

Relatively less attention will be paid to the more frequently described cases of individual pathology, either of the neurotic variety (the guilt-offender, the substitutive delinquent, the compulsive delinquent), or of the aggressive variety (particularly the primary behavior disorder of the oedipal type). There is little we could add to the many excellent analyses of such cases of which the psychoanalytically oriented literature abounds (Aichhorn, Bettelheim, Redl, Friedlander, Bowlby, Ophuijsen and others). We shall include a discussion of these varieties in two places: once in Chapter 1, when dealing with problems of classification and distinction between comparable units of behavior; and again in Chapter 3, when these varieties will be compared with psychopathy (and, more sporadically, in other chapters as well).

The reader will find certain repetitions in the book. These had been unavoidable, since each of the seven chapters actually was meant to be an essay in itself. This becomes evident particularly in Chapters 1 (on classification), 2 (on waywardness), 3 (on psychopathy) and 6 (on adolescent varieties). Two of the remaining chapters (4: on drifting, 5: on aggressiveness) depend on the others and are, in fact, supplemented by them. The cases in Chapter 7 come to exemplify the more theoretical analysis of all other chapters.

It will be noticed that half of the book is devoted to waywardness and psychopathy. This may be due in part to the fact that the author had previously published two books on these subjects (26, 32). But it also reflects his opinion about the importance of these two concepts.

It has often been claimed that the overwhelming majority of delinquent children succeed, later in their life, to adjust to the demands of society. This is due to the fact that the largest number of delinquent children in every country of the world come from the socially underprivileged strata of the population and belong to the "waywardness" type. They require more years for their social maturation than others. Hence, it is of the utmost importance from the point of view of educators and social planners clearly to recognize the conditions that are responsible for the emergence of waywardness. We must see in this form of maladjustment a social pathology that requires socio-educational methods of prevention and treatment rather than a forerunner of adult criminality. Nothing would be more mistaken and, indeed, more dangerous for the welfare of society than seeing each wayward child as requiring *individual* treatment. We should never lose sight of the need for a system of preventive and rehabilitative measures to deal with waywardness, its social roots and impacts.

No less decisive for a correct evaluation of juvenile delinquency in its theoretical and clinical aspects is that of psychopathy. The concept has been misused, for many decades in the past. Today, we know that only very few delinquents will be found to be psychopaths provided we apply rigid criteria of definition. Of these few only a small percentage will be found in young age groups, before adolescence. What then, it may be asked, is the reason for devoting more than one quarter of a study on juvenile delinquency to that variety?

The answer is that the most disquieting phenomena of adolescent delinquency in modern society closely resemble constitutionally conditioned psychopathic behavior patterns as described in clinical studies. Two questions, then, arise: Can psychopathy in general be reduced to other, non-constitutional (psychogenetic) patterns as studied by a number of psychoanalysts? Can the psychopathy-like behavior of adolescent delinquents, which may be due to the influence either of certain social class conditions or of modern insecurity and value ambiguity, be diagnosed as psychopathy?

Certain forms of aggressiveness and of drifting are, as we said, of a constitutional type (either of the psychopathic or of the feebleminded variety). In this case, as well, the analysis of psychopathy may prove to be helpful. We shall also add a number of case descriptions to make the theoretical analyses more meaningful. This will be done in the last chapter.

The book is based on a number of previous studies: a paper on the problems of classification which appeared in Hebrew and in English, a Hebrew study of waywardness, and an English book on psychopathy.

Special thanks are due to the following publishers for their kind permission to use texts previously published by them:

Archives of Criminal Psychodynamics, Washington, 1957
GRUNE & STRATTON, New York: *Psychopathy*, 1959
Megamoth (Hebrew Quarterly), Jerusalem
SZOLD FOUNDATION, Jerusalem: *Waywardness in Children*, 1947.

Jerusalem, Israel CARL FRANKENSTEIN

Contents

CHAPTER ONE

On Classification

1. A Critical Analysis of Three Examples

Many attempts have been made in the professional literature dealing with the varieties of asocial and antisocial behavior to classify them by way of analyzing their causes or clinical pictures. On the following pages we shall examine the basic concepts of some of those attempts in order to clarify certain methodological issues that seem to us vital for a proper understanding of classification in psychopathology. We shall present three examples of what seem to us basically wrong approaches. A fourth method will then be suggested which we consider more adequate : it will be based on defining the essential characteristics and causes of the different clinical pictures to be classified. This is the phenomenological method. It is *not* identical with descriptive approaches, as psychoanalysts want to make us believe when they contrast the method with theirs, that of so-called psychodynamic case-analysis. On the contrary : when it comes to classifying clinical pictures, the psychodynamic approach to individual cases is meaningful only as an integral part of phenomenology.

In order to define essential characteristics we must compare with each other the clinical units of asocial and antisocial behavior. Here, however, we face our first difficulty : if those units are too large, that is, if each of them or even only one contains sub-units, essentially different from each other, it is unavoidable that the differentiating categories formulated on the basis of unit-comparison will be too large as well. How, then, can we avoid the danger of comparing overcomprehensive clinical units? It may, of course, be argued that there is no limit to dividing and sub-dividing behavioral entities, and that every division, hence also every definition of essential characteristics of differentiation, will forcibly be tentative only. But this undoubtedly correct qualification does not affect the need for comparing behavioral units as clearly separated from each other as possible, if we want to suggest a viable system of classification. To the extent that our scientific understanding becomes more differentiated, our methods of classification, it is true, will have to be corrected; but every

1

such correction is based on a previous method of classification and only definitions of essential characteristics will help us in our endeavour to make such definitions more differentiated.

Two other arguments are often voiced : (a) that the very act of distinguishing between clinical units is already an act of classification; and (b) that in every first distinction between behavioral units* the definition of essential characteristics of each of these units is based on comparing with each other *not* these larger units but the *sub*-units contained in each of the former. Thus, for instance, must we compare with each other the varieties of psychopathy, if we want to recognise its essential elements as distinguished from those of waywardness or of neurosis. Or another example : We must compare with each other the varieties of neurotic delinquency before we can distinguish between psychoneurosis proper and neurotic delinquency. In other words : implicit classification precedes explicit classification.

These two claims are actually parts of one. The concept of "essentiality" is relative to the frame of reference which we choose. When the latter is "social behavior", the essential element of neurotic disorders, for instance, is : "an attempt to get rid, through projection, of the pressures resulting from excessive and unrealistic internalization", and, in this respect, it will be meaningful to compare neurosis with psychosis. When the frame of reference is "the synthetic and organizational power of the ego", the essential element of neurotic disorders is more appropriately defined as "the compromise character of the symptom". In this case, we shall have to compare with each other not only the phobic, the compulsive and the hysterical varieties of neurosis but also those of neurotic delinquency. The same applies to primary waywardness : when the frame of reference is "social behavior", the concept of "externalization" (35) will be appropriate as essential characteristic of the behavioral unit, and we shall compare its manifestations with those of socially or culturally conditioned externalization. When we compare clinical pictures from the point-of-view of "ego-strength", we shall prefer to emphasize the extreme ego-weakness of the wayward child or adult, and shall try to answer how it differs essentially from ego-weakness in mental retardation or in brain-injuries. When we compare with each other the varieties of psychopathic behavior under the viewpoint of "social behavior", we define their essential characteristics as "ego-inflation" and "incorporation of the non-ego"; when we compare them under the viewpoint of "ego-strength", we find their common essential element to be "absence of polar relation-

---

* As, for instance, in the field here considered, between primary waywardness, psychopathic, neurotic and organic delinquency, etc.

ships both to the ego and its functions" (32). In the first case, psychopathic behavior disorders may be compared with other forms of egocentricity, in the second case with varieties of autism.

It is this method of using different frames of reference that leads to growing differentiation between clinical units and sub-units. The criteria of distinguishing between them, in the early stages of classification, are the results of observation and generalization and not of systematic comparisons or etiological analyses. In the psychopathology of behavior, for instance, we find in this stage the crude distinction between emotional, intellectual and physical deviations, and to the extent that sub-units are being suggested, they are the results of chance observation rather than of systematic thinking. Thus, we find, in the areas of mental retardation, distinctions according to the degree of retardation and, perhaps, also to personality-types, but not yet according to causes. Physical disorders appear, in this early stage of classification, as divided into the groups of (acute or chronic) diseases, of deficiencies (of sensory or inner organs) and of orthopaedic handicaps. Sometimes, metabolic or neurological disorders are mentioned as separate sub-units. Emotional disorders are then divided into neurotic, psychotic and psychopathic disorders, sometimes differentiated by the additional distinction between constitutional and experiential causes. All these disorders or deficiencies represent, in the early stages of behavior research, primary units, partly as causal factors, partly as describable clinical pictures. This lack of distinction between causal and descriptive concepts, so characteristic of this type of classification, continues to be felt in present-day psychopathology as well. A few examples from the area of delinquent behavior will prove our claim.

In her study of juvenile delinquency K. Friedlander (38, p. 184) mentions the method of classification as it was accepted in the "Institute for the Scientific Treatment of Delinquency" in England. There, distinction was made between "offences committed by : (a) mentally defectives, (b) borderline defectives, (c) psychotics, (d) borderline psychotics, (e) psychoneurotics, (f) persons with character disorders (including psychopathic personalities and sex perverts), (g) persons with behavior problems, (h) persons with organic disorders, (i) non-delinquents, (j) normals, (k) alcoholics.

This is obviously neither a classification of clinical pictures nor one according to differential causes. In the first case, it should have been based on a phenomenological comparison of syndromes, each capable of resulting from a variety of causes. In the second case, it should have been based on causal configurations, rather than on isolated and accidental disorders, and evidence should have been adduced to the effect that delinquency is essentially different in each of the eleven types. Moreover, each of the concepts is much too large and much too general to designate either a causal group or a significant behavioral unit. It would not be difficult to enlarge the list through methods of quantitative differentiation and combinations. Thus, we could distinguish between the various forms of asocial or anti-social behavior, as it may appear in different types and on different levels of intensity, in neurosis, psychosis, psychopathy, mental retardation, etc. And we should certainly take into account the various causes, or, better, causal configurations responsible for the emergence of the deviations said to be, in turn, responsible for delinquent behavior. In this way, causal differentiation would make possible at least a more comprehensive and a more adequate method of classifying varieties of delinquency, a method based on configurational thinking. Besides that, we should not forget those forms of delinquent behavior that are primarily the result of developmental processes. Others, such as a primary wayward-ness, are omitted from the list. Such and other deficiencies are, however, unavoidable in any method of classification which relies primarily on more or less limited observations and inductive thinking.

K. Friedlander herself distinguishes between three major groups of juvenile delinquency, one comprising cases of antisocial character forma-tion, a second comprising cases of organic disorders, and a third one—those of psychotic ego disorders (38, pp. 186 ff.). In her first group are included cases of delinquent behavior caused:

a) by the antisocial character formation alone (children beyond control, wayward girls, aggressive adolescents, habitual criminals in adulthood);

b) by a lesser degree of antisocial character formation reinforced by severe environmental or emotional stress, usually due to unconscious conflicts (first appearance of delinquency at adolescence);

c) by a slight degree of antisocial character formation, strongly re-inforced by neurotic conflicts (kleptomania, pyromania, certain sexual offences and occasional crimes);

d) by a certain degree of antisocial character formation combined with neurotic acting-out of phantasies (Reich's instinct-ridden character, Alexander's neurotic character, Aichhorn's imposter type, Henderson's predominantly inadequate psychopath).

Her second group, that of organic disturbances, comprises cases of delinquency due to toxic influences (alcohol, drugs, etc.), mental defect, brain-injuries, pre-adolescent encephalitis, epilepsy, dysrythmia. Her third group, that of psychotic disorders, is self-explanatory.

We object, as already said, to basing classification on isolated causal factors and not on causal configurations. Moreover, it should not be forgotten that we are not concerned here with classifying pathological phenomena as such but varieties of asocial and antisocial behavior. Let us take the example of behavior disorders following two cerebral pathologies, for instance chorea and encephalitis. The fact that in both cases the central nervous system is negatively afflicted is unimportant and extrinsic to the classification of delinquent behavior; what we need here is : comparing with each other the similarities and differences between behavioral syndromes which may result from these two pathologies, and comparing the syndromes with similar ones in which cerebral disorders are causally irrelevant. In other words : we suggest a phenomenological approach to classification (which includes, of course, causal analysis) rather than basing it on causal thinking only.

Moreover : it is doubtful whether the clinical pictures included in each of the four sub-units of K. Friedlander's "antisocial characters" are indeed homogeneous enough to justify their inclusion in one group. The aggressive adolescent described by Aichhorn (2) and the wayward prostitute described by Friedlander (38, pp. 116 ff.), for instance, appear, together with the habitual criminal, in her first type of antisocial character formation. But the fact that certain causal factors can be found to operate in the case history of each of the three types does not justify their inclusion in one group; the differences between their essential symptoms are so obvious that we must ask : which additional causal factors must enter the causal equation in order to produce in one case the aggressive youth, in a second case the prostitute girl, and in a third one the habitual criminal.

Or consider the third sub-unit of the antisocial character : all its representatives have, it is true, one characteristic in common, a rather high degree of compulsiveness based on strong neurotic conflicts. But can the latter qualifications ("based on strong neurotic conflicts") indeed be applied to all cases included in this sub-group? A phenomenological analysis may reveal that the compulsiveness underlying the delinquent behavior in this group has, in some cases, a strong organic element, in others a quasi-psychotic coloring. What is, we must then ask, the clinical meaning of compulsiveness in each case? Here again, it is the phenomenological behavior analysis of different cases of compulsive delinquency that may make possible a more adequate classification than one based on etiological considerations only.

The fourth group of Friendlander's antisocial character formation would seem to deserve most severe criticism. Here, the so-called "inadequate psychopath" is equated with the delinquent who acts out his phantasies in offences. Such a definition, however, does not take cognisance of the constitutional nature of psychopathy; it tries almost to eliminate the essential differences between neurosis and psychopathy. On the other hand, the use of the clinical term of "psychopathy" requires a previous comparison with each other of the delinquent and non-delinquent forms of psychopathic behavior. In this way, we would further not only the cause of conceptual precision but also of classification. And we would discover that most varieties of psychopathic behavior are not included at all in Friedlander's list.

Another argument would have to be directed against the absolute separation of the "antisocial character" from organic or psychotic disorders. Feeblemindedness, at least in its higher grades, is in many cases a most important auxiliary factor in Friedlander's first type of antisocial character formation. In other cases, organic or psychotic disorders may be results and not causes of antisocial character formations. Alcoholism or drug-addiction, too, may appear both as manifestations and as results of antisocial character formation of the first or the fourth type but not as its causes.

Thus, we see that Friedlander's method of classifying delinquent behavior, though undoubtedly superior to the first-mentioned (that of the Institute for the Scientific Treatment of Delinquency), suffers from a similar weakness: both are wanting in phenomenological differentiation. Causal analysis is certainly indispensable for the understanding and the treatment of individual cases, but the very principle of causal analysis, namely that we must discover, in each case, the unique configuration of partial causes, makes causal analysis unsuitable to serve as sole or even as principal basis for the classification of clinical pictures. Classification of behavioral patterns as such is an attempt to bring isolated phenomena together into abstract groups. But it is precisely for this reason that we should *not* base it on etiological differentiation only: *isolated* causal factors are but abstractions; hence, units of classification based on them will always tend to be overcomprehensive; *configurations* of partial causes refer to individual causes only; hence, units of classification based on them will always tend to be too narrow.

This point can be clearly exemplified by a third method of classification, one based entirely on case analyses and on abstraction of partial causes. We refer to the method used by Pearson in his book on Emotional Disorders in Children (79, pp. 281 ff.).

He starts with cases of asocial and antisocial behavior resulting from the child's *protest* against overaggressive adults or against inadequate social ideals, against extreme frustration or against overstimulation by the environment, cases in which protest may bring about unplanned and ineffective *escape* from the oppressing environment.

A second group comprises, according to Pearson, cases in which delinquent behavior in the child is the result of *imitating* the delinquent patterns prevailing in the socio-cultural environment of his adults.

Then follow the groups of cases in which delinquency is caused by *mental retardation* and the accompanying ego-weakness, by *cerebral injuries* and the accompanying inability to control impulses, or by *psychoses* and the personality disruptions characteristic of such disorders, by *unconscious guilt feelings* and punishment needs, by *defective super-ego* developments, usually called psychopathic antisociality.

In the last group we find those cases of delinquency which, according to Pearson, are due to *frustration of erotic needs*. This group is divided into three sub-groups :

a) perversions;

b) offenses indicating neurotic regression, as a rule of compulsive character (kleptomania, pyromania, symbolic offences);

c) antisocial reactions to disappointments and frustrations in the child's relationships with his parents :

i) offenses committed in order to take revenge on the disappointing parents;

ii) offenses committed while the child escapes from the parents into "daring" independence for which the child is, of course, far from being ready;

iii) offenses committed by over-protected and therefore insecure children who try to convince themselves that they are strong;

iv) offenses committed by children whose love-needs have remained unsatisfied and who therefore regress into the sado-masochistic stages of their libido-development and express their suffering aggressively;

v) offenses committed by educationally effeminated boys who react to their passive drives by asocial or antisocial acts.

Most of the last-mentioned reactive types of delinquency with their mainly overcompensatory character are not essentially different from the first-mentioned protest- or escape-types, though the degree of consciousness may be lower in the reactive group. The regressive sub-group of the reactive unit does not seem to belong to the other ones; in any case, it seems more justified to group these offenses together with compulsive and guilt-offenses. The weakness of the causal thinking underlying Pearson's classification is obvious. It is no mere coincidence that case description plays a central role in it, though only to the extent that it gives relief to the causal role of this or that *partial* factor (so much so indeed that the impression is created as if the case not only exemplifies but actually *proves* the exclusive causal responsibility of that partial factor). Truly clinical case-analysis based on configurational approaches to causation would be, of course, of little use to classification. What we need is neither isolation of partial factors nor clinical analysis but—definition of *essential* causes, essential for each of the behavioral units to be included in a scheme of classification.

To sum up : classification of clinical phenomena aims at organising them in groups and sub-groups according to their essential similarities and differences.* "Essential" is the trait without which a phenomenon would cease to be what it is. Hence the need for discovering, through comparative analyses of concepts and syndromes, the essential characteristics of each clinical picture; one of the tools of comparison being an analysis of essential causal connections.

2.   How to Distinguish Between Clinical Pictures : A Fourth Example

We have so far tried to define and to explain the meaning of classification and its methodological principles. For this purpose we submitted to critical analysis three examples which seemed inadequate. Now, we shall analyse another example with a view to clarifying the concept of "essential characteristics". We have chosen an example which is based on phenomenological comparison and shall try to examine its inner consistency. We hope that our analysis will help us in our endeavor to formulate criteria of distinguishing between different units of behavior.

We have chosen the unit called "Primary Behavior Disorder" in its oedipal and pre-oedipal forms. We base our analysis on the writings of the psychiatrist Ophuijsen (77) and one of his pupils, Hamilton (49).

The word "primary" designates not only the fact that the disorder starts already in the early stages of the child's life, but also the fact that it is not "secondary" to constitutional, organic or psychotic defects. But the word is liable to mislead, since, according to Ophuijsen and Hamilton, the PBD "results" from the child's early experience that he cannot trust his parents. In other words : the disorder is, in fact, secondary, and it would therefore be more fitting to call it "early" and not "primary". It is

---

* Obviously, we need not discuss here methods of classification as used in police and court reports and statistics, since they use external criteria only, such as the object or the seriousness of the offense.

primary only in relation to the child's ensuing emotional and moral development.

His inability to trust his parents prevents him from introjecting their images, and he will therefore be unable to establish meaningful inter-personal relationships or to understand their essence. Already early in his life he will act out, without control, his impulses. His impulsiveness will sometimes be accompanied by habit disorders (enuresis, encopresis, thumbsucking, exaggerated masturbation, etc.), sometimes by conduct disorders (stubbornness, temper tantrums, negativism, etc.).

Hamilton suggests that the type of the accompanying disorders is determined by constitutional factors, passiveness supporting the appear-ance of habit disorders, activeness that of conduct disorders. But neither the symptom-distinction nor its explanation with the help of hypothesized constitutional factors are convincing, and the authors themselves offer another interpretation of the differences between the accompanying symptoms. We are told that the relative frequency of neurotic signs depends on the period of development in which the child experiences rejection and frustration at the hands of his parents: A child who did experience parental love at the beginning of his life, though perhaps not convincingly enough to establish in his psychic structure a "basic sense of trust" (21), is liable to harbour strongly ambivalent feelings towards his parents, and such feelings in turn are liable, sooner or later, to arouse inner conflicts which will find their expression in neurotic symptoms. Later, in the oedipal phase, the parents' attitude towards the child changes, and he is forced into the disappointing experience that they reject him. In this case, primary behavior disorders are liable to be his reaction rather than neurotic disorders, if the change in the parents' attitude was due to economic pressure rather than to inner conflicts (see later). The PBD of the oedipal type, it is true, will be accompanied by neurotic symptoms, indicating relative insecurity and strong ambivalence in the pre-oedipal phases. But the core syndrome will be one of hate and aggression directed, implicitly or explicitly, against the disappointing parents.

(What is liable to happen when the disappointing experience of "the parents as rejecting" follows a period of full security? Such cases will be rare, since the development of a really reliable "basic sense of trust" indicates, as a rule, the prevalence of positive life conditions in the child's primary environment, so that his later rejection by the parents will be an exception. In other words: rejection in the oedipal phase is usually preceded by some measure of instability in the child's relationship with his parents. When the relationships are positive and a radical change occurs nevertheless, the child is liable to express his disappointment by feelings of ambivalence and by inner conflicts so intensive and extreme that a neurosis rather than a PBD is likely to be the reactive result.)

It thus follows that there will be found practically no case of oedipal PBD without an admixture of neurotic symptoms. In this respect the pre-oedipal case essentially differs; when a child prematurely, that is, before his ego had a chance to pass through the first stages of its crystallization, experiences the loss of his parents' love, the PBD is liable to appear as an uncontrolled expression of impulses, without any admixture of neurotic signs.* Here, a comparison of the pre-oedipal PBD with psychopathy would seem to impose itself, and we shall try to do so later.

Since every neurosis is accompanied by behavior disorders of some kind, the question arises : what their meaning is in contrast to that of the so-called "primary" behavior disorders. The former must be seen against the background of the central problem of neurosis, that of anxiety. We must therefore ask, which factors account for the relative weakness of anxiety in the emergence and development of the pre-oedipal PBD. Ophuijsen offers a partial answer only (which we have already mentioned) : when economic stress, so he suggests, causes the parents to reject the child, PBD is liable to be the result; tensions between the parents are in this case less responsible for the child's rejection than they are in the causation of neurotic reactions. But he does not try to explain how economic stress specifically determines the causal effect of parental rejection. And yet, it is precisely this specificness that makes causal categories meaningful within any system of classification.

In another place (31) we have tried to explain how poverty is liable to operate as a factor of externalization, that is, as causally responsible for the emergence of an attitude towards the world as conglomeration and accidental meeting place of external factors. This externalizing effect limits the child's ability and readiness to relate any experience to himself. Hence, the weakness or even the absence of anxiety, that is, of fear of ego-loss (27). In this case, even parental rejection is liable to appear in the child's mind as an inevitable characteristic of reality as such rather than as expression of personal aggressiveness, specifically directed against him. Such a child will start, already at an early age, to react aggressively to his reality, almost by way of imitation and generalization, as it were, without personal relatedness either to himself or to any specific individual in his environment. And even the place of oedipal conflicts is then likely

---

* Though Ophuijsen and Hamilton claim that even in this case certain neurotic symptoms may appear when the child passes through the oedipal phase and is subjected to the experience of what Ophuijsen calls "the parents as a couple".

to be taken by external, non-directed reactions, to external, non-internalized images. *The extent and the form of externalization are, indeed, most important differential factors in any attempt to classify asocial and anti-social behavior patterns.*

Let us now examine the inner consistency of the term "Primary Behavior Disorder", in the light of the symptoms mentioned by Ophuijsen and Hamilton. The most important symptoms are: "lying, truanting, stealing, disobedience, running away, destructiveness, fighting, sexual activities, etc. . . . constant conflict with the environment and the absence of guilt" (77, pp. 35 f.). The child does not react to punishment or to threat of punishment. There are practically no signs of internalized aggressiveness. The latter appears as protest or, better, as externalized reaction to the real or imagined aggressions coming from the environment, but not as defence. Unambiguous neurotic signs may be rare or even absent (in the pre-oedipal phase of PBD) but habit disorders, such as encopresis, enuresis or thumbsucking may be abundant as already mentioned, as indicators not of inner tensions and regressions and not of certain unspecific constitutional type factors, but of neglect and ensuing fixation to early phases of development.

The latter qualification obviously refers to the pre-oedipal form, which thereby essentially differs from the oedipal form with its coexistence of behavior disorder with neurotic symptoms beginning to appear at the fifth or sixth year of life. It would therefore seem justified to question our right to include the two units of behavior, the oedipal and the pre-oedipal "types", in one clinical picture.

Here we come back to the central question in our discussion: how to define criteria of the classification of clinical pictures. Partial similarity of symptoms is certainly not sufficient to include two syndromes in one clinical unit, even when this partial similarity between symptoms is paralleled by one between causal factors. *It is precisely when we are faced with such partial similarities that we should ask whether they do not cover essential differences.* Let us exemplify the principle underlying this statement by a comparative analysis of the two forms of PBD.

1) Aggressiveness from an early age on is common to both. But signs of inner tension and neurotic disturbances (such as feelings of insecurity, depressive moods, etc.) can be found in the oedipal form only. The pre-oedipal form is characterized by more generalized aggressiveness and by absence of personal relatedness in the aggressive acts, while, in the oedipal type, the parents are meant.

2) A second common trait (which Ophuijsen himself does not mention

specifically) would seem to be the polymorphous character of the asocial and antisocial symptoms, as against the compulsiveness of neurotic delinquency. This polymorphous character of symptoms, that is, their tendency automatically to spread, as it were, over all life-areas, indicates weakness of the ego in its organizing and synthesizing functions. But such ego-weakness may be the result of a process of defective development from the start, or it may be the result of a developmental arrest or of regression. In both cases, it accounts for the tendency of symptoms to "spread automatically", in the absence of ego-selection; but in the pre-oedipal form, this ego-weakness is based on its *inability* to relate to the environment, because it did not have time to crystallize functionally before the pathogenic disappointment took place; in the oedipal form the ego weakness results from the *loss of relational ability*, following the pathogenic disappointment.

3) Causal analysis, too, reveals essential differences. Parental rejection is, according to Ophuijsen, the main causal factor responsible for the emergence of both forms, and in both it is economic stress, rather than inter- or intrapersonal tension that accounts for the child's rejection. We added that poverty determines that "climate of externalization" in which the child is bound to grow up, without the experience of personal relationships. The differential causal factor, according to Ophuijsen, is the time-factor : in the one form, the disappointing rejection occurs in the anal, in the other form—in the oedipal phase. Is this time-differential causally an essential factor? It is evident that it depends on the answer to this question whether to interpret the two forms as sub-units of one clinical picture or as two different clinical pictures.

We tend to accept the second alternative : to the extent that the child *did* succeed in establishing personal relationships with his environment in the first years of his life, later rejection by his parents is liable to cause severe disappointment, protest and regression; but all reactions are liable to be interspersed with strong ambivalence feelings, through which the child will then continue to express his relational ability, even after his disappointing experience, that is, after the former channels of expression have been closed. It follows that, even if some symptoms of the reactive behavior are similar in both forms, we should ask in which respect their meaning differs, in the light of the child's essentially different life experiences.

4) Another way of proving the heterogeneity of the two forms of PBD is to examine the case histories quoted in Ophuijsen's and Hamilton's studies. Let us first sum-up again the details of comparison : The pre-

oedipal type excels in his general uncontrolled impulsiveness, which is not related to the images of his near environment. The oedipal type directs his aggressiveness against what Ophuijsen calls "the parents as a couple"; his mind is related to the personal tensions in his family environment (and in this way he expresses his relational ability, though distortedly). The pre-oedipal type is also called the "true criminal" who does not negate his actions, although he knows, of course, that his environment condemns them. The oedipal type is also called the "neurotic delinquent" who tries to provoke punishment in order thus to receive a confirmation of his negative world-perception. (We shall later see in which ways he essentially differs from the neurotic delinquent.)

Both show egotistic demands, inability to accept routine or discipline, an always ready tendency to be offended and hurt, to blame others and to see the adults as his enemies. Both feel always attacked and discriminated, and they "take revenge" through their asocial and antisocial behavior. Both want that everything be "theirs" without being ready to give anything in return. Both frequently react with rage where others would have reacted with envy. The difference between the two, as already said, is primarily one between their relational ability, which is much less developed in the pre-oedipal type.

So far the summary of comparisons. But when we look through the case material quoted by the authors, we find in *both* types many neurotic traits (see for instance, 77, pp. 49 ff.). Aggressiveness and thievery are accompanied by severe sibling rivalry, over-activity, enuresis, onanism, strong guilt-feelings, tics, pavor nocturnus, etc. Besides, we are informed that practically all children described are of at least normal intelligence; their parents are described as neurotics and not only as inconsistent or rejecting. Exaggerated love-needs and anxiety feelings which are mentioned in most cases indicate basic insecurity and strong inner conflicts. *There is not one case description of a pre-oedipal type* where inner tension and neurotic signs are absent. Should it be argued that the absence of "pure cases" proved the tension-creating influence of the oedipal phase or the universality of anxiety and ambivalence, the distinction between pre-oedipal and the oedipal forms of PBD would seem to lose its justification: perhaps it would be more correct simply to distinguish between different degrees of inner tension and between different forms of neurotic reactions? Perhaps the term PBD is superfluous, and it would be sufficient to distinguish between neurosis and neurotic delinquency, on the one hand, and between the latter and psychopathy, on the other?

Ophuijsen and Hamilton are obviously of a different opinion: not only do they contrast PBD with neurosis, they also conceive of the two forms as of two sub-units. We accept their distinction but claim that they did not have at their disposal the proper case material for an adequate analysis of the pre-oedipal type. They were unable clearly to recognize the essential characteristics that *distinguish* between the two types but saw the pre-oedipal as a variety of the oedipal form only, in accordance with their case material.

It is not difficult to understand why this was bound to happen. Who are the children in the group of pre-oedipal PBD? They have been hurt deeply in the roots of their personality before the ego had time to grow into an organizing center and to fulfil its function as guardian of its identity and development. These are the aggressive children who grow up in the slum quarters of our cities without proper care, and whose heart is full of resentment and hatred (unless they reach adequate educational institutions where they find what they need, gradual rehabilitation of trust in trustworthy adults and systematic reconstruction of their partialized personality).

Not only is their pathology essentially different from that of the children in whom aggressiveness is a defence against the "suspect", the "treacherous" adult (the cases of oedipal PBD); not only do they differ from guilt-offenders and other neurotic delinquents (see later); they are also essentially different from the wayward children, on the one hand, and from psychopaths, on the other.

In the second part, which will be devoted to an analysis of wayward-ness (pp. 39 ff., compare pp. 150 ff.), we shall understand why children who grow up, from the earliest years of life on, under conditions of poverty and neglect, do not reach, as a rule, child guidance clinics from which psychiatrists and clinical psychologists draw their case material as basis of diagnosis and classification. But it is precisely in methods of classification based on clinical observation, case analysis and inductive thinking that absence of contact with certain groups of cases is bound to be dangerous: including such groups in one of the other groups of classification is bound to distort the system of essential characteristics which we need for differentiation between clinical pictures.

It would seem that the absence of clear distinction between the oedipal and pre-oedipal forms of PBD, neurotic delinquency and waywardness is bound to limit the usefulness of these clinical concepts for the purposes of classification. There exist other forms of delinquency as well, in psychotics, psychopaths, mentally retarded and brain-injured, and many children become delinquent by way of protesting against aggressive or frustrating adults, of escaping from a depressing environment or of imitating delinquent behavior. But in the psychotics, psychopaths, brain-injured and mentally retarded, delinquency is but an epiphenomenon of the basic pathology. And protest, flight or imitation are but precipitating causes of delinquency; the latter will result, in this or that form, only when these precipitators act on a pathogenic structure.*

Another question is: how to distinguish between separate clinical pictures and sub-units of one picture. Is the pre-oedipal PBD a separable unit, or is it a sub-unit of PBD? Does the distinction between the four forms of feeblemindedness (the aggressive, the paranoid, the submissive, the apathetic type—see 36) still allow us to speak of the feebleminded delinquent, or must we distinguish at least between aggressive and passive varieties? Will the answer be similar with regard to the forms of psychopathy, or to perversions? Is neurotic delinquency one clinical unit or must we distinguish at least between guilt offences, compulsive and symbolic offences? What are the criteria that will determine the answer to such questions? How shall we define and compare with each other the essential characteristics of each of these clinical pictures?

3. CRITERIA OF CLASSIFICATION

What questions should we ask when we wish to understand the essentials of a certain form of—normal or abnormal—behavior? The answer depends of course on our psychological theory: the behaviorist, the psychoanalyst, the Jungian, the structuralist—each will give a different answer, will select different criteria, in accordance with "his" theory. I refer the reader to my study *The Roots of the Ego* (34) in which I have tried to explain my psychological premises. According to the basic concepts employed there I shall now suggest a list of questions to be asked when we try to compare with each other the varieties of delinquency mentioned so far (waywardness, primary behavior disorders of the oedipal and of the pre-oedipal types, delinquency out of guilt feelings, compulsive delinquency, substitutive (symbolic) delinquency, as well as perversions,

---

* We cannot speak of the delinquency of the one who protests (escapes, imitates), although the three factors play an especially important role in the delinquency of the adolescent, as we shall try to show in the sixth chapter. There we shall see that the meaning of each of the three factors in adolescent delinquency differs essentially from what Pearson has in mind: protest and revolt not against aggressive or frustrating adults but against a social order or against adulthood as such; escape not from a depressing environment but from the danger of oedipal revivals; imitation not of delinquent adults but group-patterns of behavior. In other words: when we speak of revolt, escape or imitation as being causal factors of adolescent delinquency, we have in mind a complex system of reactions to social and mental factors.

psychopathies and the delinquent behavior of mentally retarded children):

1) What is the degree of the ego's organizational strength, as it manifests itself in the planning of the delinquent act and in its execution according to certain inner directions? The question may also be formulated differently : *What is the degree of ego-participation?*

2) A relatively high degree of ego-participation is compatible with a relatively low degree of conscious directedness towards the delinquent act (as, for instance, in the substitutive offences of the neurotic); in other cases, a relatively low degree of ego-participation may appear together with a higher degree of ego-directedness (as, for instance, in the delinquent acts of the guilt-offender). *What, then, we must ask, is the degree of conscious directedness towards the offense as against the intensity of ego-participation?*

3) But whatever the degree of ego-participation in the act and of conscious directedness towards the act may be, the ego may or may not identify itself with that act, may or may not emphasize the importance of its function in the execution of the offenses. In this respect, psychopathies and perversions essentially differ from neurotic delinquency (to give only one example). *What, then, is the degree of ego-emphasis?*

4) The last question leads to the following ones : *What is the amount of allotropic aggressiveness as symptom and as motive of the delinquent behavior?* The answer to the two parts of the question will not necessarily be identical, and the proportion between the intensity of aggression as symptom and as motive is one of the essential characteristics of each variety.

5) The same applies to the proportion between aggressiveness and anxiety as conscious or unconscious motivator of delinquency. *What is the degree of anxiety?*

6) *What is the intensity of guilt feelings after the offense?* It might be meaningful here to compare the intensity of guilt with ego-emphasis (see point 3).

7) *What is the intensity of inner tension* (as determined by inner conflicts, usually between conscious and unconscious tendencies)?

8) *What is the extent to which man is determined heteronomously by the non-ego,* in its three different meanings, that is, by the environment, the organism, the unconscious?

9) *What is the delinquent's rigidity and compulsiveness?* The answer actually follows automatically those to questions 1, 2 and 8.

10) *What is the delinquent's relational (in)ability?* How does it influence his behavior?

11) *How does the delinquent behavior affect the thinking processes,* their contents, their effectiveness? How does it influence intelligence?

12) *What is the relationship between the two life-tendencies,* that towards staticness and that towards expansion?

Although the list could be enlarged, and particularly by adding the causal factors that are essential to each of the clinical pictures, the above mentioned questions would seem to be sufficiently specific to allow constructing the "profiles" of each of the various behavioral units, and to answer the question of how to distinguish between main and sub-units.

In most questions appears a quantitative formulation; but so far we have no proper tools for giving exact quantitative answers. Besides that, analyzing the *form* in which each of the differentiating qualities appears in each clinical picture is no less important than indicating their degree of intensity. It is therefore preferable to use in our answers verbal descriptions rather than (necessarily artificial and simplifying) mathematical formulae.

We shall now try to analyze each of our twelve criteria of clinical comparison. Let it be clear that our analysis does *not* refer to normal behavior; each of the criteria has a different meaning when it serves the analysis of normal, and when it serves the analysis of disturbed behavior.

1) *Ego-participation* depends on the structurization of those qualities and attitudes that appear in our developing personality, primarily through the activation of defence mechanisms: the earlier this process of structurization starts, the better are the chances for the results of these defences to become integral parts of the emerging ego-structure. There will then be no need to activate the mechanisms specifically in defence of otherwise dangerous or even unbearable positions. The ego will, then, be free to participate "naturally", as it were, in the execution of its acts. We find this constellation in the aggressive forms of psychopathy and to some extent also in the pre-oedipal types of PBD, in whom aggressiveness crystallizes as an integral part of the ego.

In this respect, the oedipal type differs; he must constantly be on guard to protect his conception of the world as being hostile. In each variety of disturbed behavior that requires permanent defences, ego-participation will be divided between the seeming or real "danger" and the symptomatic action, irrespectively of whether this action is a neurotic manifestation or an offence. It follows that ego-participation is lower in oedipal PBD, with its inner tensions, than in the pre-oedipal variety of PBD, with its early structurization of aggressive behavior-patterns, and this in spite of the fact that the very activation of defence mechanisms requires a fairly high degree of ego-participation. For similar reasons the latter is higher in character neuroses than in psychoneuroses of the phobic, the compulsive or the hysteric type or in neurotic delinquency, irrespectively of whether we speak of symbolic, substitutive or guilt offences. The differences between ego-participation in perversions and in manic compulsive delinquency (kleptomania, pyromania, etc.) can be explained in the same way; although in both cases the almost absolute heteronomy of the offences is evident, the degree of ego-participation is higher in the pervert, in whom anal factors of determination surpass in causal weight later (oedipal) factors of traumatization.

However, not only the period of structurization or the extent of finality help us define the degree of ego-participation, but also the intensity of the non-ego's determining power. This statement may seem to be a tautology, especially when we reduce it to its structural meaning, as we have tried to do elsewhere (see 34, pp. 29 ff.). There, we have elaborated why the ego's openness towards the internal or the external non-ego, not accompanied by adequate organizational ego-strength, is a basic condition of every disorder. But we believe nevertheless that it is justified to interpret ego-participation as a function of the determining power of the environment, the organism, the unconscious; the ego cannot possibly delineate its dependence on the non-ego. This dependence is a function of the latter's intensity no less than it is a function of structural elements.

If we want fully to understand the differential meaning of our statement for the purposes of classification, we must properly distinguish between the three areas of the non-ego : being determined by the external environment (through conditioning, as in primary waywardness—see 26), by the organism (through increase of stimuli from within, as in brain-injuries—90), by the unconscious (through the interference of autonomic complexes, as in psychoses—53)—these, too, are factors determining the degree of ego-participation : it is practically non-extant in cases of organic automatism; it is low but can be developed in cases of environmental conditioning; it is likely to be fairly high though nevertheless paralyzed by the need for constantly activating defense-mechanisms against inner threats, as in cases of neuroses and psychoses.

2) In a later part of our discussion, where we shall analyze the concept of compulsiveness (see pp. 128 ff.), we shall also emphasize the differential

significance of the relationship between ego-participation and *conscious directedness towards the offence*. The two factors are equally weak in primary waywardness and in brain injuries (in which it is almost nil). They are equally strong in certain forms of psychopathy and in the pre-oedipal form of PBD. Ego-participation is more intensive than conscious directedness towards the offense in certain extravert forms of psychopathy and in the substitutive (neurotic) delinquency, while in other forms of psychopathy (f.i. the "oscillating" type), in guilt-offenses, in most perversions and certainly in compulsive delinquency the first factor is weaker than the second one (the same is true for the psychopathoid adolescent delinquent whom we shall describe later—see pp. 209 ff.).

Obviously, the terms "equal", "stronger", "weaker" are of relative significance only, since the absolute intensity of both factors differs in each clinical picture : when the pervert, for instance, shows less of the first than of the second factor, both are nevertheless fairly strong; not so in neurotic delinquents, in whom both factors are fairly weak, in spite of the relative superiority of one of them.

3) The proportion between the two first factors receives its significance for the classification of asocial and antisocial forms of behavior through the third factor only, *ego-emphasis*. The pervert and the psychopath excel in the intensity of ego-emphasis, the neurotic and the compulsive delinquent and certainly the brain-injured and the mentally retarded of the passive variety—in its extreme weakness. Between these two extremes we find all the forms of delinquency that are characterized by aggressiveness.

4) When we speak of *aggression*, we must distinguish between its meaning as cause and as motive. There are cases, in which aggressiveness plays a central role as motivator though phenotypically it may be not in evidence (for instance, in some perversions). In most clinical pictures, however, the phenotypical and the motivational intensity of aggressiveness are more or less equal.

5) Different is the proportion between aggressiveness and *anxiety* : there is no definable relationship between the two in most of the clinical pictures of delinquent behavior that we discuss here. We find units characterized by weak anxiety (weak at least as motive) and strong aggressiveness, as, for instance, the PBD, mainly the pre-oedipal variety, or certain psychopathies. In other units we find strong anxiety at the root of the delinquency, accompanied by relatively weak aggressiveness (as motive), for instance in neurotic delinquency, mainly delinquency from unconscious guilt-feelings. In the organic cases we often find strong anxiety as motivator of antisocial

behavior, here as a rule organic anxiety, while aggressive drives do not play a decisive role (to exclude so-called "shame-rage"—see Cannon: 15).

6) *Guilt feelings* after the offense are usually weak in all the units discussed here, including that of the guilt offender who eliminates his guilt precisely through the punishment he seeks and receives for his offenses. Only the compulsive delinquent and sometimes also the pervert show signs of guilt-feelings at the time of committing the offense and afterwards.

7) The factor called *inner tensions* is almost identical with that of anxiety as motivator of the offense, whether the tension is caused by primary aggressiveness, whether it has caused anxiety. Where anxiety is weak, tension is weak, too (as, for instance, in primary waywardness, in pre-oedipal PBD, in mental retardation or in psychopathies). The two are equally strong in compulsive delinquency, in guilt-offenses and in brain-injuries (where anxiety is of an organic nature). In perversions and in symbolic offenses, too, tension and anxiety are usually fairly strong.

8) The most important qualification is that of *heteronomy*. Here, intensity is still less important than in the other varieties: dependence on external factors of determination, external with regard to the ego, or, as we would prefer to say, dependence on the non-ego, is common to all forms of abnormal behavior, delinquent, neurotic or externalized behavior. But the proportion between environmental, emotional and organic factors of determination constitutes one of the most important criteria of distinction between the various forms of asocial and antisocial behaviors.

Organic factors of determination operate not only in the impulsive and uncontrollable behavior of the brain-injured or, to some extent, in that of the mentally retarded; the ego probably depends on organic factors of determination also in certain perversions with their periodic character (see Fenichel's theory in the matter—24) and perhaps also in cases of compulsive delinquency (although such factors of determination have not yet been explored comprehensively). But in contrast to the brain-injured and the mentally retarded in whom unconscious factors do not play any causal role, their weight is decisive in perversions or in compulsive delinquency. In the other varieties of delinquency we find combinations of environmental and intrapsychic factors of determination (such as complexes or affects).

Thus, we find, for instance in the oedipal PBD and in the psychopathoid conditions of the adolescent (see pp. 209 ff.), dependence on the environment and, almost equally, on the unconscious; the pre-oedipal form of PBD, the aggressive and, still more so, the so-called oscillating forms of psychopathy or primary waywardness are characterized by a relatively strong or even an exclusive influence of environmental factors of determination. In the last-mentioned varieties of delinquency, the ties between consciousness and the unconscious are almost entirely disrupted. Although the experiences of early disappointment in pre-oedipal PBD and in psychopathies have entirely disappeared from consciousness, they do not arouse any specific anxiety (as complexes or unconscious affects would do in neuroses). And it certainly does not require repeated emphasis that in waywardness no motivational contact with the unconscious exists.

9) The concepts of *rigidity and compulsiveness* will be explained in greater detail in one of the following chapters of the book (see pp. 128 ff.). There, it will be mentioned that although rigidity constitutes one of the essential elements of compulsiveness, it appears also in forms of abnormal behavior that are *not* characterized by compulsiveness. And again, we can call the relationship between the two, rigidity and compulsiveness, one of the differential characteristics of the various forms of asocial and antisocial behavior. There exist forms of behavior, such as psychopathy in its varieties, or primary waywardness, in which both, rigidity and compulsiveness, are absent. Others are characterized by a large measure of compulsiveness, hence also of rigidity, such as compulsive delinquency and the various perversions. In other cases in which compulsiveness is absent, such as in the different types of PBD, in the delinquencies of the mentally retarded or the brain-injured, rigidity may nevertheless be present. In these cases, the rigidity is a result of stubborn maintenance of a certain world-perception or lack of differentiatedness or of integrational failures (usually of some organic nature). Rigidity in PBD should *not* be interpreted as a means of defense (while we must interpret the "anticipatory" *aggressiveness* in oedipal PBD as a defense against the "danger" of interpersonal relationships); rigidity is in this case the un-avoidable result of ever-recurring aggressiveness, almost the outcome of "self-conditioning". Similarly, the rigidity of the brain-injured is to be interpreted *not* as a defense against organic anxiety (according to Gold-stein—45), but as an unavoidable outcome of the organic deficiency. In other words: rigidity is in these cases a quality of the basic disorder and not of the offenses in which the disorder finds one of its expressions.

Much more complicated is the relationship between rigidity and compulsiveness in the clinical picture of symbolic-substitutive delinquency. Here, rigidity finds its expression in a quasi-compulsive bond to a certain pattern of relationship: the delinquent experiences the different figures in his environment as representatives of a "near", a "significant" reality; he distorts them projectively, eliminates all that may distinguish between them in order to express his desires, his anxieties, his aggressiveness against strangers as if they were near-ones. But the very fact that these many figures, whose actual differences he tries to "eliminate" projectively, *are* indeed different from each other, the very need to distort them, again and again, *prevents* compulsiveness. In this respect he differs from the guilt offender in whom compulsiveness is evident (and it is not by chance that so many students of delinquency combine this type with the compulsive offender in one unit).

10) *Inability to establish and maintain objective relationships* with environmental figures has no great value as a differential criterion in classification: there is not one single form of asocial or antisocial behavior in which such inability would *not* be present (although it is more in evidence in PBD, in perversions, in brain-injuries and in psychopathies than in waywardness or in the varieties of neurotic delinquency). But the human objects of relationships have a different meaning in each of the various clinical units of delinquent behavior, according to the central function which the ego allocates them; in PBD they represent a hostile and frustrating world; in waywardness they are almost impersonal parts of a material world; in neurotic delinquency they are symbolic objects without definable individual physiognomies, to be used for the needs of distorting and unifying projections; in perversions they turn into accidental objects of distorted sex drives, again almost without individual physiognomies; in the varieties of psychopathic delinquency they become the absolutely impersonal objects of incorporation, of unlimitedly egocentric misuse.

11) How is the *intelligence* affected by each of the various units of delinquent behavior? In oedipal PBD and in psychopathy, intelligence remains, as a rule, unaffected, since both, the constant interpretation of the world as an enemy whom one has to beat, and the interpretation of the world as object of incorporation, are likely to help develop the intelligence, at least functionally. Different is the fate of intelligence in waywardness, in which negative factors of conditioning account for the decrease of intelligence in the course of time (though the decrease remains, as a rule, reversible). In the various forms of neurotic delinquency and in perversions we often find a negative influence of the pathology on the individual's cognitive efficiency, it would seem for two reasons: the exclusive concentration of mental energy on the substitutive, the symbolic,

the "representative" meaning of environmental images and processes may prevent objective learning (hence the many cases of pseudo-feeblemindedness); and whenever most emotional and spiritual energy is being spent on heteronomous offenses (and unconscious factors of determination direct the individual in his tendencies and actions) the mind is liable to glide away still further from the areas of rational activity.

12) Our last question refers to the connection that exists between the clinical picture and the relative weight of *the two life-tendencies*, that towards staticness (systematization or inactivity, feeling of completeness or indolence) and that towards expansion (change or destruction, activity or hyperactivity, enlargement of boundaries or lack of systematization). In another place we have dealt at some length with the problems of those life-tendencies (34, pp. 7 ff.). Here we only pose the following double question: does the relative prevalence of one tendency prepare the ground for the emergence of a certain type of misbehavior, although the internal and external life conditions would allow for a different development? (the question of the life-tendencies as the decisive determinant of behavior). Is a certain behavior capable of strengthening one of the two life-tendencies, irrespectively of whether this reinforcement operates parallel with an existing structural constellation or in opposition to it? (the question of the behavioral pattern as determinant of the structural constellation).

There can be no doubt that, the more a child becomes accustomed to certain patterns of behavior, the more is his basic life-orientation likely to change : structurally given introvert reaction-patterns, for instance, are liable to make room for opposite patterns, when the child adopts an externalized or an aggressive life-style, as the result of environmental or experiential factors of determination. The same applies to changes in the relationship of the two life-tendencies : a prevalence of the life tendency towards staticness may make room for an opposite prevalence, when life-conditions drive a child into a life-style which is characterized by an excess of external stimulation and of external (and/or aggressive) reactions to such stimulations. Such a change is liable to occur in clinical pictures of which ego-weakness is characteristic (waywardness, brain-injuries, mental retardation and—perhaps—also compulsive delinquency) rather than in other types, as for instance, primary aggressiveness or psychopathic states.

But for the completion of the "profiles", is the first question likely to make more meaningful contributions : which structural tendencies and "preferences" prepare the child for which forms of asocial and antisocial behavior, in addition to environmental and experimental factors of determination?

The weakness of one of the two life-tendencies does not necessarily prove the prevalence of the opposite one. For instance: the tendency towards staticness may be weak, as in waywardness, and yet, the tendency towards expansion may not be particularly strong (as is the case in waywardness, in contrast to PBD or to perversions). The two tendencies may be weak at one and the same time, as is the case whenever lack of structure characterizes a condition (for instance, in mental retardation). The tendency towards expansion may be weak, as in brain-injuries, and yet, the opposite tendency will not necessarily be strong (as is the case in brain-injuries, in contrast to guilt-offenses). Just as in waywardness weak staticness appears together with non-existence of expansion, or in brain-injuries weak expansion appears together with weak staticness, we also find the opposite constellations: a strong tendency towards staticness may be combined with lack of expansion (f.i. in compulsive delinquency); and a strong tendency towards expansion may be combined with lack of staticness (f.i. in psychopathies).

4. Unit or Sub-unit?

Let us now return to the question which we have asked before (see p. 15); when are we entitled to speak of two separate clinical pictures, rather than of sub-units of one and the same picture? What, for instance, would be our answer with regard to the following:

— the oedipal and pre-oedipal forms of PBD;

— neurotic delinquency in its three forms: delinquency out of unconscious guilt feelings and punishment needs, substitutive (symbolic) delinquency, compulsive delinquency;

— the aggressive forms of delinquency in the mentally retarded as against delinquent acts committed by the passively seduced (or induced) retarded;

— the aggressive, the paranoid and the passive forms of delinquency in psychopaths?

(a) Behavior disorders

We refer to what we have said about the two forms of PBD (pp. 8 ff.): about the much higher degree of structurization in the pre-oedipal disorders, on the generality of aggressiveness against the world, as against its specific directedness against the parents in the oedipal type, on the multitude of symptoms of inner tension and neurotic manifestations in the oedipal form as against the absolutely external character of tension in the pre-oedipal type. Let us add the dependence on the unconscious and the strong anxiety in the oedipal as against the absence of anxiety in the pre-oedipal form of PBD. In the light of all these essential differences we should ask whether the common characteristics (a high degree of directedness towards the delinquent act, ego-emphasis, aggressiveness, inability to establish objective relationships with the human environment and the weakness of guilt-feelings) justify comprising the two forms in one clinical picture. From an etiological standpoint we could formulate a different question. Does the time-factor constitute an essential difference? Is the disappointment in the parents which comes to confirm the basic suspiciousness, something essentially different when it appears very early or in the oedipal phase only?

It would seem that the differences are more essential than the common traits. The latter can be found in other clinical units as well, such as the perversions or the aggressive forms of psychopathy, but no one would suggest that these be included, together with PBD, in one unit. Hence, we have no right to base on those common traits the construction of one clinical picture with two such units. However, it is not only the fact that the common traits appear in different patterns of abnormal behavior as well, but *primarily the recognition of the differences between the two forms of PBD that requires, so we believe, a clear distinction between two separate clinical pictures.*

When a child grows up in the spirit of "aggressiveness from within", of negation, he never comes to experience the forces of danger and threat that make his very existence doubtful. He does not *suffer* from suspicions, from doubts, from fears, from insecurity. He negates the world not in order to justify anticipation of aggression feared to come "from there", but in order thus to express his desire to be independent and to control all possible sources of danger. This is his way of distorting differentiation between the ego and the external non-ego. His illusion of being capable to control the non-ego by aggression and negation enables us to distinguish between him and the paranoid who does *not* believe in such a chance. The primarily aggressive does not experience the non-ego as a source of disappointment, as the oedipal type of PBD does. The reason for this difference is the weakness of ambivalence in the so-called pre-oedipal type, and weakness of ambivalence, in turn, reflects the absence of the experience of what Ophuijsen calls "the parents as a couple".

On the other hand, he does not resemble the psychopath either, with the latter's ego-inflation and non-recognition of the non-ego, which for him is but an object of incorporation; and he certainly differs from the wayward child who freely moves in the polymorphous appearances of his world, reacts to its stimuli and recognizes its right of existence, although he, the wayward, is unable to accept the limitations which the non-ego tries to impose on him.

Thus, it is evident that the so-called pre-oedipal "type" of PBD constitutes a clinical unit in itself and does *not* belong, together with the oedipal "type", in one comprehensive unit. Causal similarities often mislead us not less than similarities between symptoms: even when a child grows up, from his early years on, in economic stress and without security with his parents, doubts their reliability as educators and providers, even when in one of the early stages of development something happens which confirms the child's insecurity, the experience of disappointment may have a different meaning in the two cases.

In the so-called "pre-oedipal" type, the disappointing experience participates, as it were, in the crystallization of the ego which thus acquires a negative relationship with the environment, a naive and primary relationship which does not, in turn, require the activation of defence mechanisms. Through his aggressiveness and through his destructions the child tries, as already said, to master the hostile and disappointing world. But this attempt does not prove that he feels himself threatened by the danger of becoming dependent on this or that environmental figure, a danger from which the oedipal type tries to escape.

In other words: when a child feels rejected by his parents, whose economic situation deteriorates, and he becomes for them "an object among other objects", this disappointing experience has no personal meaning, if it appears in a very early period of his development; the earlier parental behavior changes, the more it determines the child's world conception rather than his patterns of *self*-conception. If so, it may not be correct at all to speak here of "disappointment"; it would perhaps be more adequate to interpret what happens in the child as a transition from suspiciousness to negative "knowledge"; from now on, the child "knows" that the world is one of aggressiveness, in which the individual cannot possibly survive unless he himself forms patterns of aggressiveness.

What characterizes the antisocial behavior, which is liable to emerge on the basis of the here mentioned negative experience, is an aggressive *relationship* to the world, contrary to psychopathy, in which aggressiveness *lacks* all relationship, since the world has ceased for the psychopath to be a subject. This difference explains, among other things, the fact that primary aggressiveness is and remains accessible to adequate treatment, though it may be prolonged and complicated: every treatment and every attempt to change certain pathological patterns of behavior presupposes the ability to see in the human environment an environment of subjects.*

(b) Neurotic delinquency

The similarity between neurotic delinquency and the oedipal PBD has been emphasized quite frequently : the latter shows so many neurotic traits (inner tensions, changing moods, depression, resentment) that Ophuijsen himself considered calling it "neurosis with signs of acting out in the center" (77, p. 37). On the other hand, we have seen, in those methods of classification which we submitted to a critical analysis, that committing offenses out of unconscious guilt-feelings appears as the common characteristic of all forms of neurotic delinquency. However, the clinical identity between guilt offenses and compulsive (manic) or substitutive† (symbolic) offenses has never and nowhere been proven.

These are but a few examples of the weakness of differential thinking which we often find in clinical psychology with its almost exclusive case-orientation. Since every case "belongs"—obviously—to more than one clinical picture, the impression is created, as if the limits between the various units were unstable, or as if almost every unit could be characterized by concepts that actually "belong" to another one. But this seeming unclarity is based on a misunderstanding : classification must aim at maximal (abstract) exactitude, at extreme formulations and not at "imitating" reality. Without such an emphasis on what divides one clinical picture from the other, there is no justification at all for formulating differential clinical concepts.

Elsewhere (33) we have compared neurotic delinquency in *all* its forms with waywardness, psycho-neurosis and PBD; there we did not distinguish between substitutive, compulsive and guilt offenses. On an etiological level we thought that the time-factor would be sufficient to distinguish between the compulsive delinquent (with traumatization in the anal phase) and the substitutive delinquent (with disappointment in the oedipal phase). We tried there to define the *common* traits in all forms of neurotic delinquency : as exaggerated though unrealistic conscience, as constant effort, on the part of the child, to create through his offenses a hostile and tense environment (and in particular a hostile family environment)

---

* In the wayward child in whom the weakness of this subjective modality of relationships is the result of negative conditioning, depends the success of treatment and of re-education precisely on the educator's ability to re-condition him and to develop in him this subjective modality of world conception and relationships.

† Substituting a neutral for a near figure at which actually the aggressiveness or the revenge is directed.

which would satisfy his guilt feelings and would justify his anxieties, and as an ever recurring attempt to prove to himself that he is negative and bad.

But between compulsive and substitutive delinquency an *essential* difference exists with regard to the amount of continuity in the aggressive and destructive acts or in the thefts : compulsiveness manifests itself in the ever recurring committal of the same kind of offenses, while substitutive delinquency finds its expression in ever different isolated acts, according to the temporary increase of negative affects against the parents; when these affects decrease, for some reason or another, and for some time, delinquency will have a "rest". In addition, guilt-feelings after the act are strong in intensity and acuity in the compulsive offender; not so in the one who is driven into his acts, from time to time, through the need to give expression to his feelings of resentment or revenge, but remains conscious of the very existence of such feelings, though not of their hidden objects.

What is the essential difference between compulsive and guilt offenses? From the point of view of continuity and systematization of delinquent acts the two types are equally different from substitutive offenses, particularly when we compare with each other adult representatives : both, the compulsive and the guilt offender, show some amount of "specialization". But when we compare their attitudes towards the environment, we encounter essential differences : the compulsive offender is much more removed from reality than the guilt offender; he lives in his almost hallucinatory world and finds in it all his satisfaction (though mixed with anxieties). The guilt offender, on the other hand, finds his satisfaction *not* in his acts but only in the punishment which he receives for them; he tries very hard to remain within his social contexts, and seeking punishment is, paradoxically, one of the manifestations of this attempt. The compulsive offender resembles the compulsive neurotic (just as the oedipal PBD resembles the non-delinquent and non-compulsive neurotic). He can also be compared with the aggressive (the pre-oedipal PBD) : in both, the root of the disorder is in the anal phase; in both, we find a much higher degree of structurization than in the oedipal PBD or in the guilt-offender. But on the other hand, there exist essential differences as well : as we have already said, the compulsive offender is much more removed from reality than the aggressive who tries to master the hostile world through his aggressions and destructions. From the latter point of view, the aggressive resembles the guilt offender who uses reality for his unconscious needs.

How, then, do we answer our question of classification? What are the differences between the compulsive, the substitutive and the guilt offender? Do they justify or even require differentiation between three separate clinical pictures, or can we speak of one only, that of neurotic delinquency, with three sub-units?

In the light of our preceding analysis the compulsive and the guilt-offender would seem to represent two different clinical pictures; in the first, the period of traumatization precedes that of the second; hence, we find delinquency much more rooted in the structure of the individual when we consider the first than the second type with the strongly defensive nature of his offenses; compulsive delinquency can be interpreted with the aid of causal categories much easier than guilt offenses which lend themselves better to finalistic interpretation (like all forms of defensive behavior). The quasi-hallucinatory nature of compulsive delinquency is clearly contrasted by the relatively realistic nature of defensive delinquency. Although in both cases conscious directedness towards the offense is stronger than ego-participation in its planning and execution, both elements are stronger in compulsive delinquency than in guilt-offenses which are characterized by the extreme weakness of ego-participation.

(Differentiation between the two forms of delinquency becomes more complicated under the impact of the type-factor. The more the representatives of the two delinquent forms resemble each other in their type-conditioned reaction patterns, the more are their essential differences liable to lose of their distinctness: the compulsive delinquent, whose offenses are primarily meant to satisfy his instinctual demands, may become addicted, under the influence of passive type conditions, to certain habits. These, in turn, are liable to undermine his health, and his delinquency may then become secondarily a tool for the satisfaction of masochistic tendencies, as if he were a guilt-offender. The latter may become habituated, under the influence of strong extravert type-conditions, to a kind of offense that provokes, and strengthens, compulsiveness. But these are exceptional cases; for, the very pathogenic process which leads one individual to compulsive delinquency and another one to guilt offenses is the result not only of experience but also of structural factors, one being the prevalence of certain type-conditioned tendencies.)

And finally, again a few words about the substitutive delinquency which we have compared above (see p. 28) with compulsive delinquency. There we have said that in the first case, like in that of guilt-offenses, the pathology is rooted in the oedipal phase, and, in both cases, systematization of offenses and guilt-reactions after the act are infrequent, all in contrast to compulsive delinquency. On the other hand, substitutive delinquency differs from the two other forms which we have discussed here : ego participation is stronger, not as in the two other forms weaker, than conscious directedness towards the act, the environment has more important functions of determination, compulsiveness is much less pronounced in substitutive than in the two other forms of delinquency. One could therefore define the former as an independent unit, unless we would prefer including it with guilt- or with compulsive offenses in one larger unit. We tend to accept the first answer.

(c) *The passive (drifting) offender*

It is difficult adequately to classify the different forms of delinquency as they appear in psychopaths or in the mentally retarded before having analyzed in detail the essence of both, psychopathy and retardation. We have done so in the third chapter of the present volume as well as in another study (36). There, our analysis refers to the clinical pictures in their generality, that is, to their essential elements as expressed in the social, the emotional and the cognitive behavior of the psychopath or the mentally retarded, and not specifically to their delinquency; on the contrary : we see there that many of them are in no way delinquents, irrespective of whether they behave in a socially acceptable way or not.

In other words : when we deal with the classification of delinquencies, we refer to one aspect only of psychopathy or of mental retardation, to that of their pathological impact on the social behavior only. Our analysis will show us that the three forms of abnormal behavior relevant to our discussion are : the aggressive, the paranoid and the passive varieties. In both, psychopathy and mental retardation, we find representatives of these three forms of deviant behavior. The question requiring answer and decision within a discussion of the problem of classifying delinquencies is, whether the contrast between asocial and antisocial behavior provides us with an additional or even a decisive criterion? Let us quote from another source (34, pp. 143 f.) :

"The *asocial* individual does not participate objectively, through polar relationships, in social tasks that require ego-transcendence, either because he is *able to live without* the non-ego, or because he is *unable to live with* the non-ego. The *antisocial* individual needs the non-ego, though for destructive purposes only, either to prove to himself and to his environment that he is independent or in order to take revenge.

"The asocial, as a rule, does not hurt others intentionally, although he may do so inadvertently. Here we find waywardness in children and in adults, who as vagabonds, drunkards, happy-go-lucky solipsists enjoy their existence; here we find extreme introverts living outside or beyond reality; here we find egocentrics withdrawn from social contexts, display-ing antisocial, yet not primarily aggressive behavioral manifestations.

"While all these patterns indicate ability to live without the non-ego, escape from the world out of fear of its threatening superiority, neurotic immaturity and infantility, or other forms of neurotic reality distortion and the ensuing acts of unlawfulness, indicate *in*ability to live *with* the non-ego, to establish and maintain dialogic relationships with the en-vironment and the unconscious. Here belong those representatives of waywardness and delinquency whose life is a continuous quest for a long-lost paradise of completeness, of maternal unity (and we should be careful not to diagnose them too quickly—as psychoanalyists tend to do —as cases of reaction formation and early repressed aggressiveness).

"But none of these forms of deviant and delinquent behavior should be classified as expression of *antisociality*. The difference between asociality and antisociality can be defined as one between two modalities of differentiation between the ego and the non-ego; it is inadequate in the first case, while it is normal but frightening in the second. Hence the passiveness, the indolence and the avoidance tendencies in the asocial individual; the intentionality, the hatred and the ego emphasis in the antisocial individual."

When we now return to our discussion of the various forms of delinquency in psychopaths and in the mentally retarded, we must pose the following question: Should we distinguish between asocial and antisocial behavior and base on this distinction a definition of separate clinical units? Or are the characteristics common to all varieties of psychopathy, on the one hand, and the characteristics common to all varieties of mental retardation, on the other hand, more essential than the differential characteristics of asociality and antisociality?

In our study of *Impaired Intelligence* (36) we have suggested that a distinction should be made between four types of retarded individuals: the apathetic, the submissive, the paranoid and the aggressive. To the extent that mentally retarded individuals of one of the two first men-tioned types develop delinquent behaviors, they will show signs of lack of structure and definable "style", of automatic reactions to accidental and changing stimulations. It is reasonable to presume that, in these cases, asocial symptoms will be more frequent than expressions of antisociality; even where isolated acts of seeming aggressiveness appear, they will lack intentionality and will therefore fail to indicate truly antisocial tendencies.

In psychopathic individuals, too, passive forms of delinquency are not infrequent. We have in mind the oscillating type who reacts to the most contradictory stimuli, as if he could incorporate in this way the infinity of existence; the drifting psychopath, that is, the vagabond, the addict, the sex pervert; the unstable psychopath who "mirrors" the behavior of people in his environment. The manifestations of delinquency in these passive psychopaths resemble those that appear in the apathetic or the submissive types of the mentally retarded, although what distinguishes between them is ego-inflation : even in the passive forms of psychopathy we find ego-inflation, in contrast to the ego-nullity of the retarded. Obviously, this contrast gives a special color to each of the delinquent manifestations in both, the psychopath and the retarded, particularly when we consider the degree of directedness towards the act : it is much higher even in the passive forms of psychopathy than in any form of mental retardation.

But in spite of this difference it would seem justified to speak of one behavioral unit, *that of the different forms of passive gliding into asocial behavior*, with their low degree of ego-participation. Of all other forms of delinquency only that of primary waywardness can be compared with this passive delinquency. But even among them do we find essential differences, especially when we compare with each other their young representatives : the wayward child is characterized by the *polymorphous nature* of his asocial behavior symptoms, the naive *enjoyment* of his street life, the *reactive* character of his actions and feelings, *avoidance* of all objective tasks of learning and of working. All these qualities indicate a certain measure of vitality, which *cannot* be felt in the passive delinquent, neither in the retarded nor in the psychopath. Instead of the polymorphous nature of offences we find *contrariness and lack of consistency* in the actions of the passively drifting delinquent, instead of reactivity —*automatism*, instead of naive enjoyment—*malcontent*, instead of avoidance—*non-perception* of social contexts and functions. It is therefore justified to distinguish between waywardness and passive drifting into delinquency, at least when we compare with each other their *young* representatives.

(d) Young and adult delinquents

The next question refers to the *aggressive forms of delinquency* in the psychopath and in the mentally retarded : should we consider them one separate comprehensive unit, or are the essentials of psychopathy and those of mental retardation different from each other to such an extent that the common trait, aggressiveness, is insufficient to constitute one group?

But before trying to answer this question, we must discuss in brief the limits of classification. It has been mentioned (see p. 17) that each of the criteria so far used has a different meaning when we deal with socially adequate and when we deal with delinquent behavior. Here we add: Is "delinquency" one and the same phenomenon irrespective of whether we speak of juvenile delinquency or of adult criminality? What is between waywardness in a child and waywardness in an adult? Do all wayward adults belong to the before mentioned group of passive (drifting) delinquents, or do they belong to different groups of waywardness? What about oedipal PBD and primary aggressiveness? Do they exist in childhood only or in adults as well, though perhaps under other names? Can we speak at all of psychopathy or perversion in childhood? Are they not typical of adults only? Do the compulsive and the guilt-offender appear in every phase of human development or in childhood and adolescence only? It is evident only from posing these questions that the answers cannot be the same to all.

Elsewhere (26, 34) we have discussed the difference between waywardness in children and in adults. In adults, we have said there, the polymorphous nature of symptom manifestations is absent, there is much more "specialization" in one type of asocial behavior; naive enjoyment of waywardness is less evident in adults, their behavior is *not* the result of an uninterrupted chain of conditionings through poverty and educational neglect from the beginning of life on, but is often enough caused by an experience of disappointment in a fairly late stage of development and by an ensuing regression. Let us add here that reactivity either is not one of the characteristics of the wayward adult: he is much more "dulled" in this respect, and his avoidance of social functions and contexts, too, is much more "dulled" than that of wayward children, less accentuated, less vital.

It would therefore seem that adult waywardness is essentially different from waywardness in children and that the former is almost identical with the unit we shall describe, in the fourth chapter, as "passive drifting into asocial behavior". Here, however, new causal connections become evident: not only the passive varieties of psychopathy and of mental retardation but also neurotic or quasi-neurotic reactions to later experiences of severe disappointment may account for the emergence of the life-style which so much resembles that of the wayward.* Moreover, the many cases should be mentioned in which the early pathology persists into the period of adolescence and later, though with changed symptoms. True enough, structural passiveness is a common element in all these causal connections, and it explains the "choice of the pathology" and its

---

* In this context we wish to mention those cases only in which conscious or unconscious quest of the unknown mother produces vagabondage or alcoholism.

result, adult waywardness; but this behavioral pattern may be the result of the most diverse causal factors. This is one of the outstanding differences between the life-periods : *whereas in childhood and adolescence, that is, before the processes of structurization reach their relative end, each behavioral unit is specifically connected with its essential causes, this connection grows weaker with advancing age, when the crystallized behavior itself becomes a causal determinant of the continuing development.*

Thus, primary aggressiveness merges, as it were, with oedipal PBD—two separate units in childhood, each with its specific causal constellation —and a new behavioral unit comes into existence, *delinquency out of hatred.* It may well be that a more deep reaching analysis of individual cases will reveal certain differences in the aggressive, destructive behavior of adult criminals, according to the period in which their aggressiveness started in early childhood, or according to the degree of generality of their aggressiveness as against their specific hatred of parents and other "near" figures. But these differences no longer prevent us from speaking of one single unit of classification, that of delinquency out of hatred and negation of society.

On another plane we find delinquency out of unconscious guilt feelings and substitutive delinquency; not only have they representatives in all phases of development, in children or adolescents as well as in adults; there are no major differences between the essential characteristics of these delinquencies in childhood and in adulthood. These are indeed unambiguous clinical units. (Though we should add that substitutive offenses occur much more frequently in children than in adults whose stronger developed tendency towards systematization helps them become more compulsive).

Perversions and compulsive delinquency are rarely if ever found in childhood and only exceptionally in adolescence. To the extent that we do encounter, in children, signs of perversions or of compulsive delinquency, they are epiphenomena of autotropic disorders rather than indicators of an unambiguously allotropic behavior disorder.

(e) Aggressive delinquency in the psychopath and in the mentally retarded

Here we return to the question from which we started at the beginning of the preceding paragraph : have we the right to comprise in one clinical unit the forms of aggressive delinquency as they appear in the psychopath and in the mentally retarded? Is what we have said about the passive forms valid for the aggressive forms as well?

In the third chapter we shall see that egocentricity, extreme brutality, the tendency to explode, as it were, in destructive acts, and even the paranoid variety of psychopathy receive their specific significance through those characteristics of the disorder that we shall define as ego-inflation, absence of anxiety and extreme predominance of expansion over staticness. (When the latter characteristics are absent, the former negative qualities have an altogether different clinical meaning; we find them in other pathologies such as psychoses, brain-injuries, etc.) In the psychopath, the objects of aggressiveness are not objects of personal relationships, do not exist but for the purpose of incorporation, even in the paranoid variety in which stands out a negative and hostile world conception. It is doubtful whether we can call aggressiveness at all a psychopathic mode of behavior (even if his world is aggressive); for, true aggressiveness, as we have tried to show elsewhere (29), is characterized by an existential intention to eliminate from reality factors of threat and danger (but not only by an intention to take revenge).

From this point of view there exists no doubt a similarity between the aggressive psychopath and the aggressive mentally retarded : in both cases, aggressiveness is non-directed, lack of personal relationship is outstanding. And we add again : also in the paranoid form, in which attack and injury come in reaction to the "bad intentions" of a hostile world rather than in self-defense. Self-defense is characteristic of aggressiveness in PBD (where it has an anticipatory character) or in primary aggressiveness (where it serves as a tool to master the world).

Needless to add that in spite of this basic similarity there exists also a very important difference between aggressiveness in the psychopath and aggressiveness in the mentally retarded. In the former's offenses ego-inflation stands out, in the latter's—the automatic and quasi-mechanical nature of reactions. In addition, in the retarded, both the aggressive and the paranoid delinquencies are continuous, from the beginning of life on right through to the age of adulthood. In this respect, he differs from the psychopath in whom the patterns of behavior crystallize fairly late, in fact only after the end of adolescence. (This is one of the reasons why it is so difficult to diagnose a child as a "psychopath" : the clinical picture hides itself, as it were, behind other pictures until much later, when the true characteristics come to the fore.)

But the difference between the ego-inflation and automatism of reactions is essential only when we deal with *general* clinical differentiations, *not* when we classify the varieties of aggressive delinquency. For the purposes of classification, the contrast between the *expansive and the paranoid forms of aggressive delinquency is more important*, and each of the two appears in both, the psychopath and the mentally retarded.

The terms "expansive" and "paranoid" aggressiveness come to designate type-differences (extravert and introvert tendencies) in delinquency : when man lives primarily in relation to the world that surrounds him, that is, to his environment as to a world of objects, delinquency, to the extent that he will fall victim to it under the influence of this or that causal factor, will expand (enlarge) the boundaries of his ego. This aggressive expansion means : denial of the limitations which the non-ego, the attacked human and social environment, imposes on him, means : negation of the non-ego as subject. This is what we propose to call "expansive aggressiveness", whether its roots are in psychopathic ego-inflation or in reactive automatism of the feeble-minded type.

Paranoid aggressiveness, on the other hand, is characteristic of the introvert type of delinquency : when man lives primarily in relation to himself, that is to his ego as object only, delinquency, to the extent that he will fall victim to it, under the influence of this or that causal factor, will be his reaction to the world's bad intentions. His aggressive reactions, which are almost automatic, come to give expression to his existence as an object only, to his denial of himself as a subject.

It may be argued that this attitude can no longer be called "paranoid" : a person who reacts aggressively to his feeling of being attacked or persecuted, so it may be argued, considers himself capable of eliminating, through his counterattacks, all that threatens him and endangers his existence; in other words : he does see himself as a subject and not as an object only. But here we should remember that we do not use the term "paranoiac" but "paranoid"; it is precisely in the absence of the last-mentioned element (the ability to eliminate sources of threat and danger) that we see the essential difference between the paranoiac and the paranoid. The latter's aggressiveness is not purpose-directed (attack to eliminate the attacker) but solely reactive (real attacks in reaction to imagined attacks without any intention to eliminate a source of danger or threat). The paranoiac sees himself simultaneously as subject and as object, the paranoid, and particularly the aggressive paranoid, sees himself as object only and the non-ego as subject only.

If this is so, another argument may be proffered : that paranoid psychopathy is a *contradictio in adjecto* : how can psychopathic ego-inflation appear together with paranoid self perception as object only? But it is precisely through committing the aggressive offense that these two seemingly contradictory elements are being brought together. Let us not lose sight of the fact that we speak here of reactive offenses whose very execution produces and strengthens in the offender an illusion of egoity, and that this illusion in an individual without ego and without subject feelings is a sign of ego-inflation.

In the mentally retarded of the paranoid variety, this illusion of egoity is even more in evidence, and his aggressive offenses are still more reactive and purposeless.

The two forms, the expansive and the paranoid variety of aggressive delinquency, are contrasted by primary aggressiveness (the so-called pre-oedipal type of PBD). The *expansively aggressive psychopath* destroys the world around whenever the latter for some reason "annoys" him, and the *expansively aggressive retarded* destroys and attacks anything in automatic reaction to external stimuli; whatever they may be. But in both, aggressiveness is *not* a means to master the environment, as it is characteristic of primary aggressiveness. The *paranoid psychopath* as well as the *paranoid retarded* react to the world's presumed badness with destruction and aggressive offenses, and both inflate themselves through the very acts of committing their offenses. But we *cannot* connect their aggressive offenses with conscious or unconscious intentionality (as expressed in attempts to master the world, to defend themselves, to anticipate aggressiveness, to provoke aggressive reactions on the part of the environment, etc.).

Thus, it follows that we can combine in one clinical unit, that of "expansive aggressiveness", the psychopathic and the retarded varieties, and in a second unit, that of "paranoid aggressiveness", these same two varieties. And let us emphasize again what we have said already before : that there is nothing in the here suggested concepts ("expansive" and "paranoid" aggressiveness) to dilute the essential differences between mental retardation and psychopathy (which appears in all degrees of mental development). It is only within the framework of classifying asocial and antisocial varieties of delinquent behavior (the subject of our present analysis) that the essential differences between psychopathy and mental retardation are less decisive than the specific, type-conditioned, character of delinquency.

(On a higher level of abstraction we may define the two units as sub-units of *unintentional aggressiveness* as against the two forms of *intentional aggressiveness* which are: primary aggressiveness and oedipal PBD).

5. SUMMARY

Let us now summarize what we have said so far :

In children and adolescents we find *three varieties of asocial behavior* : (1) primary waywardness; (2) passive drifting into asocial habits, especially in the mentally retarded; (3) impulsive delinquency mainly in the brain-injured. We find *antisocial behavior in the following forms* : (4)

delinquency out of unconscious guilt feelings; (5) substitutive-symbolic delinquency; (6) PBD of the oedipal type; (7) primary aggressiveness; (8) expansive aggressiveness; (9) paranoid aggressiveness; (10) psychopathoid delinquency in adolescents (which we have so far mentioned in passing only).

In adults we find some of the same varieties, though in a more complex form : 1. *Waywardness* tends to merge with passive drifting, and not only certain types of the mentally retarded but also passive psychopaths constitute the population of this group of asocial behavior (in addition to those who become asocial by way of reacting to later traumatization). 2. In a second group of adult delinquent we find the *"organic cases"* who display both asocial and antisocial behavior, and epileptics or alcoholics are among their representatives (see later, pp. 137 ff. and pp. 160 ff.). 3. In a third group we find *guilt offenders and compulsive delinquents,* such as kleptomaniacs or pyromaniacs who are almost absent in childhood and adolescence. 4. A fourth group contains the *perverts* with their compulsive behavior. 5. The place of the remaining six childhood groups is taken by that of the *aggressive criminals* who try to prove to themselves and to their environment that they are independent and that they are capable of domineering everyone who wants to limit them or of taking revenge on them. It is with regard to this last group that a new attempt at classification should be made—of course after excluding the four preceding groups.

CHAPTER TWO

Waywardness

A. DEFINITIONS

1. INTRODUCTION

DEFINING, DESCRIBING AND interpreting are three essentially different operations, both noetically and methodologically. And yet, they are practically inseparable from each other, whenever their object is a social or a mental phenomenon. To *define* it means: to formulate concepts capable of delineating it against other similar phenomena. This requires intimate knowledge of its constituent elements and their constant confrontation with those of other phenomena. Theoretically, then, definition precedes description; practically, it *depends* on the latter; we cannot possibly define a phenomenon without keeping in mind its factual components. Their later explicit description is but a repetition of its implied antecedent. But without the limiting and delineatory activity of defining, let us say, a behavioral unit, its later description would run the risk of being inexact and inadequate. Theoretically, a definition is valid only to the extent that it is free of all elements of explanation. Practically, its precision and usefulness depend on the number of (causal or finalistic) elements of interpretation it contains. True again: these interpretational elements are implicit only, until they come to the fore in the "theory" based on definitions. Theoretically, but theoretically only, describing and interpreting are two distinctly different operations. But practically it will be impossible to find one single description of a social or a mental phenomenon in which the selection of details has not been determined by an underlying theory. This is equally true for psychoanalysts, metaphysicists or structural psychologists. Some may pride themselves in explaining the described facts genetically, others will prefer linking them with hypothetical entities, but no one will ever describe his observable facts in "theory-free" terms.

2. FIRST DEFINITION (also a comparison with criminal behavior)

This short preamble is certainly justified when we speak of a behavioral entity as ambiguous as that of "Waywardness in Children". English and American authors do not like the term. They prefer the more general concept of "juvenile delinquency" (as against adult criminality). They have written innumerable essays and textbooks on the subject, in which causes have been analyzed, varieties classified, behavior patterns described. But nowhere do we find waywardness as a separate clinical unit. Cyril Burt, f.i., one of the most comprehensive of these authors, tends to include the manifestations of what we here propose to define as "waywardness" among the symptoms of "juvenile delinquency" (13). Even its legal definition comprises these manifestations (11). Only in the classification of adult offenders do we sometimes find the wayward as a separate sub-group, though even this division does not lead to a more differentiated terminology (1). Neither does the French language use a special term for what is sometimes called "petite criminauté"; quite inadequately, so we must add, since the difference between waywardness and criminality is, as we shall try to show, not one of degree (quantity), but one of essence. And terms like the Russian "besprizorny" or the English "neglected" designate one of the socio-educational causes of the phenomenon rather than the phenomenon itself.

What we have in mind is an *attitude*, not a series of offenses, which is but one of the manifestations of this attitude. The simultaneous appearance of many, often self-contradictory, symptoms is the first characteristic of the form of asocial behavior which we call waywardness in children. We have already mentioned (see p. 33) that not only the criminal but also the wayward adult essentially differs from the wayward child insofar as he, the adult, specializes, as it were, in a certain type of asocial or antisocial behavior. *The polymorphous nature of wayward behavior in children*, delinquent or otherwise (see later, pp. 69 ff.), is contrasted by the relative frequency of one type of offenses in adult criminals.*

Every society endeavors to produce in its members certain inter-dependent attitudes that are compatible with each other. A traditional society will, of course, be more successful in these endeavors than a society passing from one cultural system to another, or a society which has to cope with the problems of mass-immigration. Law and education are the primary instruments through which common attitudes are being produced and reinforced, the first through limiting man's freedom, the

---

* "To a certain extent, each offender selects his own type of offence," says D. Abramson (1, p. 22). This statement is not contradicted by the fact that many criminals have committed one crime only in their whole lifetime, though as a rule for external reasons only.

second through making him free within these limits. Both aim at subordinating man to trans-individual values whose servant he shall become, in his personal relationships, in his work, in his thinking, in his evaluations. Hence, the ethical value of objectivity, of genuineness, of responsibility, of empathy.

Such a norm of social behavior not only is not contradicted by the demands for self-recognition and self-realization, but in fact depends on it. Normative behavior is made impossible when man is too much determined by the forces of his unconscious which may then interfere with his behavior in the forms of affects, complexes, resentments, immaturity, egotism, etc. Deviant behavior may be the result of such determination by the unconscious, the inner non-ego (34). More: the very incompleteness of norm-realization in average man's behavior, his very lack of self-awareness, his very dependence on unconscious determinants come to prove the need for self-recognition and self-realization.

Totalitarian societies may subsume under the concept of asocial behavior such attitudes as individualistic self-isolation or egotistic neglect of the group's welfare, even when the laws are kept and no direct damage is caused to the environment. Non-totalitarian societies, however, do not know of such all-inclusive and unambiguous definitions of social versus asocial behavior. They are much more indifferent and accept even the most aggressive individualists as representatives of social value. They distinguish between social and normative conduct, expect and require a minimum only of service and obedience. This minimum can be recognized from written laws as well as from unwritten customs. On the other hand, they accept deviations from their average requirements as ethically valuable, as long as such deviations are consonant with the norms of ego-transcendence. They may misjudge reformers, revolutionaries, discoverers of new truths when those violate society's boundaries of tradition; they may even eliminate them as foreign bodies or as sources of threat. But such reformers or fighters for new values in the non-totalitarian societies will never be included among representatives of asocial behavior. And yet, it would be wrong to regard this as proof of permissiveness or generosity; on the contrary: the exclusion of ego-transcending "delinquents" from the realm of asociality only comes to prove the narrowness of the latter concept; it only relates to those forms of behavior that are characterized by non-fulfilment of society's minimal requirements for an "orderly" life.

Asociality, then, appears where man in his actions and reactions does not feel himself bound to, guided or restricted by, the inner agent of moral direction, that we call "conscience", "superego" or "inner authority", or by the agents of external societal restriction. For an understanding of the varieties of asocial behavior, of which waywardness is one, and perhaps the most important, representative, this double independence is of primary importance; it is an expression of what we shall have to describe as "lack of structure" in the behavior of the asocial individual.

The criminal, at least the "ordinary" (not the compulsive or the otherwise abnormal) criminal, identifies himself with his actions (3). His ego, far from being delivered to the mercy of—unconsciously rooted and uncontrollable—impulses, lives in harmony with a consciously rooted and controlled principle of organization. *There is no such principle of organization in the ego of the wayward child, it is as weak and as undifferentiated as is his conscience.* The wayward, and particularly *the wayward child, does not repress his impulses* but lives with them without conflict. In this respect he resembles, and at the same time differs from, the "ordinary" criminal who does not repress either, but shows much more conscious identification with his attitudes and actions. The criminal is, therefore, much more than the wayward, capable of delaying or even of giving up, at least temporarily, certain satisfactions. He does not resemble a child as does the wayward, in more than one respect.

And yet, *the wayward is not a child either*: *he knows well of the existence of social norms,* even recognizes them as legitimate, and recites well their implicit and explicit tenets. He may be too weak in the synthetic functions of his ego, too little differentiated in his power adequately to distinguish between the elements of truly polar relationships. He may not be able to recognize the objective significance of social demands or even to accept them as realities which mean and imply certain definite and defineable obligations, whether actual or potential. But unlike in a normally developing child, the wayward's inability to live "with" the social non-ego (see pp. 30 ff.)* does not operate as a challenge (to change, to develop, to become a being capable of social intercourse). Even his anticipatory plays do not serve growth or change but are reinforcers only of asociality.

His is a world of things material rather than of humans or of ideas. In this respect, too, he differs from the criminal whose planned actions would not be possible in such a world of "things", of external happenings and reactions. The criminal endeavors to remain within the fold of that very society whose laws he violates consciously. The wayward neither

---

* There we spoke of the inability to live with the social non-ego or the ability to live *without* it. The latter ability, however, requires more systematization than a child as such would ever be capable of. It is a characteristic of wayward *adults* rather than of children.

belongs to that society of humans nor does he feel a need to belong to it. His offenses, on the other hand, are not the most important expressions of his "life without a social non-ego", but are epiphenomena only of his waywardness, which has more, and indeed more essential, symptoms, as we shall try to show later.

In the chapter on classification we have included among the criteria of differentiating between the varieties of delinquent behavior such factors as "ego-participation" and "conscious directedness toward the act". We have added (on p. 18) that both are equally weak in waywardness. *The unplanned, reactive, unstructured character of its symptoms* is only another expression of this very ego-weakness; there is no "specialization" in the wayward child's behavior, as we find it in the criminal; its asocial manifestations are as polymorphous as are their eliciting chance stimuli. This would seem to be a more adequate formulation of the most essential characteristic of waywardness, than if we would hold "heterogeneity of impulses" responsible for those polymorphous reactions. In other words: we suggest that in an analysis of waywardness there is no room for concepts of intrapsychic factors such as "impulse" or "conflict" or "inner tension". In their stead only concepts designating automatically reactive processes should be used.

Waywardness is a variety of asocial behavior as it emerges under conditions of externalization (33, 35). We propose to come back to analyzing this concept later (pp. 55 ff.). There we shall ask how a child is being conditioned into a certain pattern of asocial behavior by a specific configuration of structural and environmental factors. Suffice it here to point out, once again, a basic difference between the wayward and the criminal: Waywardness, as a rule, *results from a continuous process of being conditioned* (in children from birth on); criminal behavior as a rule results from an interaction between intrapsychic deficiencies and environmental handicaps (starting usually at a certain well circumscribed moment in life). Waywardness is not a final but rather a transitory result of conditioning; criminality is much more the end-result of a certain causal development.

3. WAYWARDNESS AND MENTAL RETARDATION

Two concepts used so far in our attempt to define waywardness require clarification and qualification: lack of structure and reactivity. Both may be said to be equally characteristic of mental retardation, in its congenital as well as in its secondary, environmental varieties. And yet, waywardness and mental retardation are far from being identical units of behavior.

True enough : each one may be one of the causes of the other (which makes a comparison still more difficult). But we find many mentally retarded individuals, particularly of the submissive or the apathetic types (36), who can easily be drilled into some form of social adequacy and will never glide into waywardness; we find many retarded, particularly of the aggressive or the paranoid types (36), whom we shall encounter in other sub-groups of delinquency (see our later remarks on the so-called expansive and paranoid forms of aggressiveness, pp. 176 ff.), but again not among the wayward. And even those mentally retarded individuals whom we do find among the wayward, differ from both, the intellectually normal wayward and the non-wayward retarded.

How are these differences recognized? When an intellectually normal wayward child reacts to a variety of changing stimuli he will do so consciously and will enjoy his doings, his deeds and misdeeds, at least as long as society leaves him at peace. He will undoubtedly not be guided by the selective forces of a well integrated self. But it is he who acts or reacts, and it is he who enjoys his actions or reactions. Not so the mentally retarded, when his intellectual insufficiency accounts for waywardness : he is not aware of his stand outside society or of the illegitimacy of his actions; on the contrary, he lives out his impulses as if they were part of the social system in which he is embedded. It is his mental insufficiency that prevents differentiation between ego and non-ego, between his needs and social norms.

This is the essence of what we might call the feebleminded variety of lack of structure. If being structured means, as we have said elsewhere (34), being "organized" according to the principles of mutual relatedness between parts of a whole, both to each other and to that whole, then, obviously, the feebleminded is unstructured. But on the other hand, the wayward child's actions in their non-selective reactivity are unstructured as well, as we have said above (p. 42). They, too, lack whole-relatedness insofar as they are not *directed* by a center of synthesis, the ego. They are, however, *related* to that ego, at least after their reactive emergence, in each case separately and always anew. In this respect, the wayward's lack of structure differs from that of the mentally retarded : whereas the former's offenses, as well as all other expressions of his behavior, are *reactions* to environmental chance stimuli, the latter's behavior is more adequately described as a *result* of these stimuli.

Between the non-delinquent and the delinquent retarded another essential difference can be found : the latter shows considerably more unrest, excitability, hypermotility, than the former. This may be the result of certain physiological factors which we tend to translate into the language of typology : there exists undoubtedly a close correlation between submissiveness or apathy and a relatively low degree of excitability and unrest, on the one hand, and between aggressive or paranoid tendencies and strong excitability, on the other. But all four types can be found in different classes of delinquents, among them also the wayward. The more excitable and aggressive types will, of course, display an emphasis on other symptoms than the more indolent or the more submissive types, and each will glide into waywardness on different paths; but the chance groups of wayward children are heterogeneous enough in their composition to permit entrance to many types, through many alleys, in many functions.

Paradoxically, it is lack of structure that explains the different outcome of development in the cases of a mentally normal and a mentally retarded wayward child : the former, as we have mentioned above (p. 33), may become a socially well functioning adult, with or without the help of educational interventions, in which case we speak of "delayed maturation" (42); he may also glide into a "criminal career", mainly under the influence of antisocial individuals or groups that may have gained control over him at a critical stage of his development; or he may remain wayward until he reaches adulthood and adopts the patterns of adult waywardness, which as a rule show different causes and different symptoms than waywardness in children (pp. 33 f. and pp. 150 ff.). It is his typical lack of structure that accounts for the *unpredictability of his development and its outcome*. The mentally retarded, on the other hand, will remain "faithful" to the patterns of his social inadequacy as they are determined, primarily, by his type-conditions.

In the first chapter (on classification) we maintained that the various forms of passive drifting into asocial behavior in the mentally retarded, on the one hand, and in the psychopath, on the other, have so much in common that it would seem justified to combine them into one clinical unit of asociality. Waywardness, we added (p. 32), differs from that unit, particularly when we speak of children and juveniles : the polymorphous nature of symptoms in the behavior of the wayward, his ability naively to enjoy his street life, the reactivity of his actions and reactions, and his avoidance of all objective social contexts indicate a certain *vitality*, in contrast to the passively "drifting" retarded or psychopath. The clinical unit of passive drifting, we concluded, is characterized by the contradictory and the automatic nature of actions, by the individual's malcontent and nonperception of social contexts—all indicating *lack* of vitality.

But let us emphasize once more what we have mentioned at the beginning of this paragraph (p. 44): that mental retardation and way-wardness are at the same time causes *and* results of each other. This complex question does not interest us in the present context for the bearing it has on the etiology of waywardness but only as an additional indicator of certain essential elements of definition. Mental retardation is difficult to assess in wayward children, not only because they are *per se* discriminated against in any test examination,* but also because their patterns of behavior are liable to injure their native abilities. Poverty breeds both waywardness and mental retardation; both reinforce each other, because they prevent value orientation in any task situation that transcends immediacy; ego-weakness accounts in both cases for what might be called an inductive spread of symptoms, one producing another, instead of each being produced by a central cause. Where this symptom is absent we should not diagnose waywardness.

Another characteristic may be formulated as the result of our com-parisons: Externality of hero-figures, of values, of norms, and their subsequent easy exchangeability which exclude autonomy, are again common qualities of the wayward and the mentally retarded; they make them into ineffective individuals, doomed to continued failure, dependent on, even addicted to, unstructured behavior, which provides them with many illusions of ego-strength. However, the wayward child *remains aware of the discrepancy between his "universe of excitements and satisfactions" and the surrounding norms of behavior*, although the latter constitutes for him an ego-alien reality. The mentally retarded, on the other hand, and particularly the asocially drifting feebleminded, identifies his universe of ever-changing and unstructured happenings, including his own actions and reactions, with reality *in toto*. There is no awareness of discrepancy between "his" and "their" reality in his mind.

4.   WAYWARDNESS AND NEUROTIC DISORDERS

The unending discussions of the conceptual relationship between these two units suffer from a threefold semantic inaccuracy: no differentiation is made between asocial and antisocial behavior, between neurosis and neurotic delinquency, between the various forms of the latter. Our purpose here is limited: we intend to compare the essential characteristics of one form of asocial (not of anti-social) behavior, that of waywardness in children and juveniles, with those of non-delinquent neuroses of the

---

* Their scholastic weakness and the unreality of the test situation both account for many of their failures.

phobic, hysteric and compulsive types, on the one hand, and with those of the three forms of neurotic delinquency, on the other. We intend, thus, to clarify the essentials of waywardness by a confrontation with two abstractions, one being that of neurosis, the other being that of neurotic delinquency. But we are aware of the fact that these are abstractions only, since in reality the sub-groups of both, neurosis and neurotic delinquency, represent separate clinical entities (reference is made to the first chapter, on classification).

The first abstraction, that of "neurosis", is facilitated by the fact that all its varieties have indeed certain causal and symptomatic traits in common : phobic substitutions, hysteric conversions, compulsive system-formations, all have in common rigidly defensive tendencies against over-strong pre-oedipal or oedipal affects directed towards and/or against the parents or their substitutes. Development of neurotic reactions and symptoms presupposes overstrong dependence on the primary objects of relationship and failure to separate the ego from the human non-ego in order to build up an independent subject system. When psychoanalysts speak of excessive love-needs and basic insecurity (for, how could excessive love-needs ever be satisfied?) they mean the same : inability adequately to evaluate the relative significance and determining power of both, the parental subject-position and the own object-position.

But overdependence and insecurity must not necessarily produce *neurotic* reactions to relational inability in the pre-oedipal or oedipal phases of development (thereby reinforcing insecurity and overdependence). Behavior disorders, not only of the "primary" but also of the neurotic delinquency type, may be the outcome of the same reaction-patterns : there must be, it is true, more moral awareness of the norms of relationships (of their ideal type), and there must be at least as much guilt as aggressiveness to produce neurotic delinquency. The neurotic, we have said elsewhere (33, 34), is uncertain of the love of others, the neurotic delinquent is certain of his own badness and unworthiness. This certainty, in turn, reflects some kind of ego-transcending identification with values.

If so, waywardness *is almost the opposite of neurotic delinquency* in its various forms (see the detailed comparison in 33, pp. 122 ff.). It should be clear, by now, that we do not use the concepts as Aichhorn did in his famous study (2) on what he called waywardness (Verwahrlosung) and what in fact is delinquency of the generalized hate type (PBD) or of the neurotic guilt type. But when he claims that the neurotic differs from the wayward insofar as the latter enjoys his style of life while the former suffers from his fears, his somatic disorder, his compulsions, it is obvious that he has in mind neither hate- nor guilt-offenders. For neither the one nor the other enjoys his delinquent acts, both suffer no less than the non-delinquent neurotic, though for different reasons. Non-suffering, or even enjoyment, is characteristic of that type of asocial behavior only which we here call waywardness and whose symptom-manifestations we shall describe later (a clinical unit which Aichhorn did *not* describe at all).

What characterizes waywardness in contradistinction of neuroses, is *absence of repression, of inner conflicts, of inner tensions, of anxiety.* It is, as we shall see in the paragraphs dealing with the etiology of waywardness (see pp. 52 ff.), an expression of externalization, in our case, of growing up under conditions of want and neglect. Hence, we object to all attempts to equate symptoms of neuroses with those of asocial and antisocial behavior, as found in psychoanalytically oriented studies, particularly of earlier years (e.g. 89, 92). (It is noteworthy that most of these simplifying statements are preceded by such pioneering psycho-analysts as Alexander (4) or Reich (84) who clearly recognized the essential differences between the individual's development towards neurotic and towards asocial behavior.)

From the history of individual neuroses we learn that early repressions of feelings, of impulses, of attachments may help form such a child's conception of what is permitted and what forbidden, more than the natural processuality of introjections which normally determine the development of our moral concepts. The intensity and the time of these repressions depend on structural predispositions as well as on parental attitudes. Neurotic developments are then unavoidable. Their most essential characteristic is the exaggerated, forcible, unnatural and artificial nature of later introjections, introjections that then no longer relate to objective reality images but to their unreal, pre-repression representatives within. In other words: the neurotic *does* introject his parental images but affectively and unrealistically, at the expense, as it were, of inner freedom. The neurotic will not be able adequately to interpret what his conscience allows him or forbids him to accept; his interpretation will always be determined through the uncontrollable interventions of his unconscious, his post-repression universe of concepts, of fears and of expectations. His ego lacks autonomy, realism, synthesis, cannot orient itself in the many contradictions between his mostly unconscious impulses and feelings, his distorted and distorting conscience and his incomprehensible, defensively constructed reality.

The *wayward*, on the other hand, grows up almost without repressions. *His love-needs are not excessive*, as are those of the neurotic. His growth conditions are such as to make *personal relationships meaningless*. And instead of introjecting his parental images, he imitates their attitudes. He is not plagued by directives of a conscience which come from his conscious mind and his unconscious. He is able to yield to the most contradictory impulses, for the sake of some immediate satisfaction and without feeling himself impeded or restricted by inner or outer laws. Evidently then, the wayward child is not a neurotic, and no neurotic can be neurotic and wayward at one and the same time.

And yet—we know of not a few neurotic children who, upon reaching the age of adolescence, try to overcome, to "leave" their neurotic involvement, often of long standing, by jumping into asocial (sometimes even into openly delinquent) behavior. It may well be that their ego, perhaps under the influence of peer groups, begins to demand its own demands for recognition and status. Their lack of realistic intercourse with the social non-ego, however, will inevitably produce ego-alien as well as reality-alien symptoms of asocial or antisocial behavior. And when such an adolescent glides into truly wayward patterns of behavior, the latter will often resemble those of adults rather than those of children (unless it may be a transitory phenomenon, an episode only).

It may sound paradoxical to say that, although a neurotic cannot be both neurotic and wayward at one and the same time, a wayward child may show not a few neurotic signs. We do not have in mind here such seemingly neurotic symptoms as enuresis or encopresis or thumb-sucking, which are *not* expressions of regression to libidinally determined points of fixation in the child's early stages of development, but simply residues of infantile behaviour due to faulty training. We rather think of later emerging signs of inner conflicts, reflecting, as a rule, the wayward child's encounter with a transference figure, sometimes an educator, sometimes a love object. The wish to live up to such an educator's or such a love object's expectations may produce inferiority feelings and anxieties which, in turn, may then account for the appearance of neurotic symptoms while the waywardness continues unabated (though no longer as naively as before).

An altogether different question is that of the relationship between waywardness and neurotic delinquency, primarily of the substitutive or the guilt offense (less of the later compulsive or the perversion-) types. And again, we are *not* concerned here with waywardness as a possible *outcome* of neurotic delinquency, that is, as a chance result of gliding into groups of street children and of getting accustomed to their patterns of behavior. We ask how waywardness differs, for instance, from unconscious guilt feelings and punishment needs, and what additional elements of definition we may derive from such comparative analysis.

Psychoanalysts claim, from the days of Freud and Reik on, that unconscious guilt feelings over equally unconscious oedipal strivings may result in committing numerous offenses and that the punishment the offender is liable to receive is what he seeks. Although every phobic displacement, every hysteric conversion, every compulsive self-restriction can also be interpreted as satisfaction of unconscious punishment needs, the difference between purely neurotic symptoms and offenses is an essential one : not only is the guilt offender's awareness of being bad, that negative moral certainty, much more conscious than the ordinary neurotic's uncertainty of being loved and his wish to be good; the very fact that injury must be inflicted on others betrays much more intensive contact-needs than neurotic withdrawal symptoms. Is not this intensity of contact-needs comparable with the wayward's constant contact with environmental realities to which he reacts?

The answer is in the negative. Not only because of the absence of ego-transcending value-identifications as they characterize, we have said (p. 27), the guilt-offender, but also because of the absence of all—conscious or unconscious—intentionality in the behavior patterns of the wayward child. Here, then, we have formulated an additional element in the definition of the behavioral unit called "waywardness": the directly reactive character of the wayward child's contacts with his environment excludes intentionality no less than his ego's primitive (undifferentiated) *"identity" with this environment.*

Comparison with the substitutive (symbolic) offender reveals a similar element : Displacing aggressive tendencies from the near-ones who are really meant to a neutral object proves the intensity of primary relationships; this neurotic offender tends to establish even stronger ties with his "near-ones" than the normal child. The wayward child, on the other hand, excels in the *impersonal character of his relationships* in general and his primary relationships in particular. We shall come back to analyzing this characteristic (which externalization (33, 35) and waywardness have in common).

Needless to add that the wayward shows no signs of compulsiveness. Even the patterns of behavior which he develops and to which he becomes accustomed cannot be interpreted as expressions of compulsiveness, and the relative frequency of "delayed maturation" (42) proves it.

But whatever the form of neurotic delinquency may be, from all differs the wayward in every respect : he does not "specialize"; he prefers chance groups to individual responsibility; his ego is much weaker in his organizational functions (although we may add that he does not need much ego-strength since he is not threatened by unconscious wishes, fears, images); he feels no guilt, neither before nor after committing his offenses; when he attacks, he sees before him the attacked object only (object, not subject); even brutality does not betray any pervert tendency, it is but an external sign of his independence urges; his sexual promiscuity is impersonal; he steals because he needs something immediately, not because he wants to take revenge, or because he must conceal hidden love or punishment needs; he knows not anxiety, though he may fear being caught.

5. WAYWARDNESS AND PSYCHOPATHY

Since the third chapter of this present study will be devoted to an analysis of psychopathy including comparisons with other clinical pictures of asocial and antisocial behaviour, we shall come back to waywardness in that context. Here it will be sufficient to point out (a) that psychopathy is not identical with destructive and delinquent behavior* and (b) that even in the dissocial varieties of psychopathy we must distinguish between actively aggressive, "sociopathic" (78) and asocial, drifting patterns (for details see the third chapter). It is obvious that only the latter lend themselves to a comparison with waywardness.

But here again, a comparative analysis would seem to be premature, for two reasons: psychopathy is rarely if ever clearly recognizable before the end of childhood; a comparison between the two units of asociality (waywardness and psychopathic drifting and instability) should therefore be reserved for our later discussion of *adult* forms of delinquency (see also the fifth chapter of this study); and secondly: we shall try to explain in the chapters devoted to an analysis of psychopathy why it is much easier to show what psychopathy is not than what it is. Very few cases can be diagnosed as unequivocal cases of psychopathy, although ideally its essential elements can be defined.

This will be done in the third chapter. Ego-inflation, absence of anxiety, of guilt, of tension, of contact with the unconscious, of relational abilities, predominance of the life-tendency toward expansion will be shown to be common elements of all forms of psychopathy, the actively destructive as well as the passively drifting or oscillating types. The latter differ from the former not only symptomatically but also structurally. Thus, they show relatively less ego-participation in their directedness

---

* W. James (58) goes so far as to speak of the genius resulting from a "coalescence" between "a superior intellect and a psychopathic temperament".

towards the action; their dependence on their changing environment is more in evidence than in the active, the aggressively "expansive" as well as the paranoid, types of psychopathy.

But without going into the question of the meaning that attaches to their general as well as to their special attitudes and character qualities, we can compare the wayward with the passive types of psychopathy, and not only in adults. Such a comparison is meant to yield additional characteristics that may be included in a definition of waywardness.

The wayward child, far from being ego-inflated, is *undifferentiated* and unable to organize his field of action. His reactivity is sharply contrasted by the psychopath's narcisism. For the latter, the surrounding *reality is an object only*, rather than a stimulus-sending, an eliciting subject. The wayward is *educable*, can be rehabilitated, though he may have to pass through a period of intentionally induced neurosis. The psychopath, in the course of years, may lose some of his ego-inflation, particularly when he is subjected to strict and restricting discipline, and this for a considerable length of time; but he will never become a neurotic; on the contrary : he may gradually develop into a full-fledged psychopath after many years of seeming character neurosis.

The passive psychopath, with his typical instability and drifting life-patterns, though delivered to the mercy of ever-changing impulses, is not identical with the wayward, the main difference being that even the passive types of psychopathy are ego-inflated in the manifestation of their instability, their drifting, their mirroring imitations, their asociality. The wayward, on the other hand, far from being ego-inflated, *lacks all awareness of being an ego.* True enough, it is he who enjoys his doings, and he who reacts; but his experience is free of every sign of identity reflections. He may even build up a series of self-images, under the influence of changing "heroes", but none of these images satisfies him sufficiently to stick to it for any length of time. Hence, we may say that whatever appears to be a sign of ego-emphasis is but a pathetic (more often ridiculous) endeavor on the part of the wayward child to convince himself and others of his strength. It certainly does not prove inflation (cf. also the fourth chapter).

B.   THE CAUSES

6.   INTRODUCTION

Most etiological studies on juvenile delinquency are based on comparative measurements of isolated and partial factors. Mention is made in this connection of constitutional tendencies or defects, on the one hand, of environmental disorders such as faulty parental attitudes, inadequate schooling or work conditions, lack of constructive leisure-time facilities, poverty, on the other hand. Good examples of this approach are contained in the works of Cyril Burt (13) or of Sheldon Glueck (44), not to mention those of earlier research students or of criminologists. These quantitatively oriented studies do not ask *how* a specific factor operates on the individual's growing personality to produce a certain behavior, but: which one is more highly correlated with delinquency. Although most modern research students have replaced all monistic ambitions by pluralistic thinking, each of their (more or less frequently found) factors stands in its own right; its causal effect may be reinforced by others but does not depend on them.

We do not want to repeat here what we have said elsewhere (34) on the advantages of a configurational approach to the problems of causation over the pluralistic equalization of partial factors. One insufficiency, common to all these attempts, stands out: that the behavioral entity to which they refer (in our case adult delinquency or criminality) is much too large to make the findings meaningful. Lack of proper distinction between the various forms of delinquency is liable to discriminate against highly important factors that may be responsible on the whole for relatively few cases only, since the clinical picture to which these cases refer is infrequent. Were there more clinical differentiation to precede quantitative studies, the correlation coefficient of such an "infrequent" causal factor would be very high. In other words: even the measurement of isolated and partial factors requires prior distinction between different forms of asocial and antisocial behavior in children and juveniles.

The configurational approach to the problems of causation, with its underlying holistic claim,* is strangely contrasted by the principle of maximal division of behavioral units into sub-units. But the contradiction resolves itself easily: the configurational approach actually refers to individual cases only, whereas with regard to clinical pictures and their sub-units the identification of *essential* causes in their abstract partiality is more important. Hence, it may be said that subdivision into smaller and secondary units of behavior, on the one hand, and formulation of essential causes, on the other, have one element in common: partiality.

In the professional literature many attempts have been made to bridge the gap between individual cases and clinical units or sub-units by

---

* The claim that all partial factors, including their specific causal antecedents and their results, must be related to each other within one constellational whole if we want to understand the connection between an individual case and its causes.

relegating quantitative research to criminological and statistical studies, while reserving qualitative approaches for the analysis of intrapsychic factors and developments. Good examples of the latter approach may be found in William Healy's studies (50): "The only safe way", he says, "to ascertain the driving forces which make for social offense, is to get at the mental mechanisms antecedent to the behavior in question." In another study (51), he compares juvenile delinquents with their non-delinquent siblings and comes to the conclusion that feelings of not being loved and of being rejected, rather than personality defects, account for the delinquent developments, particularly when no positive factors are at work from within to counteract frustrations from without.

No satisfactory answer, however, is suggested either by Healy or by others starting from the same basic premises to the questions of *differential* causation: "attempts to achieve compensatory satisfaction . . . to obtain revenge" or similar aims are said to explain the delinquent acts. But we are told neither why these acts make the compensatory satisfaction possible nor whether this interpretation holds good for all or for certain varieties of delinquency only. In fact, Healy's compensation-theory much resembles A. Cohen's psycho-sociological status theory (19) which admittedly applies to certain types of delinquency only.

A different answer is suggested by W. Reich in his early essay on the "impulsive or instinct-ridden character" (84), again a specific variety of delinquency only, similar in some respects to waywardness and yet essentially different from it. He believes that conscious rebellion against social norms may take place when the super-ego has not turned into an organic part of the ego but has remained partial and isolated. This, in turn, happens, so he claims, whenever manifest ambivalence in relation to parental figures has not been modified by way of identification. Weakness of repression, of guilt-feelings and of anxiety are then symptomatic of the delinquent's behavior. We shall see later (pp. 128 ff.) that Reich has psychopathic rather than wayward behavior patterns in mind when he speaks of the "impulsive character".

More comprehensive is the answer suggested by F. Alexander (5) when he says that every delinquent act "must be explained as a psychological process ending in a certain type of motor activity, but both, personality and sociological, factors are active at the same time; either of them may be predominant in one case, negligible in another . . . What is the origin of those character trends which make an individual receptive to the criminal influences of the environment?" His first answer is rather vague and non-specific: it is, he says, the individual's inadequate reality principle. Five factors determine this inadequacy: constitution, early acquired reaction-patterns, family conditions, the wider environment and what he calls the "ideological trends of civilization". When will asocial and antisocial rather than neurotic behavior symptoms make their appearance? Whenever earlier "emotional dissatisfaction in the family situation is combined with social discontent", he answers, "antisocial rather than neurotic symptom formation is likely to result". But since in some cases environmental frustrations *alone* account for delinquent developments, in others neurotic symptoms are *replaced* by offenses, the type-factor is being adduced by Alexander to explain these differences: introversion and neuroses, extraversion and delinquencies are apparently correlated to each other.

But again: a closer examination of Alexander's case material clearly proves that he has had in mind adult recidivists of good intelligence, most of whom suffered from mental conflicts rather than from their adverse environment; hence, his interpretations are *not* applicable automatically to other forms of delinquency such as the child's waywardness. And yet, it can be said that Alexander has paved the way to a differential under-standing of the *varieties* of delinquency by emphasizing the different configurations of constitutional and environmental forces.

What is the specific causal constellation, we now ask, that may be held responsible for the emergence of waywardness in children?

7. THE ESSENTIAL CAUSES OF WAYWARDNESS

Many of the symptoms of externalized behavior in children and juveniles, which we have described in previous studies (34, 35), closely resemble those of waywardness, as described elsewhere (26). In both patterns we find ego-weakness, non-selectivity *vis-à-vis* conduct manifestations, heteronomy, lack of anxiety, of guilt feelings, of inner tensions. But externalized patterns do *not* necessarily include acts of unlawfulness, though it is of course much easier for an externalized individual to glide into delinquency than for others who have reached a higher level of internalization of values (and of "living from within"). And to the extent that the latter develop into delinquents, their "choice" will certainly not be waywardness but rather primary aggressiveness, primary behavior disorders or neurotic varieties of delinquency (see the first chapter, on classification).

In contrast to the child who grows up under conditions of poverty and educational neglect and who develops *non*-delinquent patterns of exter-nalized behavior, the wayward becomes, after some time, *addicted* to his street life and to chance delinquency. *Lack of planning* has a different meaning when it serves impulse-satisfaction and refers to the child's unlawful behavior, or when it co-exists with inhibitions strong enough to prevent delinquency. The wayward child seeks *easily resolved tensions*, in compensation, as it were, of his non-belonging to the generally accepted social contexts, and, as a result, often glides into more or less pernicious *street groups*. The non-delinquent child of poverty, on the other hand, seems to be protected against the danger of committing offenses by a more realistic evaluation of his own activity. In this respect, the wayward again differs : he indulges in *illusions of activity*.

On the etiological level we find qualitative rather than quantitative differences in the configuration of partial factors which *prima facie* are identical. Common to both units of behavior are : educational *neglect* in an atmosphere of *impersonal family relationships* and a general *orientation towards the "haveable"* (35), combined in many cases with disorientation due to *cultural ambiguity and value discrepancies* between the parents and the children as well as within the parent's mind, in other cases with *family disruption* and insufficiency, again in others with *low intelligence* and the ensuing inability to resist seduction. But it would be wrong to see the differential factors in the *degree* of intensity at which each of these social elements must operate to produce waywardness. On the contrary. The more radical the neglect or the value discrepancy, the more radical the family disruption, the lower the child's intelligence— the *less* likely is waywardness to be the result.

The *qualitative* difference, on the other hand, which we believe to be responsible for the emergence of delinquent behavior in the externalized child, manifests itself first and foremost in the combination of the above mentioned basic causal factors with others. Thus, we find *extraversion, relative absence of compensatory abilities, strong needs for group approval, hypermotility*, on the one hand, *indolence, rather than rejection* in the parents' educational attitude and *moral laxity* in their behavior, on the other hand, to be significant qualifiers of the basic (common) causal factors.

Wayward behavior in children requires an amount of naive vitality that will never be available to an introvert. The illusions of activity which, we have said, are characteristic of the wayward child and juvenile cannot emerge but in individuals with *extravert tendencies*, unimpeded, as they are, by introvert self-reflexion, self-criticism, hesitation, fears. (We speak of "illusions of activity" rather than of activity, because ego-weakness and chance addiction, so typical of the wayward child, preclude genuine, that is, ego-rooted, consciously directed, activity.)

But extravert tendencies pave the way to delinquent behavior of the waywardness type only when they appear in children with *weak powers of integration, including* (though not identical with) *relative absence of compensatory abilities.* It is the latter factor that determines the causal significance of extraversion : only when the child does not know the many satisfactions that can be gained through socially acceptable achievements —in compensation of the inevitable sufferings through a life in poverty and neglect—are extravert tendencies conducive to delinquent outlets.

On the other hand, it is this very way out into delinquency and into an always eventful street-life that prevents the taking root in the child's personality of strong resentments against frustrating parents, hence also of neurotic reactions and distortions, of repressions and defences. It is the more or less exclusive privilege of the introvert to react to parental rejection or to lack of personal ties in the primary groups with neurotic or even psychotic distortions. In other words : extravert tendencies in the child account for the emergence of the many symptoms of behavior that characterize his variety of externalized reaction to his externalizing life-conditions. Fixation and regression, anxiety and repression, guilt and reaction-formation, projection and neurotic manifestations—all these are absent in the wayward child's behavior for two reasons : constitutional absence of introvert propensities and reinforcement of extravert propensities through externalized behavior.

Nowhere in the psychopathology of children can the law of circular causation (see 34, ch. VI) be demonstrated as clearly as in the area of waywardness : we have mentioned the absence of truly compensatory abilities as a determinant of the causal role of extraversion in this case. On a secondary level, however, it is precisely through committing offenses that the wayward child may bolster his ego-feeling and his sense of achievement. This, then, is *his* variety of compensation : it enables him to enjoy group approval on which he depends still more than the normally socialized child. *Strong needs of group-approval operate not only as symptoms of externalization but also as causes of the wayward child's continued search for satisfaction in his social contexts.* It is this causal factor that accounts for his inability or his unwillingness to act on his own, as an individual. Needless to stress again the circular effect of this factor : group-dependence is not only a symptom of ego-weakness but at the same time reinforces heteronomy.

(It should be added that the causal significance of the last-mentioned factor, the strong need for group-approval, differs according to the basic-elements in the causal equation of the clinical picture of which it is symptom as well as cause : it may act as a negative reinforcer of personal inefficiency, particularly when it operates in clear opposition to a generally accepted value-canon of individual autonomy. It may act as a *positive* reinforcer of what Riesman (85) would call "tradition-directedness". It acts, in the here analyzed case of waywardness, as an expression and at the same time as a reinforcer of asocial behavior, in a life not only without social responsibility but also with many opportunities for chance enjoyment. It is the impersonal nature of early relationships in the life of every externalized child that here reappears in the non-committal nature of the wayward child's group-dependence.)

Then, there is the factor of organically conditioned *hypermotility* that may account for delinquent behavior. We do not intend here to discuss the problem in all its causal implications. It is a well-known fact that many cases of "impairment of intelligence" (36) can be explained through referral to the causal factor of "minor brain-injuries" which, in turn, accounts, through the ensuing hypermotility, for the growing child's lack of ability to concentrate for any length of time on a meaningful task, particularly of learning. We do not yet know how frequently the organic impediment is present not only in the intellectually impaired but also, and mainly, in the socially inadequate child. Differential tests and other measurement techniques have not yet yielded unequivocally reliable results (the best means of proving the responsibility of organic factors still being the effectiveness of appropriate pharmacotherapy). And even those who believe they have found sufficient evidence for the presence of organic factors (minor brain-injuries) in socially maladjusted children in general have failed to subdivide their case-material into different clinical units of asocial or antisocial behavior.

It is self-evident that the risk of birth-irregularities is greater under conditions of poverty, conditions which, in turn, account for the externalizing life-conditions under which so many children from socially underprivileged families are forced to grow up. It is equally self-evident that this socially conditioned frequency of organic risks accounts for the relatively higher number of intellectually or affectively handicapped children in these families. But we should *not* try to construct correlation bridges between birth injuries and parental incompetence. There are as many parents with adequate or, as we have said elsewhere (33), "ego-transcending" reactions as there are parents with inadequate, that is, externalizing, reactions to poverty whose children may be exposed to injurious birth-processes. On the other hand, it can easily be understood that, when such children, sooner or later in their development, show disturbing signs of unrest, hypermotility, weak ability to concentrate, seeming extraversion, hyperactivity—their parents' reactions may *not* be adequate. We cannot expect that parents, who have to struggle against the odds of social inadequacy, of want and threat, will show patience with, and educationally helpful reactions to, their children's often enervating restlessness. Even when they consult experts, they are liable not to receive advice and help because of the diagnostic uncertainty and ambiguity of their children's behavior.

Here, then, we witness a secondary combination of causal factors:

1) Minor brain-injuries, suffered by the child,
2) as the result of socially caused irregularities in the birth-process,
3) produce hypermotility and pseudo-extravert aggressiveness and
4) lack of ability to concentrate on meaningful tasks,
5) resulting in unsatisfactory behavior in general and
6) in negative attitudes towards the parents in particular,
7) thus liable to provoke hostile, or at any rate, rejective responses on the part of the parents,
8) which then cause the child to avoid his parental environment and
9) to seek compensatory satisfactions in a disorderly street-life and
10) approval by his often changing groups,
11) thus getting more and more accustomed to an externalized form of living out his extraversion,
12) irrespective of whether and to what extent he had been born with, or has acquired, such extravert propensities.

8. THE AUXILIARY CAUSES OF WAYWARDNESS

The hitherto discussed personality-factors (extraversion, relative absence of compensatory abilities, strong needs for group-approval, more often than not—combined with organically caused hypermotility), in a child growing up under conditions of externalization (neglect, impersonal family relationships, orientation towards the haveable), do not *always* produce waywardness. The result of this interaction of specific personality factors with environmental deficiencies may be, and indeed often is, dissocial behavior, but not necessarily waywardness. While in many instances the configuration *may* account for it, we find in others an additional causal element, a specific climate of educational inadequacy in the family environment: *indolence* rather than conscious rejection and *moral laxity* rather than antisocial conduct.

Indolence reinforces the impersonal character of family relationships and thereby weakens the child's readiness to relate himself specifically and with bonds of mutuality to any other person in his environment. Thus, a similarly impersonal attitude comes into existence in the growing child, an attitude which, should he glide into asocial behavior, prepares him for that specific form of asociality, called waywardness. Less than in any other form of delinquent behavior, we find in waywardness personal resentment or hate, deep-rooted conflicts or reactive "solutions" of such conflicts through offenses or otherwise aggressive behavior. This absence of resentment, conflict and aggressiveness is a reflection of the basically impersonal nature of all his relationships as it results from parental indolence rather than from parental rejection.

As a second specific fault in the parents' attitude towards life in general and towards their educational functions in particular we have mentioned moral laxity rather than openly antisocial behavior. The latter is often responsible for more active forms of delinquency in children and juveniles, gradually emerging as a result of imitation or protest or both at one and the same time (compare what we have said in the chapter on classification about this variety of delinquency, pp. 15 ff.). While parental indolence reinforces impersonality, moral laxity not only leads to increased neglect of the child's needs but also to an almost complete exclusion from the family life of all unambiguously ego-transcending values. It is in this way that moral laxity, more than any other faulty attitude on the part of parents, negatively affects the child's development, not so much towards overtly antisocial behavior as towards a life without values, a life of immediately reactive satisfactions. Where moral laxity joins forces with an attitude towards the haveable, as it is often characteristic of a life in want and externalization, this configuration is conducive to the emergence, in the child's behavior, of that delinquent variety of externalization that is called waywardness. Configurated with *other* social conditions such as, for instance, affluence and wealth, it is liable to further the development of other forms of deviant behavior, as we shall show in the chapter on adolescent delinquency (see pp. 199 ff.).

We have so far analyzed the specific combinations of environmental and personality factors that can be found in the growth-history of almost every wayward child. This, however, does not mean that other elements do not participate in the causal equation of individual cases, elements known to us as pathogenic factors in other pathologies as well. Certain conditions of the natural ambiance, cultural ambiguity and value-disorientation, various forms of family disruption, parental incompetence, conditions at home, in the neighbourhood, on the street, at school or at work—each of these partial factors has a specific causal significance in the history of many wayward children. How, we must ask, develops the wayward child's ego as a defective regulator of his functions and particularly of his social behavior, through the different phases of his pre-adolescent life? And how long afterwards does the social development continue, in other words: how much more time does a wayward child need to reach relative maturity?*

Waywardness more than any other form of asocial or antisocial behavior is an *urban* phenomenon. Without the constant impact of a multitude of stimulations coming from an unstructured outside, waywardness cannot emerge. Other varieties of delinquency or criminality, and particularly aggressive, neurotic, psychopathic or psychotic varieties do *not* need to the same extent the support, as it were, of "internal-through-external" factors of determination. But without the presence of the *primary* (structural and environmental) causes of waywardness which we have discussed so far, the influence of an urban environment alone would *not* be conducive to the emergence of waywardness. What we want to emphasize with this seemingly obvious statement is the merely "auxiliary" nature of conditioning factors: waywardness should *not* be interpreted as the outcome of conditioning alone, in spite of the fact that an uninterrupted sequence of conditioning, in this case externalizing, factors is typical of its etiology in distinction from that of other forms of dissocial behavior.

Another factor frequently mentioned as being responsible for the increase in the number of wayward children is the massive disruption of family units through *wars and their after-effects*. Disruption means, in this context, not only the temporary or permanent disappearance of the father but also the general weakening of external controls. Now, it is precisely the impact of external controls that often keeps in the fold of socially accepted behavior a child who is otherwise a perfect candidate for deviant developments of the waywardness type: to the extent that a form of dissocial behavior is the outcome of conditioning (though not of conditioning alone), external controls are much more important for its delay or even prevention than they are in the case of other, more internally determined pathologies.

The same applies, of course, to a disruption of the family unit *in cultural transition* or in the value ambiguity of culture-clash situations. In this case, it is the disorientation and the ensuing helplessness of both

---

* This is the often mentioned question of delayed maturation. Many psychologists and criminologists, particularly of earlier years, have mentioned that certain types of delinquents, outstanding among them those whom we would call "wayward", need more time to outgrow immaturity. This "delayed" maturation is *not* a function of the effectiveness of treatment offered those delinquents, it is thought to be a constitutional factor. Reference is made, among many others, to authors like K. Birnbaum (8), A. Morris (71), Sh. Glueck (43). They all report cases to prove that the behavior of many wayward and delinquent children and juveniles gradually becomes more like that of socially normal individuals though it takes them sometimes up to ten or fifteen "additional" years.

parents as educators of their children that increases the latter's dependence on environmental stimulations and seductions. Waywardness with its unstructured and passive reactiveness and delinquency-addiction often results from what might be called a translation of the children's dissatisfied authority needs, a perversion of the normal internalization process: instead of transforming the father into an inner force of guidance, a diffuse multitude of substitute figures, each representing a different seductive stimulus, becomes the child's frame of reference and universe of objects for imitation or reaction.

What we have said about indolence and moral laxity rather than other forms of parental failure being responsible for the emergence of waywardness in certain children does not mean that other expressions of educational incompetence are negligible. To the extent that negative attitudes result from parents' inner conflicts, defences, anxieties or guilt feelings, they are likely, we have said, to help in the emergence of more neurotic forms of deviant behavior in children. But some of their obnoxious attitudes, for instance cruelty or sexual exploitation, are found in the case histories of not a few wayward and delinquent children; though again in configuration with other partial factors only. They may account for a defective self-conception, one of being an object only. In this case, the choice of an unstructured street life, unless it is in the order of a fearful escape, may be an expression of automatically accepting and living-out the role forced upon the child by his parents. This also explains why such a child is capable of enjoying his chance-dictated street activities, just as a normally adjusted child enjoys his generally sanctioned play activities. Even delinquent acts, thefts and aggressions, are little more than attempts to translate his object-role into that of a subject no less entitled to his subject-role than the cruel parents.

What we have said elsewhere (34) about the externalizing effect of a poverty-stricken home, a slum quarter, the street, an inadequate school or work-place applies to the problems of waywardness as well. But it would again be a mistake to look for direct causal connections. Only in configuration with the earlier analyzed essential conditions can those environmental elements add their causal weight.

Overcrowding with its concomitant noisiness, lack of privacy, and tension is liable not only to repel and eject a child from the family circle, but also, and mainly, to prejudice the development of relational abilities. Overcrowding is, in fact, one of the most potent auxiliary factors in the emergence of what we have called "impersonality". But it is not directly conducive to delinquency. Similarly, the *slum-quarter* may account for gradual structurization in the child of the illusion that the "world around" is known and familiar, because of the frequent reoccurrence of certain events or behavior patterns. But this, again, is not a direct cause of delinquency. Only when extravert propensities, hypermotility and specific parental deficiencies operate in a child exposed to conditions of overcrowding and a slum-neighborhood, is delinquency of the waywardness-type likely to be his reaction.

It is the *city-street* with its unstructured and, more often than not, incomprehensible but always attractive and seductive multitude of stimuli that will then replace, as it were, the home and the neighborhood. Offenses can, of course, be committed everywhere; but they are much more enjoyable when they are "separated", as much as possible, from the knowledge and the control of those who belong to the "area of the known". This illusion is offered by the city-street with its almost absolute anonymity. Waywardness is closely connected with anonymity, but for reasons quite different from those of neurotic escape : lack of intensive personal relationships makes possible (a) diffusion and avoidance of responsibility; (b) increased illusions of knownness; (c) floating in chance-occurrences and, at the same time, (d) primitive excitements. The street also strengthens extravert tendencies, even in a child in whom they may not be strongly developed from the start. To the extent that patterns of waywardness then crystallize, the "street" assumes yet another causal role, that of reinforcing symptoms of asociality and turning each into an additional cause. No other variety of delinquency is characterized, as we already have emphasized several times, to the same extent as waywardness by this form of circular causation. It is a reflection of ego-weakness and lack of structure. For, the stronger and the more structured the ego, the more selective is it likely to be in the "choice" of both, symptoms and causes.

Ordinarily, when the child passes, more or less successfully, through the stages of his socialization process, he comes to feel that he *belongs* to the parental home as well as to each of the institutes of learning provided for his socialization by his parents and by society. In wayward children this feeling of belonging is transferred to the street. We usually call that process *"truancy"* and speak of the child who avoids his home, his school, his work. But we should not forget that the negative form of "avoidance" (89) reflects the adult's normative view, not the wayward child's psychology. The latter does not escape from social contexts out of fear or inner tensions, as a neurotic may do. He *prefers* his own social context—which is the street. As additional *causes* of waywardness we may nevertheless mention the inadequacies of school or work-place, with their average-orientation and rigidly defined expectations and demands : once a child has chosen the street as his social context, he is bound to grow less and less tolerant of absolute claims represented and expressed by the teacher or the employer.

9. CAUSATION IN DEVELOPMENT

We shall now try to answer the question : how each of the developmental phases is liable to change its functions within the growth process of a child who is exposed to the here analyzed conditions of waywardness. We start from the presumption that this is a continuous, uninterrupted process of becoming accustomed to a certain pattern of behavior rather than a reactive process of identity formation. While Erikson would ask what each phase contributes to the crystallization of the individual's identity (21), we want to know how a defined configuration of causal factors affects (delays, modifies, counteracts) what we have called in a former study (35) the "phasal achievements". There we have given examples of such modifications under conditions of poverty and neglect, of plenty and affluence, of modern technology, of cultural transition, of life in rural areas, of the so-called levantine mentality. Can the emergence of waywardness be made comprehensible in a similar way?

Of the factors mentioned before as being responsible for this type of asocial behavior, hypermotility and extravert tendencies on the one hand, parental indolence on the other, make themselves felt already *at the beginning of life*. Externalizing life-conditions will undoubtedly impede or even prevent the emergence of nearness, hence also of anxiety-tension and of relational abilities. But these are *general* handicaps in the psychic structure of a child who grows up under conditions of extreme poverty and neglect, when the "haveable" becomes the sole value and content of the mind; they are not *specifically* affecting the infant's phasal achievements, nor do they prepare the ground for later asociality.* Strong extravert tendencies and hypermotility, on the other hand, may manifest themselves, already at this early stage, in destructive behavior, unintentional as the latter may be. The extravert's manipulations often have a destructive effect, particularly when organically caused hypermotility limits control and direction. The way out into apathetic withdrawal is certainly closed in these cases. Contact-needs will not only remain unsatisfied, particularly when the parental climate is one of indolence, they are again liable to find seemingly aggressive expressions and result in "wild" behavior.

---

* Unless we call externalized behavior *per se* asocial, which would be wrong.

Obviously, all these are not yet indicators of future deviation. But the reactions on the part of the environment, parents and others, are often such as to jeopardize the infant's elementary needs for care, rest, static-ness. As a result, the seeds of asociality are being planted: the infant learns much less the acts of observation or of manipulation than he learns how to react to outside stimuli only and how to seek substitute satisfac-tions in activity rather than in the establishment of personal contacts with the relevant figures of his environment.

The same causal factors—extravert tendencies and hypermotility on the one hand, parental indolence on the other—continue to determine the *second phase* achievements as well: instead of learning the secrets of mutuality and ambivalence, the child now comes to communicate with chance-objects rather than with personally defined subjects. The lack of compensatory abilities may also begin to make itself felt at this stage, though it becomes causally relevant in the full sense of the word later only. What we have said about the first phase holds good for the second, too: it would be premature to diagnose the beginnings of waywardness at this early stage of the child's development. But we may hold the environment's *reactions* to the child's lack of mutuality responsible for his growing exclusion from a universe of norms and relationships. Thus the little child not only starts to "turn away from", but also to "turn against" his adults, to live alone, as it were—no doubt an important preparatory factor for future asociality of the waywardness type.

It is in the *third stage* of the child's development that the additional determinants (and manifestations) of the parents' failure and incom-petence, their moral laxity and their exclusive orientation towards the haveable as well as the educational outcomes of family disruption or of cultural ambiguity (to the extent that these factors are present) take their place in the causal equation of waywardness: the ego must be available (though it may be weak and unstructured) to imitate parental behavior. This imitation is what often happens in the individual "history" of waywardness. Instead of reacting from within by way of mobilizing a variety of defense-mechanisms (outstanding among them denials, repres-sions, reaction-formations and projections), the child learns how to take over, almost automatically, his parents' attitudes and life-orientation. Indolence, however, has a different meaning in adults and in children: while it means passiveness, lack of initiative, lack of involvement in the former, it means undifferentiated response to varying stimuli, hence also seeming activeness and seeming involvement in the child. It is typical of the wayward child that imitating parental attitudes neither prepares the way to identification nor results in the emergence of identical attitudes; imitating the parents remains as external and impersonal as everything else in the life-occurrences of the wayward child.

The non-delinquent child who grows up under the externalizing conditions of poverty and neglect and becomes accustomed to an all-pervading orientation towards the "haveable" differs significantly from the delinquent. Insufficient differentiation resulting from relative weakness of anxiety and ambivalence may be common to both; but the extraversion and the hypermotility of the wayward and delinquent child are liable to produce in this third stage of his development strong tendencies to manipulate and to change reality. The wayward child is not satisfied with eliminating, as it were, objective factual dissimilarities by inadequately equal reactions, as they characterize the externalized child in general. In addition, it is this stage in which group association makes its first appearance in the wayward child's development. Although early groups obviously differ from later delinquent environments, they nevertheless prepare the ground for later group-dependence in the wayward child's behavior patterns. They also help the child invest all his compensatory needs and abilities in this growing group-dependence.

But it is in the *fourth stage* only that defective phase-achievements specifically determine the crystallization of waywardness in contrast not only to the outcome of normal developments but also to that of externalization, on the one hand, and of neurotic syndrom-formation, on the other. This is the phase during which "the choice of illness", to use the well-known Freudian term in a different context, takes place. It is said to be the phase of learning, not only in the social and the cognitive sense of the word; the child also learns how to use his habits, his reaction-patterns, his imitation through applying them to his various and varying tasks.

Normally, social and intellectual learning helps the child overcome his oedipal anxieties. Objectivization alleviates irrational fears and guilt-feelings connected with the very act of separating wholes in cognitive or emotional contexts. Under conditions of want and neglect, learning fulfills a different function altogether, one of conditioning: the child learns how to react to external stimulations without relating himself to the objects of his learning, to those who teach him or to his own ego; externalized learning means learning how to avoid internalization, hence: how to do without concepts and how to concretize symbols.

But here again, we must ask how this type of learning becomes a factor conducive to the emergence of wayward behavior. The answer is that it must not only be diverted from the normal channels of universally valid contents and purposes into an all-pervasive orientation towards the haveable and towards chance-occurrences; it must also be replaced, in part at least, by addiction to non-recognized, unstructured and non-committal groups. It is only through such group-contexts that an illusion of activeness can be produced and maintained in the wayward child, an illusion which is the asocial substitute for learning, as indispensable for the wayward as learning for the ordinary child.

For, when there is no fear or guilt over separation (primarily because of the impersonal climate of relationships under conditions of poverty and parental indolence), destroying wholes takes the place of analysis and joining street-groups—that of synthesis through learning and internalization. Destroying wholes does not always require ego-involvement, it may be as impersonal, as accidental, as external as every function in a "life from without". Nor does the ego-involvement grow and deepen through group attachments (which increasingly sanction destructive behavior and replace the socially recognized institutions of learning).

Here, a fundamental difference between the wayward and other, more complex, varieties of destructiveness becomes comprehensible : what we have called "group-dependence" (one of the essential characteristics of waywardness) accounts for the absence of unconscious motivations of aggressiveness, for the relative shallowness and for its interchangeability with other symptoms of asocial behavior. This could be called the phasal achievement of the wayward child in the fourth phase of his development.

Needless to add that individual differences appear no less distinctly in wayward than in socially normal children. This appears in spite of those common characteristics that we have mentioned (extraversion, group-dependence, hypermotility, orientation towards the haveable, relative weakness of compensatory needs or abilities). The most important among the factors of differentiation is intelligence. It is again this fourth phase in which the factor becomes most evident and significant : while low intelligence (of both, the congenital and the secondary variety (36)) increases the dangers of suggestibility and seduceability, average or even above-average intelligence often manifests itself in a higher degree of initiative or even in leadership qualities.

The unintelligent member of a group of wayward children often tends to use verbal fluency in order to inflate himself rather than to communicate with others. Non-communicative use of words thus easily blocks all avenues to objective learning, hence operates as an additional or at least a reinforcing cause of waywardness. Small wonder, then, that we find more unintelligent than intelligent children in any wayward group; its intelligent members more easily "outgrow" their asocial patterns, either spontaneously or in response to educational interventions, unless they glide into more active and more sophisticated antisocial behavior.

We learn from an analysis of juvenile court records and statistics in many countries of the world that the number of delinquents rises in the last years of childhood, in the period of pre-adolescence. But what is rarely, if ever, shown in statistics is the fact that it is precisely the here discussed waywardness type of juvenile delinquency that now "conquers the field". The other varieties that we have discussed in the first chapter show more constancy in numbers until adolescence. At this stage, neurotic reactions, socio-cultural pathologies, psychopathic conditions, deep personality disorders and other factors account for a considerable increase in the number of certain, and often rather serious, varieties of delinquency and crime. But waywardness now becomes less important, both in the number and in the seriousness of cases. What is the phase-inherent characteristic, we should then ask, that may be held responsible for this almost universal decrease in waywardness, after its sudden upsurge in the years preceding adolescence?

The approach of biological maturity makes sex plays possible and, through them, anticipatory and often premature imitation of adult behavior, aimed at the achievement of status. This, however, means that the pre-adolescent is forced into asocial behavior still more than the child, and that his exclusion from socially valid contexts becomes almost complete. Group-dependence now fulfills not only the function of an essential element of waywardness but also that of a defense against the increasing threats of punishment. The adolescent, however, must go beyond the limits of waywardness to gain status and to satisfy his needs for radicalization; only withdrawal into addiction, or truly criminal self-inflation can do this. On the other hand, his chances are equally good to glide into some kind of low-grade "normality", that is, of generally accepted asociality, similar to that of his adult environment.

We have already mentioned (see footnote on p. 61) that according to some students of juvenile delinquency "delayed maturation" causes not a few wayward children to reach a more or less satisfactory level of social adjustment, at a later age. Reactions to positive relational experiences, to consistent educational interventions or to radical changes in the social system of which they are part, may arouse self-awareness in an adolescent or a young adult; processes of individualization are then likely to be set in motion, in spite of a still low degree of ego-participation. On the other hand, the adult world with its characteristic compromises and average-orientation, facilitates adjustment even of a young individual with a weak and insufficiently structured ego to its minimal demands and requirements.

C. SYMPTOMATOLOGY

10. INTRODUCTION

If we want to describe the symptoms of a specific variety of juvenile delinquency, in our case of waywardness, we should intimately know a large number of delinquents over a period of years in order to compare with each other individual cases and to classify them according to diagnostic criteria; observation will not be relevant unless we include the child's reactions to social and educational treatment actions and to the specific problems of his phases of development.

Here, as in every other area of symptomatology, we are faced with an inherent paradox. We must learn from the case-material, by ways of observation and induction, all about the manifestations of a given pathology; and we must apply to this case-material differential criteria, as if we knew already what waywardness meant as distinguished from other varieties of juvenile delinquency. In other words: we must know what makes of a certain behavior manifestation a symptom of waywardness, what makes of the same manifestation a symptom of neurotic delinquency or of primary behavior disorder, in order to say in the end—what waywardness is. Some tentative (speculative) definition of the essentials of waywardness must precede symptom description, although this definition must, in turn, be preceded by (less differentiated) observations. (See also the remarks on this subject at the beginning of the chapter.)

The probation officer is the best suited person to collect relevant material since he is supposed to be in intimate treatment contacts with all types of delinquency. But he, too, is limited in his conclusions: he works within a certain culture only, and it is a well-known fact that the symptoms of any given pathology change from one national or socio-cultural group to the other. The student of delinquency therefore cannot rely on a probation officer's findings unless he has access to case-material from different cultures, gathered in a similar way and based on similar premises. The same applies, of course, to the social worker, the group worker or the worker in a neighborhood center. Simultaneous or consecutive work with different ethnical sub-groups and comparing with each other the observable manifestations of behavior may serve as a safeguard against the danger of drawing conclusions from observations in one culture only.

This is exactly what the present author was able to do; for more than ten years he was engaged in probation work with juvenile delinquents from rural and from urban sectors of the Arab and the Jewish population of what was then (1936–1946) Palestine under British mandatory rule (26). From thousands of cases known to him either personally or through supervisory contact with others, those were selected that could be diagnosed as wayward children. This meant: exclusion of all who revealed neurotic reactions, were clearly feebleminded or suspected of being psychopaths. It also meant excluding accidental offenders (who, as a rule, represent the majority of all court cases) and first offenders (unless they were known to have had a long previous record as wayward children, although they had not been brought before a court).

A symptom can be described as a human quality which may *express itself* in a variety of isolated or habitual actions or omissions; but it can also be described *in terms of* such actions or omissions. When we choose the first method we must be aware of the fact that a certain action may be the expression of more than one symptom. Here precisely lies the advantage of this approach over the other (which behaviorists will, of course, prefer). Committing a theft may just as easily indicate aggressiveness as it may be symptomatic of an all-pervading orientation to the haveable. Sexual promiscuity may not only indicate neurotic or psychopathic disorders rather than waywardness, but it may also, even as a symptom of the latter, betray such different qualities as excitability, aggressiveness or chance addiction. We are not concerned here with the problems of how to keep police records or how to arrange court statistics; we should rather bear the ambiguity of asocial or antisocial manifestations in mind when registering them, as indicators of a certain human quality, after carefully studying each wayward child in whose behavior they may appear. These qualities, and not the actions themselves, are the symptoms of waywardness.

What qualities do we have in mind? We speak of:

1) Immediacy orientation, limitation of the time-span, inability to delay satisfaction.

2) Lack of differentiation, easily changing responses to accidentally changing stimuli.

3) Weak ability to organize behavior, weak power to persevere in a task.

4) Allergy to any ego-transcending demands of order and discipline.

5) Addiction to groups.

6) Addiction to the haveable.

7) Seeking adult status through a variety of asocial behavior manifestations.

8) Avoidance of control.

9) Aggressiveness against parents, peers, strangers, society, objects.

Before going into a more detailed description of each of these symptoms we should emphasize, once again, that although some may be indicative *exclusively* of waywardness, most are so only if the following conditions are fulfilled : there must be more than one symptom present in the child's behavior (the polymorphous nature of waywardness); "specialization" in one symptom-area, on the other hand, immediately arouses the suspicion that we have to deal with a *neurotic* delinquent. A similar differential factor can be defined as absence or presence of inner tensions, anxieties, guilt-feelings. Other conditions of identifying a symptom as one of waywardness are : preference for acting in groups, lack of planning, reactivity.

Are the nine symptoms listed above of equal "value" (gravity)? It is self-evident that such a question cannot be answered solely on the basis of an assessment by independent judges. Cases to be known as relatively difficult and others to be known as relatively simple should be analyzed to find out to what extent the former show a higher incidence of symptoms assessed as "grave" than the latter. It may well be that grave symptoms by chance appear in certain simple cases that range far from the extreme.

The question of numbers appears in other contexts as well : Can a symptom be defined as "grave" according to the number of its manifestations? Can waywardness in a certain individual be diagnosed as "serious" according to the number of symptoms, independently of the gravity of each? It would seem that such and similar questions have meaning for the behaviorist only. We claim that even if each of the nine symptoms should be found to "have" as many possible behavioral manifestations as the next one, we should still try to find criteria for distinguishing grave and complex from light and simple symptoms. Such criteria would then have to be sought *beyond* the symptom-area, that is, in the pathology itself of which the attitudes and qualities are symptoms : To what extent, we should ask, depends the pathology (in our case : waywardness) on the symptoms in question? To what extent depends a specific characteristic on all others? To what extent does it force the individual into consistent behavior? In other words : to what extent is it subject to that specific law of symptomatology that may be called the law of "inductive spread of effect"?

It is the latter question that leads us back from an analysis of symptoms to one of behavioral manifestations, a reduction which is of particular importance in a discussion of waywardness: when lack of structure is an essential characteristic of a given pathology, emphasis should be placed less on human qualities as symptoms, than on their behavioral manifestations. This also answers our second question about the criteria for the assessment of the seriousness of an individual case: the latter, too, should be assessed as serious or light through an analysis of behavioral manifestations rather than by symptoms, where a pathology like waywardness is essentially characterized by lack of structure. It is in the light of this qualification that we are now going to describe the behavioral manifestations of each of the nine symptoms of waywardness.

11.   IMMEDIACY ORIENTATION AND LACK OF DIFFERENTIATION

The inability to delay satisfaction is found not only in the early stages of man's development, when it is considered normal and when it actually constitutes a natural challenge to education and socialization. It also appears in certain units of behavior in children, adolescents or adults which are then considered to be "abnormal". The seeming similarity between young children, feebleminded, neurotically or organically disinhibited individuals of older age, so-called primitive, that is, undifferentiated members of certain socio-cultural groups and others has led many students of "comparative behavior" (see, f.i., 93) to draw parallels between these different groups. Some go even one step further and call that common quality, inability to delay satisfaction, identical wherever it appears.

We suggest a distinction between the following four forms of the quality in question: (1) It may be due to lack of structural and functional maturation, as in young children who at the same time experience it as a "deficit" requiring adult restriction and guidance. (2) It may be due to organic impediments as in certain types of feeblemindedness or cerebral disorders. (3) It may be due to regressive de-differentiation on the basis of traumatic experiences and character-neurotic reactions. (4) It may be a symptom of non-differentiation due to externalizing life-conditions either in children or in "primitive" adults. The distinction between the two last-mentioned sub-groups is not always easy, when de-differentiation *results* in waywardness. In the majority of cases, however, the distinction will not be too difficult.

What characterizes the wayward child's inability to delay satisfactions is the naivety of his immediacy-orientation, as against the feelings of urgency, constraint and compulsion that accompany neurotic varieties of obedience to impulses. The wayward child's time-span may be called limited, although he remains capable of relating himself to recollections of the past and imaginations of the future (unlike the feebleminded whose structural rigidity excludes these enlargements of the time-dimension). The wayward child's time-limitations express themselves in the inadequacy and irrelevance of recollections and imaginations rather than in a structural inability thus to extend the time-span. Hence, the easiness with which a wayward child can react to any stimulus that may "come" from the outside and promises satisfaction. There is no inner agent "mediating" between such a promising stimulus and the action imagined or set in motion to attain immediate satisfaction. And yet: the immediacy of his reactions is essentially different from the automaticness of organically caused drivenness: the wayward child does not cease to be a reacting individual.

It is for this reason that we discuss the first and the second symptoms in one context although they are far from being identical: the wayward child's variety of immediacy orientation, as we have already mentioned, is the result of insufficient differentiation. We refer to what we have said elsewhere (34, 35) about the connection between the irregularity and impersonality of primary child-mother relationships and lack of differentiation. The latter, we said, finds its expression in the relative weakness of the ego as a co-ordinating and organizing center, in the non-selective nature of the individual's reactions and in later tendencies to identify the essentials of feelings, concepts or values with their external representatives. It is this lack of structural and functional, relational and cognitive differentiation that gives meaning to the wayward child's easily changing responses to accidentally changing stimuli as well as to his inability to delay satisfaction. Both, immediacy orientation and shallow reactivity, are indicative of lack of differentiation.

Some frequently observed behavioral manifestations of the latter are: addiction to primitive games of chance, easily changing affect discharges, expectation of quick rewards for the slightest efforts made, identification of surface with meaning, f.i. of success with strength and value.

Games of chance should not require even the slightest mental effort to offer satisfaction. Ego-participation in planning, combination, reflexion and similar mental activities actually contradicts the wayward child's undifferentiated need for ever renewed tension and quickly following relaxation. It is this immediacy-sequence that provides the child with the illusion of activity, on the one hand, and with an illusion of being accepted (by fate rather than by chance), on the other. It also justifies the appearance in quick sequence of contradictory feelings, resentment or rage at being beaten or cheated by fate, and pride or joy at being successful, that is, strong. Here, we see how a symptom-manifestation is liable to reinforce the symptom, in our case lack of differentiation; for, it is obvious that the kind of satisfaction sought and found in easy hazard-games supports the externality of feelings aroused, again and again, by success or by failure in such short-lived games. The money earned in this way is not the main motivator since it is as easily spent as it is gained, and since the wayward child has many other and more lucrative accesses to money than this one. Nor is escape from inner tension a motive, as it may be in fear- and complex-ridden adults who seek means of suppressing what haunts them by the creation of external tensions.

Another manifestation of the symptom here analyzed is the quick change of affect-discharges in reaction to experiences of ego-impairment or of ego-assertion. Where the wayward child encounters material or personal factors of frustration, restriction or injury (a "disobeying" tool, a forbidding adult, an aggressor in seriousness or in jokes) he is likely to react with "counter-aggression". It is through such counter-aggressions that he is capable of indulging in the illusion that he has restored his threatened or injured identity. This feeling of being threatened or injured is, however, so externalized that the child does not need any objective evidence of having actually restored his identity; the mere affect-discharge is sufficient for him to be quickly at peace with himself and his environment. The object of his most violent hatred may almost in no time become an accepted companion. The same is true with regard to human or material objects of attachment. They, too, are liable quickly to turn into objects of rejection or of hate. What determines their affective "value" is the amount of assertion they give the wayward child in certain more or less circumscribed situations. Attachment to him *means* being accepted, and is not *caused* by it.

Not only in relation to himself but also to outside hero-figures the same external criteria of value prevail. In this respect, the wayward is not much different from any other externalized child. It can be shown clearly in their reactions to films of adventure, crime, wars: there may be more than one "hero" in the film, according to the successfulness of each in the different parts of the story; and the value contradiction between them, f.i. between the criminal who, in the first part of the film, is shown as successful, and the detective who, in the second part, catches him, does in no way exclude admiring two "heroes". What distinguishes this externalized way of value-attribution from the specifically wayward attitude towards the film is not so much lack of differentiation in the understanding of whole-contexts (in our case the "total" story with its hidden or outspoken moral or social intentions) as it is in the effect such misinterpretations have on the self-perception of the child and particularly the adolescent. True enough, we need not exaggerate this delinquency-forming effect of film-images; it certainly does not operate through imitations (as is often claimed by social workers or educators); but it reinforces the wayward child's tendency to seek self-assertion through quickly attained status-symbols (see later). In this way the symptom-manifestation called the wayward child's film-addiction is liable to become an important additional *cause* of delinquency.

Immediacy-orientation, limitation of the time-span and lack of differentiation find their most "convincing" manifestation in the wayward child's attitude towards work : it is purely instrumental, only a means for the quickest possible attainment of the money needed for some immediate need satisfaction. This instrumentalistic attitude prevents all objective value awareness or, even worse, operates against values, by way of aggressive rejection. Values, such as industry, advancement, learning, knowledge, etc., are liable to become expressions of the "bad" because they make short-term need-satisfaction impossible and require differentiation—a constant source of frustration. In this respect, the wayward differs from the non-delinquent externalized child insofar as open rejection, and not only neglect, of social demand support and help develop asocial behavior patterns in general.

12. EGO-WEAKNESS AND RESISTANCE TO DISCIPLINE

Ego-weakness has different meanings in different pathologies. We speak of the ego's weak ability to co-ordinate its functions which normally should come to form parts of a self-consistent identity. We speak of the ego's weak ability to organize and mobilize adequate defences against ego-alien impulses. Or of its defective control over a certain line of action. We may also have in mind those cases in which lack of security or courage produces either rigid clinging to certain patterns of behavior or avoidance of any form of self-definition or other varieties of pathogenic defenses.

Obviously, the wayward form of ego-weakness is only one among many possible varieties. It means, primarily, the ego's failure to organize a consistent system of mutually related reactions. Absence of their *mutual* relatedness means absence of *ego*-relatedness. Hence, the ego, instead of standing in the center, is here little more than the ever changing result of reactions to external stimuli. If the individual child is of normal intelligence (and as long as he continues to function on his original level) the multitude of his reactions often gives the impression of spontaneity and vitality. But even such seemingly positive qualities do not prove the operation of an adequately functioning ego-center of co-ordination.

We could, of course, repeat what we have said in the preceding paragraph, since immediacy orientation and lack of differentiation are in fact often considered identical with, and not only indicative of, ego-weakness. But within a symptomatology of waywardness we prefer to analyze ego-weakness separately in order to emphasize its essential concomitant, which we propose to call "allergy to all ego-transcending tasks or demands". It is this latter symptom that gives the behavior manifestations of both their special coloring.

Let us consider the most typical and most frequently quoted attitude of the wayward child—lack of perseverance at school or work and addiction to the street. We could, no doubt, describe them as expressions of immediacy-orientation as well. But we would then not be able to recognize the essential difference between externalized behavior in general and that of the wayward child with his delinquency-proneness in particular. Developmentally or structurally caused limitation of the time-span accounts for the externalized child's *inability* to carry out a task which requires delay of satisfaction. But it is active *rejection* of all limitations imposed in the form of societal demands that accounts for the wayward variety of truancy from school or work. In other words: ego-weakness includes, in this case, avoidance of all forms of ego-transcendence.

The wayward child's patterns of truancy cannot be explained either as the outcome of *shame* of imagined and feared failure (in competition with peers) or as the outcome of *escape* from objective tasks (out of uncertainty as to the meaning of the subjective field); it does not reflect rejection of symbols (for the benefit of a universe of things and events) or avoidance of growing-up. The wayward child does not suffer from school-phobia or from distorting compulsions. He is simply conditioned by his early and continued experiences of want, parental orientation towards the haveable, indolence and moral laxity into a life-attitude in which ego-transcendence has no place. His essentially extraversive tendencies and his hypermotility account for the active nature of his truancy: the street, for him, is not a refuge but an attractive fair where things never cease to happen, without committing him to any ego-transcending effort. Ego-organization, paradoxically, means—ego-transcendence. The wayward child's "allergy" to every form of discipline excludes adequate reactions to, or self-confrontation with its demands, exactly as somatic allergies exclude adequate reactions to certain environmental factors of irritation.

The same organizational inability and the same allergy to discipline express themselves in the wayward child's acts of aggressiveness and in his property offenses; they lack every element of planning and personal responsibility. While the manifestations of aggressiveness will be dealt with separately, we shall include a discussion of the wayward child's property offenses in the next paragraph.

13. GROUP-ADDICTION AND ORIENTATION TOWARDS THE HAVEABLE

We do not intend to go into an analysis of the often-discussed problem of the groups and their functions in the different phases of the child's growth process. Suffice it here to say that normally the child *uses* his groups, consciously or unconsciously, for the intrinsic aims of his development. He may learn, as Piaget has pointed out, how to manipulate and thus to master and to modify rules and laws within peer-groups (80), a highly important achievement towards autonomy. He may learn social behavior, often even cure himself of unhealthy isolationist tendencies through participation in group activities. He may satisfy overt or covert needs in a variety of group-contexts. Sometimes he may be dependent on groups, at other times he may avoid them. Age, sex, individual propensities and cultural patterns are among the most decisive differential factors that determine the role of groups in a child's life. But when we speak of group-*addiction*, we have in mind a deviation from the norm, whatever the age, the sex, the personality, the culture of a child may be.

The term "addiction" is being used here not in its literal meaning, as we know it from the field of psychopathology : we do *not* wish to include the wayward child in that large group of neurotics for whom the group symbolizes either an "impersonalized mother" or an anonymous field of ego-diffusion. A neurotic may be driven into group-dependence by anxiety, in this case meaning fear of ego-loss at the hands of a threatening parent figure; compulsive avoidance of egoity then forms an integral part of group-addiction. In certain psychopathic types we find it as a secondary symptom of ego-inflation, in certain maniacs as a secondary symptom of perversions. But when we speak of the wayward child's addiction to (ever changing) groups, we have in mind, first and foremost, his unwillingness and his inability to act on his own initiative. His permanent quest for reactive behavior implies a preference of group-settings, because so much more is likely to happen in groups, and so much easier is the reaction likely to be.

This facilitation of external happenings seems to be a more essential factor in the wayward child's group-addiction than the more obvious factor of escape from responsibility. Needless to emphasize that external "division" of responsibility for an offense (of trespass, theft, sex or aggression) among those who may have committed it jointly, alleviates fear and helps avoiding all forms of a more personal reaction (e.g. of guilt); and everyone who has had contacts with juvenile offenders of the waywardness type can quote many cases to prove this point. But this may be a "secondary gain" only, a by-product, as it were, of the main achievement, which is : enlarging the scope of possible happenings. We should beware of using finalistic categories to explain the wayward child's behavior : he is not guided or motivated by "intentions", neither by conscious nor by unconscious ones. He reacts, and therefore he finds himself in groups (rather than seeks them).

These are frequently changing chance-groups, formed not for a certain defineable and defined purpose, but forming themselves through the accidental association of unforeseen and unforeseeable circumstances. Nothing could be less correct than to identify such groups with the so-called gangs. None of the essential elements of a gang is present in the wayward children's chance groups : they have no leader, no rules of membership, no organizational distribution of functions, no code of behavior, no sanctions, in brief, no systematization. They happen to be, just as they disappear, only to reappear in different forms, with different members. A school mate, or a neighbor, or just someone roaming the streets may join such a group for some time. "Leaders" are not necessarily those who have ideas or initiative; on the contrary : wayward children's groups are often "led", though not for long, by verbose dullards or by youngsters with more variegated street experiences; who just happen to be "there", available, as it were, and who may be drawn into their roles of seeming leadership by chance-circumstances rather than by their own intentions or by the trust or the appeal of others. And, as already said, there is no permanence either in the group-composition or in the so-called leaders' leadership.

But roaming about the streets, examining windows or cars, getting involved in chance happenings; going together to see a film of adventure and discussing later some exciting scene, speaking about the successful strength or slyness of someone "known", a neighbor or a family member

—these are the preliminaries only to more serious business: stealing, destroying, sexual adventures. These, too, are activities carried out in groups: their content is not so much adventure as it is—the haveable. What does this mean in the context of waywardness?

Elsewhere (33, 35) we have analyzed externalization under conditions of poverty and the life-attitude possibly resulting from it. We emphasized as the main expression of this attitude man's non-selective and un-differentiated perception of the universe of objects as "haveable": whatever is wanting, is seen not in its objective significance and not as something that is reachable and may be obtained if only the proper steps are planned and taken. On the contrary: whatever is *not* available, appears in man's mind as something that suddenly, without transition, *may* be available by chance rather than by effort or merit. Externaliza-tion leads to a relative disconnection between cause and result and to blind faith in chance.

In the wayward children's groups, on the other hand, faith in chance is replaced by pseudo-activity of many kinds. The child of these groups regards a chance that may offer itself as an irresistible challenge, an invitation to do something about it. But in order to strengthen the objective character of that chance stimulus, or, better, in order to create the illusion of its objectivity, he needs the readiness of others to react to it identically. When this readiness is achieved, the trespass, the theft or the sex offense is carried out. The value of the object stolen does not determine its attractiveness; it may be high or low. The momentary strength of a sexual urge is irrelevant; it may even be absent in certain members of the group. The intensity of destructive or aggressive ten-dencies is not the decisive factor; it is more often than not the result rather than the cause of an act of trespass or destruction. It is the group-setting that creates in each case the illusion of urge and motive.

If this, however, is the structure of the wayward child's delinquency, can we then still speak of an "orientation towards the haveable"? Does he not commit at least some of his property offences by himself and solely in order to satisfy his primitive needs for whatever he may happen to have not? Demanding or taking money from his parents before he is ready to steal from strangers, snatching objects from a window-sill, an inviting room or a shop, sometimes even carrying out a (real or seeming) plan—are not these acts more realistically motivated than it would seem to be the case in the light of our preceding remarks on the "illusory" nature of a wayward child's delinquency?

The answer is that the wayward child or adolescent is undoubtedly often motivated by purely material needs; but he then seeks satisfaction not so much for the sake of these needs as for that of his ever changing needs for adventure, enjoyment, illusions. "Want", for him, has a different meaning than for adults who live under conditions of poverty. What he needs most are adult status-symbols. They and not material goods are for him "the haveable".

Even when he takes part, with others, in a seemingly well organized theft, he is liable to forget that the planning and organization are means only for the attainment of a material good. He "plays" at stealing more than has the actual theft in mind. It is the limitation of his time-span that makes it impossible for him to be an effective thief. This is the reason why it is so easy to catch these children while they commit their offense. Delinquency, to be effective, requires more than seeking adult status.

14.   SEEKING ADULT STATUS

What is the meaning of the wayward child's ever-present desire to live "like an adult"? Needless to emphasize that his tendency to seek adult status is devoid of all realism. His "allergy" to order, discipline and any other demand of ego-transcendence, his inability to persevere in a task, or to delay a satisfaction make it, of course, impossible for him to translate his external status-imitations into adequate (preparatory) actions. Imitating adult behavior provides the youngster with an illusion of *"having"* adulthood rather than of *being* an adult.

It is this distinction between "having" and "being" that explains the non-committal character of his life-style, on the one hand, and his often mentioned ability to enjoy whatever he does. External fears, e.g. fears of being caught in an offense and being punished for it, may, of course, restrict his usually positive feeling of life being a sequence of enjoyable tensions, happenings or actions. And frustrating failures are abundant in his life. But neither fears nor frustrations will ever be capable of convincing him that it would be preferable to change his life-style, which exempts him from being : through having the haveable symbols of adult status he avoids ego-transcendence, he avoids establishing and maintaining relationships with tasks or with persons, in other words, he avoids being a person conscious of his motives and choices.

When he smokes cigarettes, even in large numbers, he is not an addict nor a neurotic with oral fixations, but is an actor unaware of the fact that he plays a role, that of an adult, and more often than not his acting is rather poor and unconvincing. He is liable to steal in order to satisfy his needs for cigarettes, once he has become accustomed to the habit. Then, he may behave like an addict, though this, too, will be a kind of acting. He can be "cured" much more easily from the habit than a real addict, since there are no deep-lying personality-conflicts to be resolved.

Other symbols of adult-status in the same area, such as drinking or dope-taking (which appear much less frequently than simple cigarette smoking) are, of course, more dangerous since they affect more quickly not only the individual's will power but also his physical health. As a rule, they emerge at a later age only and have their own, specific, causal roots either in an individual's earlier (pathogenic) fixations or in some kind of social pathology which is liable equally to affect youngsters from different social or ethnical backgrounds irrespective of their individual pathologies. Many are known to have become drug-addicts in this way. Even then, however, addiction should not be interpreted as a *symptom* of waywardness but rather as one of its possible results under conditions of a more or less deep-rooted and widespread social craze.

Sexual activities, too, are an expression of that same desire for adult status. A wayward child, growing-up under conditions of poverty and neglect, of indolence and moral laxity, comes to witness and to learn, already early in his life, that sex is not only a welcome pastime but also a symbol of power. He comes to learn and to know that, in order to enjoy this pastime and power-symbol, he must accept sex as something devoid of all personal involvement or relationship. This, however, means re-inforcement of the code of externalization. He simply has to imitate "his" adults' behavior to feel grown-up, and again is saved the trouble of "being" and "becoming".

Needless to add that he is as non-selective in his sex-activities as in the other areas of his behavior. A boy or a girl, of whatever age, if only willing to serve, if only an easy object of seduction, an adult using force or cajolery, paying or paid—all are equally valued objects of a wayward child's or youngster's sex-activities. Nothing could be farther from truth than to speak of perversions when he is caught in some seemingly unnatural practice; as a rule, it is but the outcome of some chance occurrences; it has nothing in common with those truly pervert tendencies of an adult in which psychoanalysts see indications of distorted castration fears.

The absence of ego-involvement is particularly well demonstrated by the fact that the wayward child's sex offenses are usually committed in groups or at least in cooperation with someone else. The instrumentalistic nature of sexual relationships may, of course, characterize other behavioral pathologies as well,* but the preference for group-settings is indicative of this wayward variety only. Status-symbols of adulthood with their illusional character can be obtained and acted out in groups; needs of overcoming feelings of inferiority through compensatory behavior or of bolstering a basically weak ego through pseudo-achievements are easier satisfied when the individual acts alone.

Here may be the place to add a few words about the wayward type of prostitution. We are, of course, not concerned, in the present context, with the problems of child-exploitation (although waywardness may sometimes be the *result* of a child's and particularly of a young girl's sexual exploitation). What we have in mind here is prostitution as a side-effect of promiscuity and promiscuity as an expression of status-seeking. The weaker the ego's power of differentiation, the easier will it be for a girl to misinterpret as evidence of love even the crudest attempt to win her favours. Being desired means for the typically wayward girl— being grown-up. This strange identification of adult status with sexual attractiveness (illusory as it may be) characterizes the wayward variety only of promiscuity. This is true particularly when material advantages are offered that then allow the girl to indulge in fantasies of independence, that is of adulthood.

There exist still other symbols of adult status, but they require a higher degree of ego-differentiation than a wayward child would be capable of attaining even at a later stage. Driving a "borrowed" car is one of them. It becomes more frequent with adolescence only; but even then the wayward youngster prefers *participation* in a joy ride to stealing and driving the car himself. At a younger age, cinema-addiction (which we have already mentioned in another context) can also be interpreted as one of the expressions of the wayward child's desire for adult status. The atmosphere of anonymity in the darkness of the hall helps him submerge, as it were, in an external equalization process; in the course of such a process the child is allowed to identify with the adult onlookers who seem to him as passive as he is himself, and in passiveness the wayward child is indeed an "expert" . . .

15.   AVOIDANCE OF CONTROL

Avoidance of control is an integral part of another characteristic, the one

---

* Certain psychopathic patterns, f.i., in which ego-inflation excludes the possibility of enjoyment within a group-setting. Another example of instrumentalistic offenses in which ego-involvement is nevertheless strongly in evidence is that of certain compulsive sex offenses: here, it is the underlying conscious and unconscious guilt-feeling that contradicts group-settings.

we have called "allergy to discipline and order". But the emphasis is different, and this difference seems to justify the use of two terms. What we have in mind here is not only the wayward child's *inability* to accept restrictions through generally valid demands of ego-transcendence (see p. 76) but his *unwillingness* to give up his illusions of adult-status. To admit guilt means admitting that the adult is superior since he has found out the truth. Therefore, the wayward child will do all in his power to delay this discovery. Let him prove his superiority, he says (at least by implication), let him try to beat me. I won't help him, on the contrary, I shall do all I can to make his superiority difficult for him.*

There are no neurotic components whatsoever in his lying, no elements of compulsiveness or of hysterical denial. It is a conscious attempt to preserve his liberty, which is always threatened by that strange logic called law. "Truth", for him, is neither absolute nor relative (an expression of *consensus omnium* or of proof); "truth" is only what has *not* been proven by the adult representatives of law and order to be untrue. Even after being contradicted convincingly by the facts of objective truth, the lie does not lose of its reality character. In other words : its existential nature is unassailable. It may prove to be ineffective functionally, but it will nevertheless continue to stand between the liar and his judge.

"Roaming about the streets", which we have discussed as one of the central manifestations of the wayward child's ego weakness and resistance to discipline, can also be understood as a means of avoiding adult control. We have maintained that leaving the parents' house for a day or even for a few days is not indicative of escape and certainly not of irrational fears but rather of being attracted by and towards the unstructured multitude of stimuli called "the street". Its attractive power, however, is rooted in the fact that its adult "rules" are unknown and anonymous, and that, as a result, they commit the child even less than his parents. Avoiding them and the possible danger of being controlled by them means liberty and freedom.

In the same way, that is, as attempts to avoid control, can be interpreted all other manifestations of waywardness. We have emphasized that wayward behavior should be explained causally, that is, as the outcome of environmental conditioning (of course only in an individual of certain given propensities). In this respect, waywardness differs essentially from neurotic disorders, which can be explained more easily as expressions of covert or overt, unconscious or conscious intentions, "using"

---

* Redl (83) has pointed out that the "child who hates", the aggressive child, mainly of the primary behavior disorder type, excels in that very skill of transferring the responsibility for finding out the truth, to the accuser.

defense mechanisms. Do not these statements contradict each other? Is not "avoidance" one of the categories of intentionality that are counter-indicated in an interpretation of waywardness?

The answer is that avoidance of adult controls is a protection around the patterns of waywardness. Adult control is liable to "endanger" the limitations of the child's time-span, his lack of differentiation, his "allergy" to order and discipline, his group-addiction and his orientation towards the haveable. Moreover, adult *control* impedes the wayward child's striving for adult *status*. Hence, *avoidance* of adult controls is a logical supplement to all the other symptoms of waywardness, is their inherent reinforcer.

It is at the same time the essential trait which allows for distinction between the asocial behavior of the intellectually normal and the feeble-minded child. Avoidance of adult control (and not merely defense against being caught and punished) is indicative of normality, is absent in the feebleminded. One could even go one step further and say that mental deterioration, this almost inevitable concomitant of waywardness, is reflected in the child's growing failure to avoid adult control.

16. Aggressiveness

Elsewhere (34) we have defined aggressiveness as "destruction of otherness and of fear of ego-loss, resulting in a perversion of identity into rigid and isolationist staticness". It requires, so we added,

"(a) a feeling of destroyability by superior forces in the environment or by uncontrollable unconscious complexes, which, as a rule, appear as parts of that environment;
(b) a need for heightening the feeling of ego-potency by eliminating the threat from without;
(c) lack of inner mobility".

If we accept these three elements of definition,* we must exclude from our discussion most psychopathic and most organic varieties of aggressiveness: psychopathic ego-inflation (see the third chapter!) contradicts feelings of destroyability; the automatism of organically caused outbursts forbids the use of such categories of interpretation as "need" or "intentionality" as they are implied in our second element of definition. In the normal as well as in the neurotic varieties of aggressiveness, however, each of the three components can be identified.

In waywardness of children, the second element is predominant, though it appears only in reaction to short-lived, quickly changing stimuli.

---

* We are not dealing here with what we suggested should be called "positive aggressiveness". See also the author's paper on the subject (29).

This accounts for the often astonishing irrealism in the wayward child's aggressive acts, which, in their extreme uncontrollability, sometimes resemble organically conditioned outbursts, particularly in children of extreme hypermotility.

A parent's refusal to yield to a child's (justifiable or not justifiable) demand for money or some object that may be "necessary" for him to show his status; an older boy's irritating playfulness or attempt to ridicule him; a word of censure or of blame coming from a stranger; a failure and the accompanying loss of status in the eyes of his peers; a chance-attack by anyone whose path he may cross—each of these may trigger off wild attacks. One feels inclined to see in them evidence of vulnerability and include them among the inevitable manifestations of ego-weakness. But we must not lose sight of those many instances in which aggressive behavior is only a means of maintaining the illusion that it is identical with—being an adult.

This holds good primarily for those wayward children who grow up in a family in which patterns of aggressiveness prevail and who tend to imitate their parents' behavior on the streets, when they have no chance of expressing adequately aggressive reactions at home. There is nothing neurotic about their many acts of assault or destruction; it is not an unconscious drive to take revenge on the otherwise unreachable parents or to injure "substitutes" that drives them into aggressiveness. They simply feel that by behaving exactly like the adults in their immediate environment, they are capable of being like them.

But more often than not we find similarly wild and destructive behavior in other wayward children as well, children who have *not* experienced extreme repressiveness at the hands of their parents or other figures of authority; children whose extravert tendencies, whose hypermotility, whose early encounter with indolence and moral laxity not only prepared them for aggressive reactions but also made them enjoy their acts of assault and destruction. With many of them, the emphasis is indeed on destruction of objects rather than on personal attacks. Destruction, here, means : disturbing the order of things, that is, living in a world which, by virtue of being destroyable, satisfies their allergy to discipline.

Finally, we should ask whether there are no signs of ambivalence in the aggressive behavior of wayward children and youngsters. We often come across juvenile delinquents who cannot live without those very parents in whose presence they feel but aggressive impulses. They need their parents to act out "on" them all their aggressiveness. But on closer examination we often find in their total behavior strong indications of neurotic complications and fixations unless they belong to the primary

J.D.—D

behavior disorder type of delinquency (see later). Ambivalence in a truly wayward child's relationships with his parents appears, if at all, only during a certain phase of his re-education or rehabilitation process, that is, when successful treatment interventions have already divided between him and his waywardness.

CHAPTER THREE

Psychopathy

A. BASIC CONCEPTS AND TYPES

1. THE PROBLEM

ONE OF THE most ambiguous and elusive concepts in psychopathology is that of psychopathic behavior. In spite of the numerous analyses that have appeared in the literature of the last decades, it seems that we have not yet advanced very much in the differential diagnosis of the clinical picture. On the contrary, it sometimes would appear as if the abandonment of the old-time psychiatrists' descriptive classifications (8, 66, 67, 88) by psychiatrists and psychologists of the dynamic schools-of-thought, and particularly by those basing their interpretations on psychoanalytic concepts, has made the task of differential phenomenology and diagnosis still more difficult. It is true that without the aid of dynamic concepts many traits of behavior are liable to be included in the clinical pictures of so-called psychopathic types (or states) which should be explained as manifestations of neurotic developments, and, because of this, many cases are apt to be incorrectly diagnosed and classified.* On the other hand, a dynamic interpretation which is not preceded by phenomenologic type-differentiation may lead to overgeneralizing the causal significance of certain psychic mechanisms.

As a result, psychopathy may gradually lose its character as a clinical unit in its own right, that is, as an entity essentially different from others. There are, indeed, not a few psychiatrists who question the *raison d'être* of psychopathy as a separate unit; they point out the qualitative similarity that exists between the causal factors which may be held responsible for the emergence of neurotic (4) or impulsive (84) character disorders, antisocial character formations (38), primary behavior disorders of the preoedipal and the oedipal types (49, 77), affectionless stealing (9), perversions, addictions and other forms of compulsive asociality or antisociality (23, 72). The tendency to do away with the concept of psycho-

---

* For an extreme example of such diagnostic inaccuracies, see (61).

pathy should not be understood, however, as an expression of semantic refinement; it rather reflects the general trend in modern psychopathology toward thinking in terms of ontogenetic development. The distinction between congenital and acquired psychopathy, it is true, made its first appearance in the days of pre-dynamic psychiatry.* But it was not until psychoanalysis had succeeded in differentiating our concepts of pathology that "psychopathy" became questionable *in toto*.

There are, however, a number of pertinent questions which should be answered before deciding whether or not the clinical concept under consideration should be abandoned. Does the fact that we are able to trace the ontogenesis of at least some of the so-called psychopathic disorders warrant their exclusion from that clinical unit? In other words, does absence of congenital causes *a priori* preclude a diagnosis of psychopathy? Are we allowed to reserve the concept for those disorders only that do not lend themselves to ontogenetic interpretations and are not amenable to treatment? Or should we attempt, rather, to discover specific structural elements that could be defined as the essential characteristics of psychopathy, elements whose presence alone would justify its diagnosis? If congenitality is considered a *conditio sine qua non* of psychopathy, only very few, if any, unambiguous cases could indeed be quoted. If only negative criteria are applied, the concept would indeed serve as what Preu has called a "scrap basket" (81), a *refugium ignorantiae nostrae*.

We maintain that it is not the lack of modifiability (whether caused by hereditary, prenatal, paranatal or postnatal factors) but ego inflation (a concept we shall try to explain) which should be considered the essential characteristic of psychopathy. We further maintain that certain congenital and early environmental factors are liable to produce a variety of types of psychopathic behavior which determine the individual's further development almost irrespective of the quality of the growing child's later socio-educational environment. To the extent that environmental factors (operating in configuration with congenital conditions) can be shown to be responsible for what we intend to call the psychopathic constitution, it would seem to be the time factor which explains the difference between psychopathic and nonpsychopathic behavior patterns emerging in the course of the individual's development. The differential question to be answered would be : whether certain pathogenic factors operate in the child's environment before or after the crystallization of the constitutional ego-nucleus?

We shall try to answer these questions by synthesizing analytic typology

---

* See, for instance, the papers published by R. Steen (in 1913) or by A. Tredgold (in 1917) quoted by M. Gurvitz (47).

(based on Jung's theory) with the principles of dynamic psychology. While doing this, we shall always bear in mind (a) that psychopathy is not identical with its antisocial manifestations but includes a variety of more passive and in any case less allotropic character disorders; (b) that its various forms can be recognized as such, that is, as psychopathic manifestations, only by way of comparing them with similar, though essentially different, pathologies such as character neuroses, primary behavior disorders, waywardness, neurotic or compulsive delinquency.

Psychopathy has been defined as constitutional inability to establish consistent (positive as well as negative) relationships and effective human ties or as a constitutional deficiency in volition and emotion (in contra-distinction to intellectual deficiencies). Lack of identification; a poorly defined ego concept; a tendency to mirror others in behavior; absence of superego awareness, of anxiety, of guilt feelings and of neurotic reactions to conflict or frustration; shallowness of fantasy material; lack of concern for objective facts; weakness of the time concept are mentioned as the main characteristics of psychopathy in children (82). We know, of course, how difficult it is to diagnose psychopathy in children before they reach puberty and adolescence and clearly to exclude alternative diagnoses. It is also a well-established fact that a phenomenology of psychopathic behavior in adults reveals additional and still more serious deviations. There, we find moral indolence, often leading to brutal crimes; lack of control over sexual and/or material desires; hysterical fanaticism, seem-ingly for the sake of a truth, a principle, an idea, but actually reflecting an insatiable need to be the center of attention, admiration or fear; the same need producing the well-known swindler and imposter type (the "Hochstapler"); narcissistic excitability; or almost unlimited seducibility. Sometimes the vagabond, the sex pervert, the addict are included in the list of psychopathic types.

In the light of these manifestations of adult psychopathy it is obvious that the first-quoted interpretation of psychopathic behaviour in children (82), though undoubtedly applicable to that of adults as well, is insufficient to make us understand why these various forms of deviant behavior should be subsumed under one general clinical concept, that of psycho-pathy. Relational inability, which is the central element in that interpreta-tion, explains the weakness of the child's identification in general and with his parents in particular. We thus understand the deficiencies in the process of introjection and of the superego formation, which in turn explain the relative absence of anxiety, of guilt feelings, and of neurotic reactions. We may also relate to that same element the intellectual peculiarities of the psychopathic child : his lack of concern for objective facts, his inability to form proper time concepts and, let us add, adequately to experience time. This is only another way of saying that the ability to relate oneself to the meaningful persons in the environment both pre-supposes and furthers the ability to relate oneself to all that is outside the ego, to the social and the material non-ego. It is not so easy, however, to derive from relational inability alone the remaining elements of the above-quoted interpretation, the shallowness of fantasy material, the tendency to mirror others in behavior, and the poorly defined ego concept. And the concept of relational inability is certainly not adequate to explain the seemingly contradictory varieties of adult psychopathy. We therefore suggest supplementing the interpretation by introducing the concept of ego inflation.

2.   THE ELEMENTS OF PSYCHOPATHY

Normally the ego develops, through the learning process, as the organizing center of the gradually growing areas of consciousness. Learning means internalizing the non-ego, transforming reality contents into conceptual, emotional *and* functional parts of the ego. The ego coordinates not only the contents of consciousness (by relating them to each other in varying contexts of meaning) but also its own functions (by relating them to each other as well as to the actual and potential contents of consciousness, according to their relevance in a given situation). The structural basis of normal ego development and ego functioning is the polarity between ego and non-ego. "Polarity" means that the ego can fulfill its organizational and synthesizing functions only to the extent that it is able and ready to be receptive *vis-à-vis* the non-ego; it means that the non-ego, in turn, is intentionally directed toward the ego in its changing actuality while at the same time being the object of its activity. The simultaneity and exchangeability of these subject-object positions is the structural condition of normal ego development.*

But normal ego development should be interpreted not only in terms of structural, but also in terms of dynamic polarity, the polarity between the two basic life tendencies, the tendency toward staticness and the tendency toward expansion. We have tried to show in another place that normally these two tendencies are interrelated :

". . . the aim of life is the creation of complex organic and psychic systems out of simpler units. This creation goes through two phases: expansion and systematization. The process of expansion and transformation can, it is true, be achieved only through

---

*These ideas have been dealt with in greater detail by the author in his book *The Roots of the Ego* (34).

the relative negation of what exists. But as long as this negation is subject to its structural aim (integration), it does not contradict the second life tendency, that toward staticness: this tendency, too, is normatively expressed in actual life only as a tendency toward the formation of new systems and never, because of the eternal processuality of life, achieves its aim . . . Both tend toward the elimination of the separateness of elementary units . . . Only when the two tendencies function in isolation, without interaction, does the tendency toward staticness degenerate either into regression or into 'petrification' . . . and the tendency toward expansion becomes a destructive and aggressive tendency toward a blind conquest of life" (27).

The fact that individuals differ in the degree of integration and inter-relatedness of these two life tendencies may of course be due, at least partly, to congenital predispositions. There can be no doubt, however, that early childhood experiences finally determine the individual's ability to give up staticness for the sake of expansion and growth. At the same time, these early experiences determine the extent to which he will be able to trust that every expansion of the growing ego's boundaries tends toward systematization and thus leads back again to staticness, though always on a higher level of development and structurality. The most important environmental factor in the development toward this inter-relatedness of the two life tendencies is the infant's experience of regularity in the sequence of tension and need-satisfaction. It is in this way that the child learns not to fear or avoid the necessary interruptions of static-ness but to trust in the return of (and to) staticness; out of this trust, he becomes more and more able and ready to leave staticness on his own and to seek expansion of his narrow boundaries. And it is in this way that staticness becomes the basis of the first feelings of identity, that is, of the ego, whereas interruption of staticness through tension and growth becomes the basis of the experience of otherness, of the non-ego.

Thus, we may say that the interrelatedness of staticness and expansion, based on the experiential interrelatedness of tension and satisfaction, makes possible the formation of the ego as the organizing center of consciousness, of facts and functions, of knowledge and feeling, of action and affect, past and present; it is on the basis of this interrelatedness of the two life tendencies that the polarity between ego and non-ego can be experienced. The formation and normal development of the ego presupposes, as we have said above, exchangeability of the subject-object positions in the interrelatedness of the ego and the non-ego.

What, then, does the concept of ego inflation, which we consider essential for the interpretation and the understanding of psychopathy, mean?

If the interrelatedness of the two life-principles is disturbed, either the tendency toward staticness or the tendency toward expansion becomes predominant. In the first instance the result may be rigid clinging to a

given state; anxious refusal or apathetic inability to grow; self-limitation
to what is known; readiness to regress whenever the life-demands become
difficult or threatening; and inability of the ego to experience itself as the
object of a trustworthy non-ego that operates as the subject-agent of
change and determination, or to experience itself as the subject-agent of
change and determination in relation to an objectively recognized non-
ego. The essential characteristic of this behavior type is lack of courage.
If, on the other hand, the tendency toward expansion is predominant,
the result may be : passive drivenness or blind aggressiveness; restlessness;
weakness of identity feeling, which may lead to a false self-definition,
acquired by way of imitation and liable to change frequently; and
inability of the ego to experience the non-ego as subject to its own
inherent constitution and to experience itself as part and partner of the
non-ego.

Among the various pathologies liable to emerge, when the life tendency
toward expansion is predominant, the clinical entity of psychopathy in its
different forms stands out. While these forms are determined (as we
intend to show) by congenitally given structural dispositions and earliest
experiences, it would seem that all have one element in common : predominance of expansion over staticness leading to what we have suggested
should be called *ego inflation*.

Ego inflation means that the ego, instead of fulfilling its task as the
mediator between inner and outer realities and as the organ and agent of
conceptual, functional and structural coordination, becomes an end in
itself. Normally, the ego fulfills its function by facing and recognizing the
non-ego as its counterpole, that is, as an independent reality; the psychopath conceives of the non-ego as of an actual or potential part of itself,
to be incorporated at will.

The relationship between the ego and the non-ego, it is true, is disturbed also in neurotic or psychotic diseases, in waywardness or in
primary behavior disorders, in brain injuries or in feeblemindedness. But
in all these pathologies, the feeling of otherness is not only not eliminated
but, on the contrary, is accentuated, and the specific forms in which it *is*
accentuated constitute the essential characteristics of the various clinical
units. The perception of the non-ego may be distorted by projections (in
neuroses), or the non-ego may engulf the ego (in psychoses); the non-ego
may be the area of chance occurrences (in waywardness) or the absolute
enemy (in primary behavior disorders); it may become almost identical
with neural irritation (in brain injuries) or with the "omnipotent", the
absolutely separated (in feeblemindedness). It is only in the different
forms of psychopathy that otherness is no longer experienced as such,

although intellectually most psychopaths are well able to understand not only the fact but also the individual quality of this otherness. The boundaries between the ego and the non-ego remain more or less distinct, and it is usually not at all difficult for the psychopath correctly to evaluate differences; often he even excels in it. But this ability, which normally helps to establish and develop the experience of distance and thus intensifies polarization, tension and relatedness, serves the opposite purpose in the life and development of the psychopath, the purpose of "egotropic incorporation".

When psychoanalysts speak of incorporation, they use the concept to indicate a fundamental condition of the normal or neurotic process of introjection, that is, the transformation of the outer world into internal contents and forces. Here the ego develops—with the help of, and in relatedness to, its functions—into what might be called a *reactive structure*. Its essential characteristics are : expansion of the ego through learning, without loss of identity, coexistence of ego-relatedness with objective validity of reality contents and values, dialogic relationship between the ego and the non-ego.

(Incorporation and introjection may be held up or even prevented by organic disturbances in cases in which the neuro-structural basis for polarization is defective. In these cases, however, not only the non-ego ceases to exist as an object of relatedness, but also the ego ceases to exist as a subject and center of organization.)

In psychopathy, however, we observe a different process : although incorporation does take place and the incorporated is transformed, at least partially, into conceptual contents of consciousness and into ego functions, this process is devoid of polarization. Now, it is precisely this polarization which, normally, leads to a more or less conscious simultaneity of the internalized contents and functions and their objective representations in the non-ego. In other words, normally the incorporated continues to exist as a separate reality in its own right, a reality to which the transformed, the internalized is specifically related and adapted. In psychopathy, on the other hand, the lack of polarization manifests itself in a more or less radical disappearance from consciousness of the objective counterpart of what is being incorporated. It exists, as it were, in the consciousness of the psychopath, as his property only, to be used and disposed of at will; but it has lost its individual independence (or its independent individuality).

This explains the psychopath's lack of concern for objective facts. Why, indeed, should he be concerned with the independent, objective significance of what has no *raison d'être* outside his "ownership"? And why concern himself with facts which have not, or have not yet, aroused his egocentric needs? Objective facts are meaningful only for those who are able to recognize their independent existence, their right and power to limit the ego. They are meaningless for the psychopath, unless they are connected with an immediate act of incorporation. His concepts, too, are related only to his needs and demands. He may be highly intelligent and capable of forming and using a most differentiated system of concepts, wherever his ego is set on a new conquest. But even an extraordinary gift for abstraction may not prevent him from failing in relatively simple intellectual tasks when these have nothing to do with his inflated ego but refer to a general, an anonymous problem.

This failure of intelligence becomes particularly evident in the weakness of the time concept, so typical of psychopathic behavior. The discontinuity, in the life of the psychopath, between past experience, present behavior and planning for the future (which we tend to interpret as inability to learn from experience, positive or negative) often strangely contrasts his intelligence. Here again we see the effect of what we have called ego inflation : intelligence, in the psychopath, is not a function of the ego, coordinated with other ego functions within a feedback system, but becomes a mere instrument of incorporation, related not so much to objective facts as to the inflated ego's insatiable needs. This is only another way of saying that even a highly developed intelligence may be defective when otherness is not experienced as such. The time concept of the psychopath is that of the present, while past and future are nothing but an extended present.

Fantasy shallowness can be explained as another expression of that same predominance of the present in the time conception of the psychopath and as an expression of his ego inflation. Normally, fantasy is "fed" by past experiences of unfulfilled desires, by anxieties and expectations that emerge in the processes of suppression and repression, by temporary withdrawal from present realities. It may fulfill a constructive function as an agent of anticipation, or it may become an instrument of regression and avoidance. But its structural basis is in both instances the ego's ability to place itself at a distance from its own actuality as well as from the non-ego. In the psychopath, on the other hand, who lacks this basic ability, fantasy elaborates, as it were, the all-pervading theme of egotropic incorporation, thus inflating still more his inflated ego. It is related to his conscious intentions, desires, thoughts and actions only, and has no dynamic connection with the contents and forces of the unconscious.

This leads us to the question as to what extent the actions and reactions of the psychopath are motivated by unconscious complexes. By saying that lack of superego awareness, of anxiety and guilt feelings, and of neurotic reactions to conflicts and frustrations are the central characteristics of psychopathy, we imply that repression does not take place. We maintain that anxiety, i.e., fear of ego loss (27), lies at the root of those psychic processes that lead to repression, introjection of parental images, to superego formation, and, at a later stage, superego awareness, to guilt feelings and increased anxiety, and, finally, though of course not necessarily, to the emergence of neurotic symptoms and reactions.

Following C. G. Jung's distinction between the personal and the transpersonal unconscious (60, 76), we have suggested in another paper (30) that the *negative* concept (un-conscious) be reserved for those contents and feelings that have never reached consciousness or have been repressed from consciousness, while using a *positive* concept ("the depth region of the psyche") for designating the so-called transpersonal forces. At this stage of our analysis, we shall refer only to the role of the personal unconscious in the phenomenology of psychopathic behavior.

If we agree that the unconscious is not identical with repressed contents and feelings but also includes those earliest organic and environmental impressions that have never reached consciousness, is it evident that no human being can ever be free from unconscious influences. These influences enter into the formation of what are called, at a later stage of development, the constitutional determinants of personality. Not only hereditary and other congenital predispositions (type, endowments and defects, reaction patterns, thresholds of perception, level of frustration bearance and love needs) but also those ontogenetic influences, that is, the deep layer of the unconscious, participate in the formation of the individual's constitution.

To what extent, we must ask, can the individual *experience* those unconscious contents that have been transformed into structure and have become part of his constitution? And to what extent would such a re-experience, should it prove to be possible, make reversible those ontogenetic components of constitution? It would seem that we are not yet able to answer this question, which is, of course, of decisive relevance in education and in therapy. Although some psychoanalysts tend to believe in the, at least theoretically, unlimited possibility of reducing the ontogenetic elements of constitution to their earliest experiential basis (by using the usual psychoanalytic techniques), the evidence so far available to prove this claim is, to say the least, still insufficient and unconvincing. We have maintained in the above-quoted paper (30) that the reduction of structure to contents and the possibility of re-experiencing the latter as such depend on the relationship between the ego and what we have called "the depth region of the psyche" and not only on the establishment of contact between consciousness and the personal unconscious. If so, other techniques than those accepted by psychoanalysis with its purely personalistic approach would be required to open, as it were, the ego to that depth region of the psyche. But here is not the place tò dwell on these metapsychological aspects of structure change.

In a discussion of psychopathy the question raised here of the role played by earliest life experience in the final emergence of the individual's constitution is of particular interest not only for the therapist but also for the psychologist in his attempts to interpret psychopathy as a specific clinical unit. It seems to be the general consensus of today's psychiatrists and psychologists that, although psychopathy has a definite constitutional basis, it is in most cases the result of earliest life experiences operating in configuration with certain congenital propensities.* We suggest the hypothesis that the core of psychopathy, ego inflation, emerges in the first year of life, with the exception of those (relatively few) cases in which it is congenitally given. We further contend that the structural condition of ego inflation is absence of anxiety. And we must ask whether this absence of anxiety is congenitally given or results from what might be called primary repressions.

Anxiety, being fear of ego loss (27), is fundamentally caused by the interruption of staticness in the life of the infant and the child. Every environmental limitation of the infant's or the child's being with himself, of his "flow of existence", but also the very process of organic change and growth are experienced by him as such interruptions of staticness. Anxiety is reinforced and intensified if, and to the extent that, the individual is unable to re-establish (to return to) staticness. This connection between interruption of staticness and fear of ego loss becomes understandable in the light of the above-mentioned facts: staticness, we said, originates in the infant's experience of satisfactory relationships with the mother, and is the basis of the first feeling of identity; being separated from the mother is the source of the feeling of otherness, of non-ego experience. If the two experiences, the "mother as part" and the "absent mother", completeness and separateness, are approximately

---

* The discussions published in the American Journal of Orthopsychiatry since 1949 on the subject of psychopathy, its causes and its differentiation from other clinical units, clearly indicate this basic agreement. Even such an inveterate environmentalist as B. Karpman, the chairman of most of these discussions, who tries so very hard to prove his "psychogenic" approach, cannot deny that such factors as "degrees of frustration bearance", "degrees of narcissism", "cerebral structures", etc., are *constitutional* determinants of behavior, hence also of what he calls "idiopathic psychopathy".

equal in intensity and follow each other in a rhythm of regular alternation, the result is the experience of nearness ("the returning mother", "the
mother as the near one"). It is on the basis of this experience that the
child's relational ability and, with it, his ability to experience anxiety,
develops (27, 34). It is only another way of saying that normally the
tendency toward staticness and that toward expansion operate in interaction and interrelatedness : the first makes the second into a meaningful
force of growth and relationship; the second prevents the first from
leading to stagnation, rigidity and regression.

We have maintained that where this normal interrelatedness is disturbed, psychopathy is liable to result from a predominance of the
tendency toward expansion over that toward staticness, provided, we can
now add, the individual is, or has become, unable to experience anxiety.
If this ability is, and remains, intact, predominance of expansion may
manifest itself in a variety of character traits or dispositions (such as
excessive suggestibility, irritability, explosiveness, aggressive reaction
patterns, etc.); though resembling symptoms of psychopathy, they have
an essentially different meaning : they either prepare the way for what
later appears as character neurosis or are otherwise contributory factors
to the formation and crystallization of the individual's behavioral type.

What, then, accounts for this differential condition, the loss or the
preservation of the infant's ability to experience anxiety? Environmental
or organic interruptions of staticness are experienced as such, that is, as
threatening, and therefore produce fear of ego loss (anxiety), because
normally the first identity and ego feeling depends, as we have already
mentioned, on a satisfactory experience of "the mother as part" (completeness). If, on the other hand, the opposite experience, that of "the
absent mother" (separateness) substantially exceeds the first one in
intensity, the child may react with apathy and withdrawal, which are
then bound to delay or, in extreme cases, even to prevent the development of the ego-nucleus and the ego as the actively organizing center
of consciousness. Here, we can speak of primary repression of anxiety in
a child born with a normal ability to experience anxiety. Some cases of
apathetic feeblemindedness and of earliest childhood schizophrenia may
become understandable as such reactions to extreme deficiencies in the
experience of "the mother as part", *when these experiential deficiencies
are supported by a congenital predominance of the tendency toward
staticness over that toward expansion.*

When, on the other hand, the *tendency toward expansion* is structurally stronger than that toward staticness, psychopathy may emerge not
only where the child is congenitally (structurally) unable to experience

anxiety (in which case the quality of environmental influences becomes almost irrelevant), but also, and more frequently, under the following conditions of traumatic maternal experiences :

1) Early experience of rejection by the mother or early loss of the mother may bar the return to staticness, thus causing a secondary intensification of the tendency toward expansive and aggressive rejection of the non-ego;

2) when the experience of "the absent mother" exceeds that of "the mother as part" in an individual growing up without maternal care or under the influence of extreme maternal indolence (apathy), the result may be primary repression of whatever fear of ego loss appears in reaction to the experience of extreme separateness;

3) lack of ego limitation by an overindulgent mother may eliminate anxiety, together with relational ability.

Irrespective of whether absence of anxiety is congenitally given or results from the structural predominance of the tendency toward expansion and from certain deficiencies in the child-mother relationship, the experience of "the mother as part" remains unconscious; it belongs to the deepest layers of the unconscious where those impressions are sunk that have never reached consciousness. And irrespective of whether the weakness of the tendency toward staticness is congenitally given or results from the absence of anxiety and from earliest frustrations, the ego does not develop (as it can only under the guidance of the tendency toward staticness) into a reactive structure, but emerges as a kind of pseudo-structure depending entirely on constant expansion through incorporation of the non-ego.*

---

* We have already pointed out that this type of incorporation is essentially different from the one leading, in the course of normal ego development, to identification and introjection. In contrast to the latter, it does not contribute to the gradual emergence and structurization of an inner world. The incorporated loses, as we said, its individuality; it ceases to exist as an independent non-ego when it becomes part and property of the psychopathic ego. But this by no means implies that the incorporated is truly assimilated and internalized. On the contrary, it seems as if the non-ego character had only been shifted to the newly established parts of the ego.

Now, it is a well-known fact that many psychopaths, in spite of their lack of capacity for identification, excel not only in their ability correctly to evaluate individual differences but also in what seems to be empathy. However, on closer examination, a fundamental difference between true empathy and its psychopathic counterpart becomes evident. The psychopath does not feel with (and within) the other on the basis of genuine self-to-self relationship but only understands the mask the other wears, the role he plays in his own eyes and *for* his environment, the more or less concealed weakness but not the essence of the personality.

3. THE CRITERIA OF TYPOLOGY

We shall now try to analyze the various forms of psychopathy in adults with a view to constructing a viable typology. Such a construction must be based on a clearly defined principle of systematization and not only on inductive methods of case observation and case analysis (like those prevailing in the descriptive classifications of pre-dynamic psychiatry). A typologic system, in order to be meaningful for the interpretation of a constitutional concept such as psychopathy, must itself be based on constitutional categories, either of the somatic variety (e.g., Kretschmer's or Sheldon's typologies) or of the attitudinal and/or functional variety (e.g., Jung's typology). Categories of ontogenetic experience are applicable only to the extent that they refer to the earliest (pre-constitutional) phases of development. (A system like that suggested by Freud would therefore be unsuitable in the context of psychopathy because it is based on his theory of the three early libidinal phases, two of which begin at, or extend into, the period after the individual's constitution has already been established.)

We regard as an adequate conceptual basis for a typology of psychopathic conditions (a) the distinction between extraversion and introversion, (b) configurated with the quality of the infant's mother experience ("the mother as part" and "the absent mother") and (c) applied to behavior which is characterized by a predominance of expansion over staticness, by inability to experience fear of ego loss and by ego inflation. On the other hand, we shall *not* include in our typologic system functional distinctions, such as those used by van der Hoop (23) on the basis of Jung's theory of the four "Funktionstypen". As long as we are unable to answer the question whether these functional types operate as constitutional determinants from birth on or come into operation only in the course of the child's individual development, we should be careful not to include them in the construction of a typology of psychopathic conditions (although there can be no doubt that functional differentiation will enable us to recognize certain varieties in the main types of psychopathy; cf. footnote on p. 118).

When we say that only the categories of earliest mother-child relationship should enter into the construction of a typology of psychopathic conditions, we exclude by implication all traumatic events which may take place in later stages of the child's life, that is, after the end of the second year when, normally, the process of primary ego formation has come to an end. The more advanced in the phases of development the child is, the greater are the chances that the same negative experiences that produce psychopathic conditions when operating at the beginning of life will lead to behavior disorders characterized by neurotic reactions and symptoms. A few examples may illustrate this difference : Primary behavior disorders of the oedipal type or neurotic delinquency may appear in reaction to the disappointing experience of sudden loss of the mother in the oedipal phase instead of psychopathic aggressiveness in reaction to the same experience taking place in the oral phase. Periodic yielding to sexual impulses immediately followed by qualms of conscience (the "forgetful sinner") may appear instead of the sexual aggressiveness and egocentric sensuality of the psychopathic type with his moral indolence. We find insecurity and fearfulness rather than psychopathic apathy in reaction to the experience of an impersonal environment according to the phases in which this traumatic condition prevails. Or we may find neurotic reactions of the hysterical, the phobic, or the compulsive type instead of what we shall describe as the "oscillating type of psychopathy" in reaction to maternal indolence.

We have also stressed that behavior diagnosed as psychopathic must be characterized by a predominance of the tendency toward expansion over that toward staticness. We have thereby excluded those disorders which, although caused by the same disturbances of the primary mother-child relationship, appear in individuals characterized by the opposite predominance (of staticness over expansion). We then find a refusal to grow up, infantilism or lack of initiative, intellectual and otherwise, instead of the imitative and shallow pseudo-attachment or the temperamental moodiness of the psychopathic variety (in cases of early institutionalization). We may find self-hatred or masochistic fantasies instead of antisocial behavior or sadistic fantasies and eruptions in reaction to early maternal rejection. Passive intake of, and rigid defense against, the non-ego or schizophrenic withdrawal from reality instead of "oscillating" incorporation of the non-ego or apathetic drivenness and instability of the psychopathic type may appear in reaction to maternal indolence. Egocentric aloofness rather than ego inflation, ineffectuality rather than paranoid excitability is a possible reaction to early separation. Maternal indulgence is liable to produce the well-known swindler and impostor type or the queer, eccentric or fanatic psychopath who knows nothing but *his* truth, if the child shows a constitutional predominance of the tendency toward expansion over that toward staticness. In the opposite constellation, however, the same maternal indulgence may produce overdependence or obsessional self-limitation.

Moreover, it follows from the aforesaid that we regard only a few specific forms of negative mother-child relationship as causally responsible for the emergence of psychopathic behavior, if they operate in the earliest phases of the child's development. These are : a more or less complete lack of maternal contact and care; indolence and apathy in the mother's attitude toward the child; overt rejection of the child by the mother; sudden disappearance of the mother; and maternal indulgence. Neither over-protection (of the anxious or the aggressive type) nor inconsistency —to mention only two of the most important causes of emotional disorders in children—are liable to produce psychopathic behavior because in both severe ego limitations and restrictions are implied. And if maternal indolence and apathy or aggressiveness and rejection appear under conditions of extreme poverty, the ensuing externalization of consciousness, that is, the individual's growing orientation toward "the haveable which he has not", again precludes ego inflation, i.e., psychopathic behavior, and waywardness is liable to result (34).

Before continuing our analysis we shall try to summarize and supplement, what we have said so far about the various forms of psychopathic behavior. The following table shows the main causal constellations in their effect on the extravert or the introvert under conditions of structural predominance of the tendency toward expansion. We have added a comparison with pathologies liable to result from the impact of the same earliest traumatizations on a child in whom the life-tendency towards staticness predominates. It is obvious that this method of abstract comparison of essentials is not meant to replace clinical observation, diagnosis and classification of cases. Its purpose is auxiliary only : to help understand the *meaning* of causal factors by seeing them in structural contexts. In an analysis of psychopathy, the advantages of this method are evident when we compare it with purely descriptive classifications or with the generally accepted method of dichotomization. A few examples will make this point clear.

Henderson (52) and Hall (48) distinguish between the aggressive and the inadequate types of psychopathy. The first type, according to Henderson, includes such heterogeneous manifestations as suicidal flight from reality and suicide as atonement, murder without a conscious goal, alcoholism as a reaction to deep castration fears or as a manifestation of latent homosexuality, sexual disinhibition caused by epileptoid disorders, and perversions followed by guilt feelings or being free from any form of ego distantiation. Psychopathy of the predominantly inadequate type, on the other hand, is said to be a precondition of certain neurotic or psychotic disorders, to manifest itself in egocentric and narcissistic character attitudes or in exhibitionism, and includes the swindler and the paranoid types of psychopathy as well.* The specific

---

* The "predominantly creative" variety does not interest us at this stage of our analysis

form of each of these two types, appearing in the individual case, can, of course, be made plausible only when we include ontogenetic experiences as differential factors of causation. But, if so, a clear distinction between the structurizing and the neuroticizing effect of individual experiences (depending mainly on the time-factor) should precede the diagnosis and typology of psychopathic conditions. Otherwise, the neurotic equivalents of psychopathic behavior are bound to be included, and the system of classification loses its cogency. Moreover, it would seem to be almost impossible to find the common denominator of all the manifestations included by Henderson under the heading of the aggressive and the inadequate psychopath respectively.

The same applies to Karpman's distinction between the aggressive-predatory and the passive-parasitic types (65)* or to D. Levy's distinction between the "deprived" and the "indulged" types (71). Although the latter dichotomy has the advantage of being based on etiologic considerations, it is much too general and undifferentiated for the purpose of classifying the various types of psychopathy and does not enable us to exclude non-psychopathic forms of egocentric aggressiveness or inadequacy. The method of etiologic dichotomization is bound to fail because it does not take proper account of additional factors of causal differentiation, such as the types of personality or the time factor. But even more important than etiologic differentiation is the definition of a suitable criterion which must guide the diagnostician and the typologist of psychopathic conditions.

We have suggested defining the criterion of psychopathy as primary or secondary "absence of anxiety and ego-inflation in an individual in whom the tendency toward expansion predominates". It will therefore be our next task to examine the various forms of psychopathic behavior by applying this criterion. Only to the extent that absence of anxiety, ego inflation and predominance of the life-tendency towards expansion can be proved to be the characteristics of a behavioral manifestation, are we justified in diagnosing it as psychopathic.

4. The Congenital Variety

It is not difficult to understand in these terms that form of psychopathic behavior which is characterized by congenital absence of moral feelings

---

* It should, however, be added that psychiatry owes more than this "typology" to Karpman (64) who has devoted many of his writings in the last thirty years to the clarification of the concept of psychopathy. Although he is one of the strongest advocates of the psychogenic (or the anticonstitutional) school of thought, he also maintains that psychopathy is *not* to be reduced to the same factors and forces as neurotic developments. Against Alexander's attempt to identify psychopathy with the "neurotic character", he argues that although cases can undoubtedly be found "in which psychopathy is symptomatic of and secondary to a basic cardinal neurosis" (cases which he classifies as symptomatic or secondary psychopathy or as psychopathoid), "there are types of psychopathic behavior which, however careful and definite the study, fail to reveal the presence and operation of psychogenic factors. Perhaps they are not there, or perhaps they are so deep that we do not get at them. In many other and basic respects, these cases differ from the symptomatic type mentioned above. I have classified these as anethopathy : primary, idiopathic, essential psychopathy."

or human considerations. Here, the drive to incorporate the world at will is not even restrained by aggressive and destructive *intentions*. Intentionality would indicate at least some residue of relational ability. In this form of psychopathy, however, the ego's identification with itself is so complete that the non-ego loses its character as *objectum* and retains only its function as the external area of stimulation. Which reality element is liable at any given moment to stimulate the ego's incorporative tendency is determined by chance constellations rather than by a reactive and selective ego structure.*

Resistance of another person or, for that matter, of any living or material object, is liable to evoke acts of brutal elimination, accompanied by no stronger feelings than would accompany the killing of a molesting fly. If uncontrollable events of fate interrupt the incorporative drives of this psychopath, he may eliminate himself with the same ease as he is ready to eliminate any other resisting object.

Sex is often the preferred vehicle of his ego inflation, though he may be far from being strong and potent. Without being a sex pervert, he will commit sexual offenses of all kinds, if only to demonstrate his freedom from ego-limitations as represented by law and custom. His antisocial acts are not the result of the manifestation of unconscious complexes and motives but conscious means of self-expansion and expression of his complete inability to enjoy even a temporary state of staticness.

Native intelligence may help him to adapt his actions to his wants, but never for any length of time and only to the extent that the very act of adaptation adds to the pleasure he experiences in a given moment. His intellectual indolence is equal only to his moral frigidity. His readiness to disregard all rules of the game (though he knows them well and understands their meaning) may make him appear stupid. And it happens indeed that his intelligence deteriorates, by misuse and disuse, as it were.

Observers maintain that the psychopath frequently shows sentimental attachment to an animal or to a child and is able to go to any length in order to help them or to care for them. This inner contradiction would seem to prove that even cases of extreme relational inability should be interpreted as the outcome of a process of deep repression, of emotional withdrawal and dehumanization rather than as congenitally given, structural deficiencies.

---

* It may then be asked how the antisocial behavior of this congenital psychopath differs from that found in brainstem-drivenness or other forms of organically caused disinhibition. Are not absence of intentionality and uncontrolled reaction to chance stimuli characteristic of those organic varieties of aggressiveness? There exist no doubt similarities between the two clinical entities, though they are essentially different, as we shall try to show in the fourth chapter.

Now, while it cannot be denied that coexistence of such sentimental attachment, brutal aggressiveness and extreme egocentricity is indeed characteristic of certain psychopathic states, we believe that it is not to be found in the syndrome we are discussing here; we believe that it is, on the contrary, one of the elements discriminating between the congenital type of moral indolence and another type of psychopathic aggressiveness, resulting from earliest maternal rejection.

5. The Extravert Types

In this second type of psychopathy, *aggressiveness* is more in evidence than moral indolence. Because maternal rejection deprives this type of psychopath, from birth on, of the experience of staticness, his ego develops not out of a primary identity feeling (which is the offspring of staticness) but by way of avoiding the experience of rejectedness through incorporating the rejecting non-ego as completely as possible. Because maternal aggressiveness is the predominant experience in such an infant's early life, his conception of relationship becomes identical with aggressiveness. He is not morally indolent but hostile. This is true at least for the *extravert's* reaction to earliest maternal rejection. His ability to experience anxiety is not absent, as in the first type, but is being "drowned" by his reactive aggressiveness. He, too, is unable to relate himself to the non-ego in a polar way, or to identify himself with persons or ideas. But his aggressiveness is not devoid of intentionality; he wants to destroy, and destruction becomes for him a source of satisfaction.

Where relatedness does not require polarization but can develop on the basis of absolute mastery over a dependent object, we find those expressions of sentimental attachment which seem to contradict the aggressive brutality and egocentricity of this psychopath. On closer scrutiny, however, this sentimental attachment can be recognized as what it really is: the symptom of a deep-rooted, though not necessarily unconscious, need to experience at least the illusion of relational ability. The psychopath may not know that what he feels for the helpless object of his care is but an illusion (this is particularly true on the lower levels of intelligence), and he will certainly not worry about the apparent discrepancy between his sentimental attachment and his destructive actions. But by saying that he is *in need* of an illusion of feelings, we imply that this psychopath is not to the same extent identical with his inflated ego, as is the first-mentioned type. Continuous experience of the world as rejecting and hostile necessitates, it is true, a life without anxiety, and there is no more effective weapon against fear of ego loss than ego inflation. But the very fact that we speak here of an individual who *feels* rejected, and reacts to it with aggressiveness, already proves that the defense can never be perfect.

To avoid misunderstanding : we are speaking here of constitutional psychopathy and not of primary behavior disorder (PBD). The un-ambiguously defensive aggressiveness with its neurotic admixtures that characterize primary behavior disorders are the result of conscious suffer-ing, conflict and repression following separation from the mother at a later ("post-constitutional") stage of development. It is the sudden loss, real of imaginary, of the mother's love, particularly in the oedipal phase, which produces PBD (77). The question then arises : when does the behavioral pattern resulting from separation (loss of the mother) at an early stage of development lead to the picture of PBD, and when to that of psychopathic aggressiveness and egocentricity (as described before)?

Here, the causal significance of the time factor becomes evident. The developmental process leading to the crystallization of constitutional patterns of behavior and reaction takes a longer time in certain individuals than in others. We cannot yet say with certainty which factors determine the tempo of this primary process of systematization. Saying that relative predominance of the tendency toward staticness is an accelerating factor, does not really advance us very much in our quest for an explanation of individual differences (it is almost a *petitio principii*). The only conclusion we could draw from such a thesis, if proven, would be that the process of ego-formation takes a longer time in a psychopath (or under conditions conducive to the emergence of psychopathic behavior) than it does normally.

Let us consider now what happens to a child who is forced to experience the sudden loss of his mother—by death, illness or any other way of separation—before he has succeeded in dissociating his primary identity feeling from the experience of "the mother as part". In this case the *ego in statu nascendi* runs the danger of disappearing together with the disappearing mother. If the life-tendency toward expansion predominates, the void thus created can be filled from without in an uninterrupted stream of impressions rather than by way of active incorporation. (Here again we speak of the extravert reaction-type only.) Complete absence of selectivity in the process of *"filling the void"* and at least relative absence of structurization are characteristics of this psychopathic type. The whole world must be at his disposal, must be his property, so that he may be able to define himself without prior experience of identity. In this way staticness is being replaced by what we have called "passive expansion", that is, by the child's tendency to let himself be expanded through the non-ego, which thus becomes identical with the ego.

Such a child may grow up to become a truly psychopathic adult, egocentric and devoid of all concern for objective facts and for his human environment. Neither past nor future has any meaning for him; he would feel lost should he be compelled to retreat, be it for one short moment only, from the situational present in which he exists. "This, too, am I," he seems to say in response to whatever happens to him. Discontinuity and inner contradictions do not disturb him as long as he feels master and ruler of "his" realities. But in each of his acts of incorporation one can feel an undercurrent of anxiety, which his aggressiveness effectively suppresses. It is this ability to fear the void and the need for regaining his threatened security by aggressive incorporation that not only separate this psychopath from the two types described before but also make him comparable to the nonpsychopathic PBD. But absence of neurotic admixtures and coexistence of aggressive and nonaggressive modes of incorporation are indications of the psychopathic disorder as distinguished from PBD with its exclusive hostility and its manifold neurotic symptoms.

On the other hand, it is not always easy to differentiate between this third type of psychopathic behavior and the fourth one, whom we suggest calling the *oscillating psychopath*. This is the person whose ego becomes the potential recipient of the most different reality impressions, whatever their source and however contradictory they may be. Letting himself be influenced exempts him from making a choice and thus limiting himself. Here, the psychopathic ego inflation finds its expression in what could be called a "basic trick" of the personality structure, by which the illusion can be maintained that the world in its infiniteness is at the disposal of the ego. The most important outcome of this attitude, and the main difference between this psychopath and the third type, is his so-called instability. While the third type, in spite of his passiveness, is predominantly aggressive (and uses nonaggressive methods of incorporation only when the non-ego happens to offer no resistance),* the oscillating psychopath is basically nonaggressive.

To call him imitative or suggestible would be incorrect, as imitativeness and suggestibility presuppose a felt need for contact, albeit in a person with a weakly structured ego. The oscillating psychopath, however, is characterized by almost complete absence of such a need. He has no identity but only identities, each changing into another in quick succession and without inner logic. Although he may, in the course of his frequent

---

* In contrast to the PBD who would in this case do everything to provoke resistance in order to maintain his aggressive world conception.

changes, adopt aggressive as well as nonaggressive roles, his thus-produced aggressiveness is easily recognized by the strange weakness of its affective accents and of its intentionality. Here, paradoxically, it is the very lack of ego structure in which ego inflation finds its expression. Not imitating but being the other (the other who represents the non-ego in its infinite-ness) provides the illusion of egoity. And egoity, here, does not mean being one specifically identifiable individual but being the all-comprising, all-including ego in which the whole world has found its place.

This form of psychopathic ego inflation becomes understandable when we consider the causal constellations that are responsible for its emergence. In his contribution to the symposium on psychopathic behavior in children, Rabinowitz (82) mentions cold aloofness of the mother, diffusion of the mother image and early institutionalization as the three main causes of psychopathy. We believe that these factors represent but one group of causes. In the interpretation of psychopathic oscillation, maternal apathy (aloofness) and absence of an unambiguous mother image (institu-tionalization) are indeed the most potent causal factors, provided, we must add, they act upon an extravert in whom the life-tendency toward expansion predominates.

Such a child grows up without experiencing his environment as com-posed of human beings that relate themselves to him and to each other. Maternal indolence is liable to establish in the child's soul the image of a world in which differences do not appear as individualities but only as chance varieties of human existence. As a result, the boundaries between what normally is the ego and the non-ego remain fluid, and undifferen-tiated intake of the non-ego replaces the normal process of ego formation. Absence of an unambiguous mother image resulting from early institu-tionalization and from diffusion and impersonality of maternal care is liable to produce a similar effect. At the same time, however, the multiplicity of mother substitutes and the routine rule of institutional life account for the emergence of another, different, attitude which is charac-teristic of the (extravert) child in an institution : we refer to his almost unlimited readiness to attach himself superficially and nonselectively to whatever person or thing happens to appear in his vicinity.

This *"shallow-attachment"* variety belongs to the oscillating type of psychopathy insofar as both egoity and relatedness are replaced by lack or diffusion of identity and by indiscriminate receptiveness. The two varieties *differ* from each other in the degree of anxiety repression and in the depth of role identification. In the institutionalized child who never experiences continuous contact with one mother figure, the early repres-sion of anxiety may be more radical than in the child who grows up in the ambiance of an indolent and therefore unreachable, but identifiable mother. Conversely, the illusion of *being* the other is more real and, though not leading to internalization, reaches deeper levels of the personality in the truly oscillating psychopath than in the shallow attachment type. And yet, the former's need for *being* the other (which reflects his lack of need for *contact* with the other) and the latter's constant attempts to attach himself to the other are but two expressions of a life without ego. The negative concept of instability, as used by the earlier German psychiatrists, is not specific enough for the purposes of a phenomenologic analysis of the two types of psychopathic behavior in extraverts which we have described here. We shall see that it is more suited to the description of their introvert equivalents, which will be discussed later.

The psychopath most frequently described in novels as well as in psychiatric casebooks* is the imposter and swindler type (the *Hochstapler*). This is the psychopath for whom playing a role is of the essence. He must always stand in the center of attention, admired or feared. He would even prefer being despised to remaining unnoticed. He could pass as a genius of human understanding and empathy were he not utterly disinterested in those whose attention, admiration or fear he does not cease to provoke. He is often exceptionally intelligent, yet completely unable to draw conclusions from his past experiences. In this respect he resembles those addicts or perverts who, each in his limited field of passion, are likewise unable to learn from warnings of the past or from their own or their fellows' defeat.

Although he, too, is as amoral as only a psychopath can be, it is not by his amorality that he is recognized. Nor is aggressiveness particularly characteristic of this variety of psychopathic behavior. On the contrary, the *Hochstapler* does not, as a rule, use aggressive methods to attain his goals, at least not in a society in which lack of consideration is condemned unless it is well covered by a coat of suavity which conceals the marks of egocentricity. From the oscillating type, whom he resembles in his seeming adaptability to contradictory roles, he differs in one important respect: whatever role he plays, he always remains the self-identical master of his actions.

But, if so, it would seem that some of the essential characteristics of psychopathy—lack of concern for objective facts, weakness of the time concept and absence of relational ability—do not obtain in this variety,

---

* With the exception of the sex deviate, of course. But the global (undifferentiated) inclusion of the various types of perversion in the clinical picture of psychopathy is unjustified, as we shall try to show later (cf. pp. 126 ff.).

and that only absence of anxiety and guilt feelings and an unrestricted need for self-expansion are indicative of its psychopathic nature. How, indeed, could the *Hochstapler* plan his role-playing as efficiently and effectively as he does without recognizing and correctly evaluating objective facts and temporal sequences? How could he succeed in his schemings without relating himself to those whom he deceives?

We suggest the following answer: This psychopath is indeed able objectively to understand and adequately to evaluate external realities and human reactions, he is able to remember past experiences and to imagine future happenings, but only to the extent that he has turned these facts, experiences and possibilities into his own "property". Without internalizing experience, he *has* it as his possession which he uses at will.

It is this attitude that explains the essential difference between him and the oscillating psychopath who, as we said, has no identity but only identities, each changing into another in quick succession and without inner logic (see p. 106). The imposter type does not seek "the illusion of egoity" by "being the other"; he is self-identical in every role he plays. His receptivity is, paradoxically, an instrument of his egotropic activity; it is selective, not all-including. For him, the non-ego is a reality to be conquered, resistance to be broken. His inflated ego would collapse if he were forced to recognize that there are facts and forces which have the right and the power to limit him. But he knows well that only by understanding the nature of these facts and forces can he hope to escape the danger of being limited by them. Only by turning them into his own, his "disposable property", can he be sure to be the master of everything non-ego. Even when defeated, as he is bound to be sooner or later, he will continue to live in the glory of his past omnipotence.

In the development of this type of psychopathy, maternal over-indulgence toward an extravert child is frequently found to be the major factor of causation. The child's early experience that the world offers no resistance to his demands is liable to turn the growing ego into an instrument of unrestricted incorporation of the non-ego. Extraversion, particularly when supported by good intelligence, accounts for the often astonishing ability of the psychopath to understand human behavior and relationships. This understanding, however, does not result from objective confrontation with otherness and is not the condition of adaptation, as in normally adjusted personalities, but is a result and by-product of playing the other.

This type of psychopathic behavior is perhaps the most perfect of all: this individual knows how to conceal his lack of concern for objective facts, his lack of identification, of relational ability and sometimes even his lack of anxiety and guilt feelings behind a convincing mask of concern and empathy, of understanding and emotions (16).

Before proceeding, we feel that we should warn against overestimating the validity of the causal connections which we have so far suggested with a view to explaining the various sub-units of psychopathy. None of the experiential patterns mentioned (maternal rejection, indolence, indulgence, loss of mother, institutionalization) will produce psychopathic behavior of one of the different types in every extravert individual in whom the tendency toward expansion predominates. Other constitutional and environmental factors must enter the etiologic equation of the individual to account for the psychopathic outcome. The most important among them are : the level of intelligence, the threshold of frustration bearance and the intensity of love needs, psychosomatic diatheses, cultural patterns and the role of the father, who may or may not compensate for maternal deficiencies. In their configuration with each other as well as with the three above-mentioned factors (of type, structural tendency and early traumatization), they determine the course of the individual's development.

We might, then, summarize the foregoing analysis of psychopathic developments by saying that each of the traumatic experiences mentioned is liable to produce a specific psychopathic behavior pattern in an extravert (and another one in an introvert) individual in whom the tendency toward expansion predominates, provided these causal factors are not counteracted by other constitutional or environmental determinants. *How* these other factors operate as counteractors is to be determined by way of analyzing individual cases rather than by way of formulating general laws of causation.

6.   THE INTROVERT TYPES

We have so far discussed the extravert forms of psychopathy only, and shall now proceed to analyze their introvert counterparts. Introversion is defined as the withdrawal of libido from the object and its direction toward the subject which thereby becomes the principal source of motivation, whereas extraversion is characterized by relatedness to the object and outward motivation (59). It might then be argued that the psychopath can neither be described as an introvert nor as an extravert. Predominance of the tendency toward expansion would seem to contradict introversive libido concentration on the subject, while ego inflation would seem to contradict extraversive object-relatedness. Such arguments, however, would be defendable only if we could maintain that introversion is identical with subject-relatedness and extraversion with object-relatedness. While these equations are undoubtedly correct as far as the normal individual is concerned, we should beware of applying them unchanged to the abnormal. We define normality as mutual interrelatedness of the two basic life-tendencies and exchangeability of the subject-object positions, based on polarization (cf. p. 90). We define abnormality as absence of such polarity, exchangeability and interrelatedness. It is, then, not difficult to conceive of pathologic extraversion without relational ability or of an equally pathologic introversion without proper ego regulation. In this sense, even a feebleminded child, almost completely devoid of the ability to transform external stimuli into inner properties and concepts, may nevertheless be an introvert. Introversion may appear in a hyperkinetic person whose capacity for systematization may be extremely low as the result of certain cerebral deficiencies. It may appear in any intellectually and physically normal individual with a constitutionally predominant tendency toward growth and change and an extremely poor organizational ability. In all these cases, introversion could still be the dominant attitude insofar as the available libido is focused on the (organizationally weak) ego.

What, then, we should ask, may happen to the introvert under conditions conducive to the emergence of ego inflation? Which forms of psychopathic behavior are liable to crystallize under the impact of the above-mentioned (or other) traumatic experiences on an introvert individual?

Where the tendency toward *staticness* predominates, introversive concentration of the available psychic energy on the subject is liable to be used again and again for the purposes of systematization only. The result may then be a rigidly closed, defensive ego which becomes more and more identical with its defensive systems. Where, on the other hand, the tendency toward *expansion* structurally prevails, introversion is liable to produce an ego whose main purpose is to relate to itself (receptively and passively) any emerging impulse and any environmental occurrence. Which personality and behavior patterns finally crystallize will, of course, again be dependent on the configuration of nature and nurture, including the type and quality of earliest traumatic experiences. The factors mentioned above in our discussion of the extravert forms of psychopathic behavior are equally important in the etiology of their introvert counterparts.

We have said (p. 104) that "maternal rejection deprives the child of the experience of staticness" and that his ego consequently "develops not out of a primary identity feeling (which is the offspring of staticness) but by way of avoiding the experience of rejectedness through incorporating the rejecting non-ego as completely as possible". But whereas in the extravert this incorporation is not only aggressive but also consciously and directly aims at the (negated) object, it takes on a fantasy character in the introvert. The aggressive and destructive impulses are not repressed into the unconscious but are being stored up; they continue to live in the individual's consciousness as sadistic fantasies, until one day they explode in an act of terrible violence, seemingly unprovoked or at least out of all proportion to the preceding stimulus.

This is the so-called *explosive psychopath* described, though rather inadequately, by K. Schneider (88) as one of his types. The sudden eruptions of violence resemble the uncontrollable fits of aggressiveness which appear in certain cases of brain injury and, more specifically, of epilepsy. Differential diagnosis, however, does not offer too many difficulties, even without the help of diagnostic tests: the psychopath, though unable to control his outbursts, is quite able to remember them in all details. Far from feeling guilty or otherwise uncomfortable about his actions, he justifies and even enjoys them in his peculiar way of inflational self-referral.

It is typical of the descriptive orientation of pre-analytic psychiatry that this form of psychopathic behavior was called "explosive", for the sole reason that sudden and unaccountable outbursts of violence are its most dramatic symptoms. From the point of view of dynamic psychology, however, it would be more correct to define as its essential characteristic the fantasies of aggressive and destructive mastery over a hostile world. Introversion accounts here not only for the fact that the aggressive impulses are not acted out directly but also for the quasi-mechanical discharge character of the unstructured outbursts of violence. The latter should be interpreted as the outcome of an inflated ego's leave of absence, as it were, from its fantasies, rather than as manifestations of unconscious forces autonomously breaking through the ego's defensive systems (as in neuroses or psychoses). The psychopath does not repress his aggressive drives; he cultivates his aggressive fantasies in order to preserve the conscious illusion of independence of, and superiority over, a rejecting and rejected reality.

Another introvert type is the *paranoid psychopath* with his never-ceasing irritability (to use Kraepelin's term), his constant readiness to feel thwarted, to blame the world for its injustice, and to fight for his injured rights. He is utterly unable to evaluate facts objectively, to relate to, or to identify with, any person or idea. From the true paranoiac he is distinguished by his lack of anxiety and by the conscious overevaluation of his own importance.

We believe that sudden loss of the mother, at an age when the child's ego- and identity-feeling still depends on the experience of the "returning mother", and a markedly introvert reaction type are the two most important conditions for the emergence of this form of psychopathic behavior. An extravert child may react to a similar traumatic experience by letting himself "be expanded" through the non-ego and thus "filling the void" (see p. 105); the introvert does not recognize the void created by the sudden disappearance of the mother. He builds up and maintains the illusion of being threatened by the danger of losing his identity; but in reality he has nothing to lose, because his identity fails to develop in the first instance as the result of the interruption of contact with his mother.

The basic paradox in the paranoid psychopath's ego inflation lies in the fact that he defines his identity as *negated* identity. In this respect he differs from all other types of psychopathic behavior, and particularly from the oscillating and the shallow attachment varieties and their introvert counterparts, the drifting and the unstable types (see later). While egoity is based, in the oscillating psychopath, on the illusion of *being* the other, and in the shallow attachment type on the illusion of being sustained and supported by the other, the paranoid psychopath, being an introvert, does not see the other but only his own negatedness. Without this experience he would not be able to feel his ego at all, while with it (and through it) he knows that the world does not allow him to be himself.

We believe that the so-called *drifting psychopath* is the introvert counterpart of the oscillating type. Maternal indolence is a major causal factor in the developmental history of both. "Being the other" provides the oscillating psychopath, as we have said, with the illusion of egoity. The same does not hold good for the drifting psychopath. Introversion accounts for a basic difference in his attitude toward otherness. The extravert incorporates the most contradictory reality elements in a positive, affirmative way; he enjoys "being the other". The introvert, on the other hand, is passive and sometimes even apathetic in his attitude toward the world; he does not so much follow the lead, or act under the changing influence of, occurring events and persons as he follows the lead and acts under the changing influence of his impulses and drives. For him, *they* are the primary representatives of otherness rather than the external events and persons which exist in his life as drive-stimulators only.

The experience of maternal indolence is liable to establish in the psychic structure of the growing child the image of an unreachable mother and thereby to render identity formation impossible. (The latter requires, as we have said before, the experience of staticness which, in turn, is mediated and guaranteed by the experience of the returning, that is, the reachable mother.) Both the extravert and the introvert tend to react to maternal indolence by giving up the normal quest for identity. But whereas the extravert does so by changing indiscriminately from one identity to another and thus building up his illusion of egoity, the introvert, with his typical withdrawal of libido from the outside world, builds up his illusion of egoity by passively and indiscriminately giving in to his impulses and drives.

The result is the *drifting psychopath* who may become a vagabond, an addict or a sex pervert. It is not always easy to differentiate between the psychopathic and the neurotic varieties of these pathologies. It would seem that the most important element of differentiation is the intensity of attachment to the "unreachable mother". The greater this intensity (which is determined by constitutional thresholds of frustration bearance and love needs as well as by the degree of ambiguity of the mother figure), the greater the likelihood of suffering, anxiety and reaction formations. In this case, the dissocial behavior may betray signs of tension, conscious avoidance of, or craving for, dependence and unconscious tendencies to reach the unreachable. In the psychopathic variety of the same behavior pattern, on the other hand, we will rarely find such symptoms. Naive egocentricity will be much more in evidence than tension. Ego inflation will manifest itself here not only in the ordinary (negative) symptoms of psychopathy—such as absence of relational ability, of guilt and anxiety feelings, of concern for realities and of the ability to learn from experience —but also in the passively drifting, impulse-dominated individual's illusion of being master of his actions. The drifting psychopath is not aware of his lack of identity, nor does he experience his driftings, his addictions or his perversions as compulsive, as an inescapable curse or as a source of suffering and depression, but, on the contrary, feels them to be true expressions of his ego, as permanently ego-syntonic, to paraphrase the term used by Fenichel (24) in his analysis of perversions. We should add that this psychopathic type is, indeed, extremely rare, and that most cases of habitual vagabondage, addiction or perversion cannot be diagnosed as psychopathic at all but are clearly cases of neurotic or character-neurotic involvements.

In the *unstable psychopath* we see the introvert equivalent of the shallow attachment variety of the oscillating psychopath. We believe that in his individual development early institutionalization is a major factor of causation. Extreme suggestibility and lability are the central characteristics of this type. He mirrors the behavior of others* in a passive, non-selective manner. But this mirroring is the outcome of a kind of automatism which does not leave even a passing imprint on the person's identity.

Here then arises the question whether this type of behavior which is characterized by an almost complete lack of ego can still be interpreted in terms of ego inflation. There can be no doubt that the latter category would not be applicable to the instability and suggestibility of the neurotically inadequate character in whom anxiety and repression of aggressiveness produce what could be called a defensive extinction of the ego feeling or its substitution by an unlimited craving for contact and dependence.† The unstable psychopath, however, essentially differs from this neurotic character in two respects : he does not experience anxiety and therefore does not repress his impulses (although their structural weakness, in contrast to the drifting psychopath, may make them seem to be repressed); and he does not use defense mechanisms for the purposes of building up and maintaining a restricted ego system. Through mirroring the behaviour of others he is able to avoid the awareness of his lack of egoity. Being an introvert, he tends to withdraw from the chance factors of influence in his environment all the libido at his disposal, which he invests in the mirroring process itself.

It is, strangely enough, in this process that the unstable psychopath finds his illusion of egoity. Hence, when we speak, in his case, of ego inflation, we mean to say that, although identity has really been replaced by an unpredictable multitude of chance influences coming from the outside, the ego *plays* identity by mirroring the behavior of others. Absence of anxiety and defense and the distinctly egotropic character of imitative incorporations are the essential characteristics indicating the psychopathic nature of this "play ego".

When compared with the oscillating type, the unstable psychopath appears to be on the one hand more passive, on the other still more egocentric. From the shallow attachment variety with its typical contact illusion he differs by the impersonally automatic character of his imitations, from the drifting psychopath by the relative dullness of his impulses.

The last variety to be discussed is the introvert counterpart of the schem-

---

* Rabinowitz (82) is not right in considering this mirroring a general symptom of psychopathy. It is characteristic only of the specific variety of psychopathic behavior which is discussed here.

† Whether produced by the impact of early institutionalization on a child in whom the tendency toward staticness predominates or by certain types of later traumatization.

ing imposter and swindler type (the *Hochstapler*). The latter, we suggested, is liable to develop under the impact of maternal over-indulgence on an extravert individual, particularly if he is of good or even of superior intelligence. What is the possible result if the same causal factor operates in the development of an introvert of equal intelligence? In other words, how is the introvert liable to react to an educational situation in which his ego is not being limited by the primary representative of the non-ego (the mother)? (We must, of course, always bear in mind that, when discussing psychopathic developments, we speak only of individuals in whom the tendency toward expansion structurally predominates over that toward staticness.)

In the extravert, absence of environmental resistance and limitation may produce a tendency to regard everything and everybody as his potential property (to be incorporated and disposed of at will); the same factor may lead, in the introvert, to the emergence of a tendency to regard himself as the owner of absolute truth. This form of ego inflation, however, should not be confused with psychotic megalomania. The psychopath who elevates and inflates a half-truth to the level of an absolute truth and who considers it his possession will demand that the whole world recognize and accept it and will be ready to oppose and negate whoever dares to oppose or overlook it (that is, him). He will fight for it aggressively and fanatically. He may be queer and eccentric in the unlimited identification of *his* truth with his ego (and whatever he does in order to implement or propagate it will bear the stamp of his inflated-ness). But he will never lose sight of its reality implications. On the contrary, what makes a truth suitable for the purposes of his ego inflation is precisely its allegedly inherent tendency toward realization, so that the owner of the truth automatically knows also the ways and means to implement it. In this respect, the psychotic with his absurd irrealism is essentially different. Whereas the psychopath possesses his truth, the schizophrenic is possessed by it. Whereas the truth helps the "queer saint", the fanatic and the eccentric psychopath, to dominate the world, it helps the schizophrenic to protect himself against *being* dominated. Whereas it requires constant preoccupation with the human environment in the case of this psychopath with his allergy to being limited or opposed, it acts as an isolating factor in the case of the schizophrenically withdrawn patient.

But, if so, we might ask whether our hypothesis as to the etiology of this last type of psychopathic behavior is correct. Is he really an introvert? Does not his preoccupation with reality indicate an opposite, extravert, attitude, that is, libido concentration on the object rather than on the subject? To answer this question, we propose to compare the "owner of the absolute truth" with his extravert counterpart, the *Hochstapler* type. Of the latter we have said that he is able adequately to evaluate reality on the basis of his past experience, but only to the extent that he has succeeded in turning facts and experiences into his own "possessions" *without internalizing them* (p. 108). Psychopathic incorporation, we have said before (p. 93), is devoid of polarization : the incorporated loses its individual independence and, thus, the precondition of true internalization and relatedness—coexistence of the internalized and its objective, external counterpart—is lost. Nevertheless, it is characteristic of the *Hochstapler* type that he continuously seeks contact with reality factors, albeit with the sole purpose of avoiding limitation by them.

Here we see the extravert version of psychopathic preoccupation with reality. The introvert, on the other hand, does not need even this form of pseudo-contact, because it is he who creates reality by defining his truth with which all facts have to fall in line. It is a purely subjective reality construction with which he is preoccupied, an image which he has designed. Moreover, his preoccupation manifests itself in two forms only : in his demands for unrestricted recognition of his truth and for subordination under what he considers the requirements of its implementation; and in his attempts forcibly to interpret and to modify external realities in accordance with his truth. This, however, means that the psychopathic form of reality preoccupation is fully compatible with introvert libido concentration on the subject.

7. Some Concluding Remarks

We have tried to define a number of psychopathic varieties by relating each to a specific form of early, preconstitutional, traumatization in the area of mother-child relationships (rejection, indolence, overindulgence, loss of mother, institutionalization). At the same time, we have taken into consideration as a differentiating factor the attitudinal type of the traumatized individual. We have not discussed the influence of the same factors operating in the development of an extravert or an introvert child in whom the tendency toward staticness structurally predominates over that toward expansion (see the comparative table after p. 101). Neither did we analyze the influence of these factors when they make themselves felt at a later stage of the child's development, that is, after the constitution is already crystallized. We did not discuss other traumatic constellations which, though not less pathogenic, are irrelevant for the interpretation of psychopathic behavior patterns, because they are either essentially tension-creating and neuroticizing or externalizing. As we did not intend to go into details of case discussions, we did not analyze the differentiating influence of other, congenital or environmental, factors, such as the level of intelligence, thresholds, cultural patterns, compensatory forces, etc. We must, of course, remain aware of the fact that without such differential analyses our construction of psychopathic types will have limited validity only (see p. 110). This limitation, however, is essentially inherent in the phenomenologic method we have chosen here in order to explain the nature of psychopathic behavior in its various forms.

We have on purpose avoided the discussion of yet another question of etiology : Are the developmental processes which lead to the emergence of psychopathy in its various forms *co-determined* by the differences of what Jung describes as *Funktionstypen*? Or do these processes *produce* functional differences?* (see p. 99.) Moreover, it may well be that the development of a certain congenitally given functional predominance is incompatible with certain traumatic situations and that it tends to disappear or to give way to another predominance under the influence of a persistent experience of either maternal rejection or indolence or overindulgence, of either mother-loss or early institutionalization. Although we feel inclined to think that there exist at least such a negative causal relation between certain functional predominances and certain early (pre-constitutional) experiences, we are not yet prepared to take a definite stand in the discussion of this crucial question of etiology.

In the summary of psychopathic types which preceded our analysis (p. 101), we placed each extravert form against its introvert counterpart with the sole exception of the morally indolent psychopath. In this type, we suggested, *congenital* absence of anxiety, in conjunction with predominance of the tendency toward expansion, eliminates type differences. Such an individual cannot be defined either as an extravert or an introvert. His libido is neither directed toward the non-ego nor toward the ego. What we call the non-ego does not exist as something to be conquered; it *is* already part of what we call the ego, even before being incorporated. Hence, it is equally correct to say that the morally indolent psychopath is both an extravert *and* an introvert. His ego exists only in the processes (not acts) of its expansion, and the non-ego only as the field of these processes.

---

* Tentatively we would suggest that predominance of the tendency toward expansion in conjunction with the early experience of a defective mother-relationship, is likely to favor the development of what Jung calls the sensation type, and to hinder the development of the feeling and the intuition types of orientation. The fourth function (thinking) is likely to be strengthened by the early experience of overindulgence and, at least in some cases of extravert individuals, by maternal rejection or by mother-loss.

Anxiety, being fear of ego loss in processes of inner or outer change or regression, depends : (a) on the degree of disconnection (nonintegration) of the tendency toward expansion from an equally strong tendency toward staticness; (b) on the relative weakness of the ego's organizational ability;* and (c) on the ego's ability to feel itself both subject and object with regard to a superior non-ego, that is, on polarization and on feeling for otherness.

Congenital absence of anxiety, then, is indicative of the opposite conditions : (a) The two life-tendencies are not only disconnected (nonintegrated) but also unequal in strength; the tendency toward expansion predominates over that toward staticness. As a result, change from within or from without is not experienced as a threat to the ego, since such a feeling of being threatened presupposes a strong (though isolated) tendency toward staticness. (b) The weakness of the ego's organizational ability reflects an extreme structural weakness of the tendency toward staticness. Consequently, it does not contribute to the ego's feeling of being threatened by change factors and forces. (c) The ego has no feeling for otherness and is unable to experience itself as subject and as object of a superior non-ego because the primary processes of polarization do not take place (perhaps owing to some organic deficiency?). Consequently, change is not experienced as such, that is, as something which happens in, and to, the ego (and therefore as something which is liable to threaten its existence) but only as a process of ego expansion.

Thus, we can say that congenital absence of anxiety is indicative of a structural defect of polarization (in individuals in whom the tendency toward expansion predominates over that toward staticness). In the non-congenital forms of psychopathy, on the other hand, a congenitally normal ability to experience anxiety tends to disappear under the influence of defective child-mother relationships (though again only when the tendency toward expansion predominates structurally). Polarization, which, in these cases, starts normally, becomes progressively weaker, until it gives way to inflational ego expansion at the time the individual's constitution is finally crystallized.

But it would be wrong to reduce the difference between the congenital form of psychopathy and the noncongenital forms to the time factor only, without adding that this factor explains at the same time an essential difference in the structure of psychopathy. *Congenital absence of polarization accounts for those cases in which the libido is not "directed" either to the non-ego or to the ego, as there exist no boundaries between the*

---

* Where this organizational weakness becomes extreme, it ceases to be a condition of anxiety; anxiety-readiness, in this case, tends to disappear.

two. Such boundaries do exist in all cases of noncongenital psychopathy (although, in the oscillating type at least, they tend to be "fluid"). In all these cases, psychopathic ego inflation and incorporation in its various forms manifest themselves in a continuous elimination of these boundaries by way of extravert or introvert libido-directedness.

It is this difference which places the noncongenital forms of psychopathy in an intermediary position between congenital psychopathy and the so-called character disorders, including in particular what psychoanalysts describe as the "narcissistic", the "impulsive", the "instinct-ridden", the "antisocial" or the "neurotic" character.

B. CLINICAL COMPARISONS

8. PSYCHOPATHY AND CHARACTER DISORDERS

(a) The psychoanalytic approach to the concept of psychopathy

The libido-developmental or the so-called psychodynamic approach of psychoanalysis accounts for the relative neglect, in its interpretations, of the etiologic role of constitutional factors. Although Freud and his pupils do, of course, recognize the fact that constitution co-determines the outcome of normal and pathologic developments, they tend to limit its role in their clinical interpretations and to regard it as a *refugium ignorantiae* rather than as a dynamic factor of determination. "Constitutional factors are not accessible to psychoanalytic approach," says Fenichel; "hence the problem is to determine to what extent a given character structure or a preference for certain mechanisms of defense can be understood *historically* as the outcome of specific instinctual conflicts of the individual" (24, p. 523).

Modern child psychiatry and psychopathology, it is true, have shown that constitution is not identical with its hereditary or congenital components but develops under the influence of earliest experiences. And it is more or less agreed among today's child psychologists that the changes which are liable to take place in the congenital personality structure during the first year or two after birth are as irreversible as prenatal or paranatal modifications of the hereditary structure (6, 10). Many orthodox psychoanalysts, however, continue to think of constitution in terms of hereditary or, at most, congenital givens, while at the same time placing the infant's earliest experiences on one and the same level with later (satisfying or frustrating) experiences. They may admit that the character structure is determined by these earliest experiences, without, however, taking into account the determining function of what has become an irreversible character structure. That function of determination they assign to the nature of the impulses which are conflicting with the ego, to the content and the intensity of the frustrating environmental factors, to the personality structure of the frustrating environmenal figures as it manifests itself in their actions and reactions, to the availability of substitute gratification at the time the frustration takes place and, last but not least, to the time factor. The last factor determines both the type of defenses mobilized and the gravity of the outcome (24, pp. 523 f.).

"Gravity of the outcome" is the most psychoanalysis is ready to concede to a theory of constitution. It is a relativistic concept indicating a difference only of degree between the various manifestations of neurotic, as well as of character-neurotic, developments. It does not allow for *essential* distinctions between clinical pictures, such as between certain forms of psychopathic behavior and primary behavior disorders (PBD), following the traumatic experience of mother-loss either at a preconstitutional or a later stage of development. Psychopathic behavior can be called "more serious" than PBD only to the extent that determination of a clinical outcome through earliest factors decreases its therapeutic modifiability and reversibility. This holds good for every form of psychopathy as against the various forms of neurotic character disorders. If, on the other hand, the time factor is held responsible only for a difference in the degree of seriousness, each outcome will be considered reversible, although the more serious one will undoubtedly require greater therapeutic efforts. The therapeutic optimism of psychoanalysis is correlative to its neglect of the constitutional factor in the etiology of behavior disorders.

In this connection it might be of interest to mention Fenichel's criticism of a thesis defended by F. Alexander, who claims that individuals who act out their neurotic impulses are, because of their alloplastic attitude, easier patients than neurotics. Fenichel refutes this claim by saying that in these cases alloplasticity, not being genuine, must first be turned into neurotic autoplasticity, if we want to effect a cure. But Fenichel does not doubt, either, the reversibility of this type of behavior disorders which he calls psychopathic (24, p. 507).

(b) *The hysterical character*

The question then arises whether the behavior disorders which psychoanalysts call "psychopathic" are correctly so designated.

Among the five character types described by Fenichel as phobic, hysterical, compulsive, cyclic and schizoid, it is particularly the second which resembles what we have analyzed as psychopathic behavior. "Hysterical characters", he says, "have been described as persons who are inclined to sexualize all nonsexual relations, who are inclined toward suggestibility, irrational emotional outbreaks, chaotic behavior, dramatization and histrionic behavior, even toward mendacity and its extreme form, pseudologia phantastica." Etiologically, "the conflicts between intense fear of sexuality and intense but repressed sexual strivings and . . . between the rejection of actuality . . . and the tendency to find the infantile objects again in the actual environment" are held responsible for the formation of this character type (24, p. 527).

Some of the traits of the hysterical character are reminiscent of the oscillating psychopath, the imposter type or the unstable psychopath, as we have described them above. But to the extent that the etiologic interpretation offered by Fenichel is correct, it would seem evident that we have before us a nonpsychopathic form of character disorder. Repression of intense sexual strivings and intense fear of sexuality indicate not only ability to experience anxiety but also superego awareness and relational ability. The latter may be thwarted by traumatic experiences but it continues to express itself in the attempt to rediscover the objects of infantile attachment in the actual environment. Suggestibility, histrionics (and perhaps also mendacity) are therefore indicative in this case of a craving for attachment rather than of incorporative tendencies. Even the chaotic behavior bears the character of a reactive syndrome rather than of a structural trait, of ego diffusion rather than of ego inflation. It is obvious that whatever traumatic experiences may help form this character type, they operate on a structurally normal ego which is being distorted gradually, owing to the impact of these experiences and their hystericizing results.*

(c) Character disorders

Character disorders in general are defined by Fenichel as consistent defense systems, in contradiction to the ego-alien nature of neurotic symptoms. They are secondary elaborations and adjustment attempts, "intended to repair the original breakdown and to prevent further breakdowns", and are characterized by their rigidity which results from the need for constant (ego-restricting) countercathexes (24, p. 405). But the concepts used by psychoanalysts for the interpretation of normal and abnormal character

---

* In passing, we wish to add that here as well as in the area of neuroses, the similarity of the experiential factors said to be responsible for the emergence of the various character types, as described by Fenichel, makes it necessary to introduce into the individual equations constitutional and structural factors of differentiation, such as type, thresholds, relations between the two basic life-tendencies, etc.

(ego) formation are identical with those applied to the explanation of the development of neurotic syndromes.

Of the two types of character traits, the sublimative and the reactive types, only the latter is relevant for the study of pathologic phenomena. Fenichel distinguishes between phobic attitudes of avoidance and reaction formation attitudes of opposition; but the latter no less than the former are only covering a basic anxiety which lies between the original (feared) impulse and the ultimate attitude (24, p. 472).

It is characteristic of the psychoanalytic approach to the problem under discussion that contradictory behavioral attitudes are considered symptomatic of the same defense mechanisms and that only the individual constellations of environmental experiences are held responsible for the variety of the outcome. Impudence and over-politeness, inefficiency and over-efficiency, arrogance and inferiority feelings, emotional frigidity (often in conjunction with over-intellectualism) and hyperemotionality, ascetic fighting against instinctual demands and over-sexuality, eccentric fighting for the implementation of an idea and intellectual apathy, all are explained with equal ease as reaction formations. Denial of anxiety may manifest itself in one case as intimidation of others, in another as active repetition of the passive experience which gave rise to the feeling of anxiety. Introjective and projective measures fulfill the same purpose. The same holds good for other defense mechanisms such as rationalization and vindication of impulses (sometimes leading even to their idealization), as against isolation of instinctual activities from the rest of the personality or pseudo-gratification of impulses with the sole aim to end "the intolerable excitement" as quickly as possible (24, p. 487).

Here again, we see evidence of the basic shortcoming inherent in psychoanalytic etiology when applied to a differential phenomenology of clinical pictures and not to an analysis of individual cases. The almost exclusive emphasis on so-called psychic mechanisms, on the one hand, and on traumatic experiences, on the other, and the almost complete disregard for constitution and structure as causal variables and determinants are liable to obliterate the essential differences between clinical entities.

(d) *The neurotic character*

We need not go into a detailed analysis of what Fenichel describes as the pathological behavior toward the id, the superego and external subjects (anal, oral, urethal and phallic character traits; character defenses against guilt feelings; pre-oedipal fixation, persistent ambivalence, jealousy, social inhibition, pseudo-sexuality and social anxiety). Of all these pathologic character formations, only two are of interest in our discussion of psychopathic behavior : the "acting-out" character and what he calls "fixation on pre-stages of love".

Of the former, Fenichel (24, pp. 506 f.) says that the patient unconsciously misunderstands the present in the sense of his past, that he tries unconsciously "to get rid of old instinctual conflicts, to find a belated gratification of repressed impulses (instinctual demands as well as guilt feelings), or at least to find relief from some inner tension. For these persons the environment is only an arena in which to stage their inner conflicts". The acting-out of neurotic impulses aims "at avoidance of displeasure rather than attainment of pleasure". Extreme tension intolerance and restlessness, but also accident proneness and "destiny neuroses" are said to be typical of the acting-out character. The latter symptom becomes plausible in the light of the fact that here instinct gratification often alternates periodically with actions which are meant to satisfy superego demands. Fenichel believes that certain psychopathic types described by pre-analytic psychiatrists are "impulsive", "aggressive" and "dependent" belong to this group.

Alexander's (4) analysis of the neurotic character differs from Fenichel's in that he considers hatred of the father an important causal factor in its formation; Fenichel stresses the etiologic role of oral frustration, thus bringing the neurotic character close to the clinical picture of "impulsive" character disorders (see pp. 128 ff.) Fenichel's analysis again suffers from insufficient differentiation of the specific causal factors which should account for the various behavior patterns, all said to be caused by oral frustration. Alexander, on the other hand, does not explain why in this case father-hatred, instead of being repressed or transformed, persists in the growing child's consciousness and leads to open defiance of all restricting father figures. This consciousness of hostility seems to be incompatible with the fact that, according to Alexander, the father image is nevertheless internalized and transformed into superego components, and that it is held responsible for neurotic conflicts and punishments inflicted by the superego.

If so, we may ask in which respect this so-called neurotic character differs from the oft-described "criminal out of unconscious guilt feelings". The latter, too, lives out his (antisocial) impulses in an ego-alien manner (satisfying his instinctual demands) and thereby causes himself punishment or even destruction (satisfying his superego demands). The latter, too, acts under a compulsion, and his actions bear, at least in outward appearance, an allotropic character. In the latter, too, insight is absent, and the ego is weakened by unconscious impulses. The employment of two different clinical terms ("neurotic character" and "guilt offender") would therefore seem to be unjustified and superfluous.

On the other hand, we find two traits in the so-called neurotic character which are relevant in a comparison of psychopathic behavior patterns with neurotic disorders. We refer to what Fenichel calls the neurotic character's "need to get rid of old conflicts" and his "tendency to avoid displeasure" (that is, his strong tension intolerance).

Old conflicts are the result of early frustrations, of the child's reactions to them and of the anxiety which is produced and reinforced by traumatic experiences and which, in turn, produces and maintains inner tensions. As long as this anxiety is allowed to persist either as such (as in any normal development) or underneath phobic avoidances or defensive reaction formations (as in neuroses and character neuroses), no human being can ever get rid of his old conflicts. The need for alleviating their intensity and pressure, however, produces those sublimations, escapes and reaction formations that are held responsible for the normal and abnormal development of the ego. If, on the other hand, the ability to experience anxiety is either congenitally absent or is being "drowned" or otherwise eliminated by certain forms of defective mother-child relationships at the beginning of life, a "need to get rid of old conflicts" cannot arise : the inability to experience anxiety is a (primary or secondary) constitutional factor which prevents the emergence of conflict experience. This is, as we have tried to show in chapter two, one of the essential characteristics of psychopathy. In other words, *a feeling of the need to get rid of old conflicts precludes a diagnosis of psychopathy*; a psychopathic inability to experience conflicts as sources of anxiety precludes a diagnosis of what Alexander and Fenichel describe as neurotic or acting-out character.

Similarly, avoidance of displeasure is a defense mechanism and, as such, characteristic of neurotic and not of psychopathic disorders. But if we translate this finalistic concept, which indicates a conscious or unconscious intention on the part of the ego to prove to itself its independence of the frustrating and limiting non-ego, into terms of structure and constitution, we obtain : inability to experience tension as such, resulting from relational inability and from a structural predominance of the tendency toward expansion.

Both, the inability to experience anxiety and conflict and the inability to experience displeasure and tension, are possible results of early, pre-constitutional deficiencies in the interpersonal life spheres of the infant. They become elements of the child's constitution and, as such, determine his further reactions and his further development. If the same deficiencies (e.g. rejection or disappointment of the child by his parents) make themselves felt at a later stage of development only, that is, after the constitution has already been formed more or less finally, behavior disorders of the oedipal type, neuroses (including neurotic dissociality and character neuroses), perversions and other forms of compulsive dissociality are likely to result.

Thus, the inclusion of disorders such as guilt offenses or destiny neurosis among the symptoms of the neurotic character precludes its identification with psychopathy. Something essentially different is meant by the latter concept. It might even seem doubtful whether actions aimed at satisfying superego demands are at all compatible with the other symptoms of the neurotic character mentioned by Alexander and by Fenichel ("misunderstanding the present in the light of the past", "gratifying infantile impulses", "avoiding displeasure and tension"). But here it will probably be argued that it is precisely this coexistence of contradictory tendencies, this simultaneity or alternation of instinct and superego gratifications, of uninhibited impulsivity and guilt feelings which not only indicates but even constitutes the neurotic character.* And we may add, with Fenichel (24, p. 531), that it is this central symptom which makes the neurotic character comparable to the cyclic personality. This, however, would in itself be a sufficient argument against including the neurotic character in the clinical unit of psychopathy with its absence of anxiety and its ego-inflation. Although the cyclic character and the psychopath are similar in one respect, in the predominance of the tendency toward expansion, they should not be identified with each other.

Finally, if Alexander is right in assigning to unlimited father hatred a major role in the causation of the neurotic character, this would again preclude its identification with psychopathy. Fear of the father may in some cases, though not as a rule, appear fairly early in life; but hatred of the father and, more so, unrestricted and conscious hatred certainly belongs to a later stage of development, that is, to a phase when the process of constitution formation has already come to its relative end and, consequently, psychopathy (being a constitutional disorder) can no longer emerge.

(e) *The pervert*

We shall now try to answer the question whether and to what extent perversions, impulse neuroses and instinct-ridden characters belong to the area of psychopathy. Most psychiatrists, whether psychoanalytically oriented or not, take the inclusion of these disorders in the clinical

---

* Alexander sees in Dmitri Karamazov the prototype of the neurotic character. We would hesitate to diagnose him as a psychopath.

entity of psychopathic behavior for granted (non-dynamically oriented psychiatrists because of their symptomatologic approach, psychoanalysts because of their tendency to reduce structural to dynamic differences). Fenichel when dealing with "perverse activities and the impulses of the psychopath (such as the drive to run away, kleptomania or drug addiction)", says: "The impulses in question have, in contrast to compulsive impulses, an instinctual character; they are felt in the same way that normal instinctual impulses are felt by normal persons. Because of this difference, perverts and impulse neurotics are sometimes not called neurotics at all but psychopaths" (24, p. 324). The way in which the term "psychopathic" is used here shows that psychoanalysts are rather skeptical as to its clinical justification. The fact that acts of perversion are often accompanied or followed by strong guilt feelings and that the pervert feels himself forced to "like" something against his will is seen as proof of the essential similarity between these deviations and neurotic disorders. (The differentiation is considered by some analysts a matter of semantics rather than of structural analysis.)

According to Fenichel, perversions develop on the basis of castration fears and are said to be attempts to prove there is no castration. Repression takes place in the life history of the pervert no less than in that of the neurotic. But it is less inductive and less universal in developments of the first type, where some impulses are allowed to remain in consciousness and thus facilitate the repression of castration fears (24, p. 328). In addition, a constitutional factor of "augmented erogeneity" of certain body zones is believed to operate as a specific causal factor in the genesis of perversions. This factor would account for the relative weakness of anxiety, while, in most neurotic developments, strong anxiety accompanies sexual gratification (24, p. 366). It is as if increased sexual excitability provided a kind of organic defense against fear of sexual gratification, though not of castration which is being repressed by way of denial.

At the same time, however, we are told that "perversions occur sometimes in combination with neuroses, most frequently, because of the common pregenital fixation, with compulsion neuroses and psychoses. All three of the following possibilities are encountered: (1) Perversion and neurosis develop alongside each other. (2) A neurosis complicates a primarily established perversion. (3) A perversion is added to a primarily established neurosis" (24, p. 365).

In the light of these remarks, it would appear that perversion is interpreted as a form of neurotic behavior. It is produced by pregenital fixations and strong castration fears, under conditions of a constitutionally increased sexual excitability, which operates as an anxiety-weakening factor. Not only the castration fear, the pregenital fixation and the frequent coexistence and combination of perversion and neuroses, but also the strong guilt feelings which often accompany perverse activities seem to support this definition. On the other hand, the relative weakness of anxiety, which is explained as resulting from a constitutional quality of the organism, may be adduced as an argument in favor of the psychopathic character of perversion.

We maintain, however, that the above-described pervert is not a true psychopath. Early traumatic occurrences, though causing fixation on the infantile level, do not produce here a constitutional inability to establish relationships or to experience anxiety. In the psychopathic pervert, on the other hand, it is this inability rather than developmental fixation which explains his infantility. In the neurotic variety, the organically conditioned increase in sexual excitability, though counteracting fear of sexual gratification, does so only against the background of intense castration fears (which, in turn, result from traumatic experiences). In the true psychopath, sexual excitability, which is usually much less pronounced, operates as an instrument of passive incorporation and of drivenness, without being directed against castration fears (the latter again being considerably less pronounced as the result of the relational inability and the elimination of anxiety). The former type is more frequently found among extraverts who, as children, had been exposed to either overstrict or overindulgent parents. Psychopathic perverts are usually introverts who have grown up under the influence of an indolent or a cold mother. In the former, the discrepancy between the two basic life-tendencies (toward expansion and toward staticness) is considerably smaller than in the psychopath (though they are, of course, equally separated from each other). The tendency toward staticness makes itself felt in the form of attempts at ego systematization or of guilt feelings, both of which are absent in the passively driven psychopath. Finally, we believe there is less specialization in the psychopathic perversions, at least in those that appear in the behavior patterns of the driven psychopath.

(f) The impulse neurotic

In impulse neuroses, the impulses are described as ego-syntonic and, though irresistible, are said not to be experienced as compulsions. These neurotics are characterized by their extreme intolerance of tension "They cannot wait . . . their aim is not pleasure but the discontinuance of pain.*

---

* cf. p 205 where Fenichel's identical analysis of the acting-out character was quoted.

Any tension is felt . . . as a threat to their very existence . . . Their impulsive acts . . . signify a striving for a goal which they simultaneously try to avoid because they are afraid of it. They make their objects responsible for not providing the needed relaxation, and they feel guilty for the aggressiveness with which they provoke their objects . . . Impulse neurotics are fixated on the . . . early phase of development, in which striving for sexual satisfaction and striving for security are not yet differentiated from each other . . . Being fixated on the oral phase, they tend to react to frustrations with violence. Their main conflict is one between this tendency toward violence and a tendency to repress all aggressiveness through fear over loss of love . . . As a rule, these conflicts were first expressed in struggles around masturbation, and masturbation was subsequently supplanted by the morbid craving . . . Objects are not yet persons, they are only deliverers of supplies, and thus interchangeable" (24, pp. 386 f.).

The principal forms of impulse neuroses are: pathologic wandering, kleptomania, pyromania, passion for gambling, addictions with and without drugs, and the so-called "instinct-ridden character". All these are "unsuccessful attempts to master guilt, depression or anxiety by activity" (24, p. 382).

There exist many similarities, both in the underlying dynamics and in the manifestations, between impulse neuroses and the oral character (see 24, pp. 488ff.), the "acting-out" character (see 24, pp. 506 f.) and the cycloid character (see 24, p. 531), their common denominator being fixation on the pre-love stage of development. Some parts of the above-quoted description would equally well apply to the so-called guilt offenses, others to the primary behavior disorder of the oedipal type (see later) and still others to perversions.

The sharp distinction between the ego-alien character of compulsion neurosis and the ego-syntonic though irresistible character of impulse neuroses seems to be problematic. Fenichel himself restricts the validity of his statement by adding that there exist many "transitional states" between the two (24, pp. 382 ff.). What are the essential characteristics discriminating between compulsion neurosis, impulse neurosis and psychopathy? To be compulsive means (a) determination by—organic, environmental or unconscious—forces beyond man's conscious control; (b) contradiction between weak ego-participation and intensive directedness of the ego towards the (compulsive) action; (c) rigidity.

Compulsiveness is evident in perversions and impulse neuroses (which we would therefore prefer to call "compulsive dissociality"). But we should add that the allotropic character of these disorders requires a relatively higher degree of ego participation than does compulsion *neurosis*, and at the same time intensifies the ego's directedness toward the dis-social action. The *second* component of compulsiveness appears here as a contradiction between a relatively high degree of ego-participation and a still higher degree of intensity of the ego's action-directedness. It is this simultaneous increase in intensity of both ego-participation and ego-directedness which may give the impression that the impulse is not as ego-alien as the compulsive symptom. But the fact remains that here, too, the degree of ego-participation is considerably lower than that of ego-directedness toward action; in other words, the second component of compulsiveness is still present.

Furthermore, we question the correctness of Fenichel's interpretations when he says that the impulse neurotic feels his impulse as ego-syntonic "at the time of his excitation" (24, p. 368) and that "these impulses, in contrast to compulsive symptoms, are felt in the same way that normal instinctual impulses are felt by normal persons" (24, p. 324). A normal person, when excited, feels his impulse as ego-syntonic and *at the same time* as part of the non-ego; he may, temporarily, *identify* with the impulse without becoming *identical* with it, that is, without losing his capacity for polarization. Not so the pervert or the impulse-neurotic who, at the time of their excitation, lose their ego identity and become mere executive organs of their impulses, as it were. In this respect, they are much more comparable to the compulsion neurotic who is as helpless in the power of his symptoms as they are in that of their impulses. Thus, we see that the *first component* of compulsiveness, too, is present in perversions and impulse neuroses.

The third component of compulsiveness is, as we said, rigidity. It usually increases in proportion to the amount of energy required for neurotic defense. This amount is greater in processes leading to the formation of neurotic *characters* than in the development of neurotic *symptoms*. When we compare compulsion neurosis with perversions or impulse neuroses, we will find that in the latter (leaving aside the most extreme cases) rigidity tends to affect the total personality less than in the former. It expresses itself in the (organically conditioned?) rhythm of periodic tension increase and compulsive tension discharge, and not in defenses as in the compulsion neurotic with his fearful avoidance of sexual gratification. But although the nondefensive nature of pervert and impulsive activities may give the impression of lesser rigidity, the compulsive and the impulsive neurotic are equally rigid in their fixatedness to one specific mode of symptomatic behavior.

The psychopath, on the other hand, unlike the pervert or the impulse neurotic, cannot be called compulsive. Although the various types differ greatly among each other in the degree of ego-participation and ego-directedness toward action, the first is in all types at least equal to the second and usually even exceeds it, owing to the characteristic ego inflation. Thus, the second component of compulsiveness does not apply. Neither does the concept of heteronomous determination seem to be applicable, as the non-ego does not exist as ego-transcending but only as potential property to be incorporated at will. Nor could rigidity be said to be characteristic of the behavior of psychopaths, with their often well-developed ability to adjust themselves to changing reality conditions (provided they are of normal intelligence) or at least to follow these changes.

Any well-developed pathology is, of course, rigid insofar as it tends to be patterned in its specific line (and even absence of inner consistency, coexistence of contradictory traits of frequent change of symptomatization can be a pathologic pattern, hence rigid in its phenomenality). But when we speak of rigidity as a specific symptom of a certain pathology, we mean not only extreme unchangeability but also that lifelessness that usually goes with either defensive self-restriction or automatism. In this respect, no form of psychopathy with its typical ego inflation can be called rigid.

(g) *The instinct-ridden character and oral fixation*

We shall conclude our discussion of impulse neurotics with a short analysis of the so-called instinct-ridden character (84), and shall try to show in which respect this, too, differs from true psychopathy.

Fenichel objects to seeing in the instinct-ridden character a narcissistic psychopath, "happily" enjoying his lack of superego directions, lack of guilt feelings and lack of consideration for others. Ambivalence toward the first objects of relationship reappears in his later personality as ambivalence of the ego toward the superego. According to Reich (84), unrestricted and undelayed yielding to impulses, that is, extreme tension intolerance, is based in this case on an active tendency of the ego to isolate the superego. Such an individual is able openly to rebel against social demands because of the partial character of his internalizations; they allow him relative freedom from superego control whenever an irresistible striving for instinctual gratification or for security makes its appearance (24, p. 375).

Lack of educational consistency or of parental love, says Fenichel, parental overindulgence and lack of educational limitation and, in other cases, identification with an aggressively impulsive father image, says

Reich, are responsible for the incompleteness of superego development which is characteristic of the instinct-ridden character. Here, again, we have a striking example of the insufficient etiologic differentiation so frequently found in psychoanalytic interpretations. It does not help us very much in our endeavor to understand the genesis of this pathology when Fenichel says that early experience of "both intense erogenous pleasure and intense environmental frustrations" in an orally fixated individual is the precondition of this character pathology (24, p. 375 and p. 479).

This formula does not answer a number of relevant questions of etiology: Is the "intense erogenous pleasure" a congenitally given factor which, perhaps, produces the oral fixation? Or does it result from earliest experience (and if so, what kind of experience is liable to create such a tendency in the organism)? Is, perhaps, the tendency toward oral fixation the congenitally given factor which produces the erogeneity? Or do both terms designate the same factor, the one (intense erogeneity) in the language of the organism, the other (oral fixation) in that of development? And how could overindulgence, that is, lack of ego-limitation, be included among factors of intense environmental frustration? Moreover, nowhere does Fenichel try to verify his etiologic equation by holding constant one of its components (e.g., the intense erogenous pleasure) while treating the two others (e.g., environmental frustration and oral fixation) as variables and asking what clinical result would then be likely to appear?

The causal factors mentioned by Fenichel and by Reich are not only different from each other but also so general and the term "environmental frustration" is so ambiguous that it seems, to say the least, doubtful whether the clinical entity under discussion can be adequately explained in this way. The factors do not in any case allow for an etiologic differentiation between perversions and impulse neuroses, on the one hand, and between the instinct-ridden character and other forms of impulse neurotics, on the other.

The same objection to insufficient differentiation can be raised in the area of symptomatology. We are informed by Fenichel that the instinct-ridden character includes: certain forms of juvenile delinquency, particularly those in which the offense betrays an unconscious need for punishment; hypersexuality without return to staticness through satisfaction; narcissism of the orally fixated individual with his conflicts between rebellion and ingratiation; rationalization of aggressive stubbornness which may produce the "fighter for a good cause"; antisocial behavior resulting from identification with instinct-approving adults. It would seem difficult to define a common denominator of these varieties of the instinct-ridden character, unless we want to see it in the inner tension between contradictory tendencies. This contradictoriness, however, is no less characteristic of the other impulse neuroses, of perversions, of the neurotic and the hysterical character, and even of many psychoneuroses or character neuroses.

It is not a major purpose of the present analysis to criticize the psychoanalytic method of defining clinical units of character and behavior disorders and of distinguishing between them. Our aim is to clarify the concept of psychopathy, as defined in this chapter, by confronting it with those psychoanalytic concepts which seem to connote similar behavioral phenomena. For this purpose, we shall now compare the psychoanalytic concept of *oral fixation* (which appears in each of the above-mentioned character disorders as a central factor of determination) with that of psychopathic constitution (which we consider essential for the understanding of our clinical entity).

In the oral stage, says Fenichel (24, pp. 63 ff.), objects do not yet exist as objects of relationships but only as food to be incorporated or as suppliers of food and satisfiers of basic needs. This incorporation forms not only the basis of later identification but also of ambivalence, as the object is liable to be destroyed and lost through the act of incorporation. Both, identification and ambivalence, can, of course, appear only after the concept of an object in its own right has been established.

Fixation on the oral level is likely to result from constitutionally strong erogeneity operating in conjunction with the experience of either excessive oral satisfaction or frustration. Excessive satisfaction may produce inability to bear even the slightest amount of frustration or to reject or give up any instinctual drives and demands and to a later preference for self-contradictory modes of satisfaction, that is, of symptoms, attitudes or activities which are able simultaneously to satisfy instinctual demands and to allay the anxieties aroused by them. Where the constitutional erogeneity is weaker, excessive satisfaction or frustration will produce other forms of behavior (characterized by less activity?) but not oral fixation. The latter, also called fixation on the pre-love stage of development (24, pp. 509 ff.), manifests itself in oral dependence and/or egocentric omnipotence feelings in an individual who is devoid of objective relational ability. He is, however, characterized not only by this inability but also by a strong need for security, born out of excessive anxieties, like every neurotic. It is, indeed, this common root which justifies subsuming all pathologies stemming from oral fixation under the general concept of neurosis.

But if this is granted, psychopathy cannot be identified with the various manifestations of oral fixation. The psychopath is not fixated on the earliest phase of his development; he does not react with anxiety to the frustrating experiences of rejection, deprivation, indolence or isolation, because these experiences, instead of being experienced as such and provoking specific reactions within a definable ego system, operate as reinforcers only of the constitutionally given tendencies.

Fixation presupposes more or less equal intensity of the two basic life-tendencies. It is this (structural) equality which explains the individual's ability to experience conflict, tension and anxiety, and his need for solving the conflict and avoiding anxiety. Generally speaking, the tendency toward expansion expresses itself in the organism's receptivity and plasticity, the tendency toward staticness in its systematizations. Development and growth are felt simultaneously as a structural need and as a threat (coming from within and from without), particularly under the influence of frustrating experiences. If the individual reacts to this feeling with a tendency to avoid change and to remain statically bound to a specific stage of development, we speak of fixation. In other words, fixation is an expression of the individual's tendency to solve tension conflicts by avoiding development and growth. This tendency, however, must be preceded by the emergence of a primary identification of the growing ego with its needs for staticness. We could also say that, whenever the normal *return* to staticness is hindered by frustrating experiences, the individual tends to *remain* static if an equally strong tendency toward expansion has supplied him with the necessary anxiety incentive.

If the tendency toward expansion is abnormally weak, the individual's receptivity may be decreased to such a degree that the threatening character of growth and of environmental frustrations is not felt intensely enough to provoke defensive reactions. If the tendency toward staticness is equally weak, apathy in its various forms will result; if it is stronger than the tendency toward expansion, rigidity will prevail; and the processes of growth and development will be devoid of their normal character of intentionality. In these cases, true fixation will become unnecessary or impossible.

If, on the other hand, the tendency toward expansion is structurally predominant over that toward staticness, processes leading to fixation will not be favored either, though for a different reason : here, constant drive to expand the boundaries of any extant state and increased receptivity are liable to give the very feeling of staticness and rest a character of danger-to-be-avoided, and any form of systematization will be delayed (cf. p. 105). If extreme environmental frustrations are absent, even a relatively weak structural tendency toward staticness may be sufficient to provide at least that minimum of synthesizing energy which is required for the process of normal ego formation (provided, of course, the two life-tendencies operate on the basis of interrelatedness). But under conditions of environmental frustration a predominance of the tendency toward expansion is liable to prevent the emergence of a structured ego, because a predominant or even exclusive reliance on expansion renders difficult, if not impossible, the experience of polarity which, in turn, lies at the basis of normal ego development* as well as of fixation.

We shall now return to the question from which we set out : how does the true psychopath differ from Reich's "instinct-ridden" character and, in general, from character deviations based on what Fenichel calls fixation on the pre-love, particularly the oral, stage of development? Although we believe that the psychoanalytic concepts of libido development (such as orality) are inadequate for the understanding of ego formation and development, and especially of the process of differentiation and polarization, we shall accept Fenichel's definitions and analyses as a basis of comparison.

Typical of impulse neurotics, including the instinct-ridden characters, we are told, is the deep-rooted ambivalence which expresses itself in their tendency to seek simultaneous gratification of instinctual and security needs, and which stems from oral fixation. The essence of orality is defined as fear of losing the nourishing object by incorporating it and as tendency to incorporate it in order not to lose it. Fixation on the oral stage is, according to Fenichel (and others) determined by the constitutional factor of over-strong erogeneity of the oral zone. And, paradoxically, it is said to presuppose a conception of the object in its own right, that is, as an object of relationship and not only of food and incorporation; for, only an object of relationship can be lost.†

In all these respects the psychopath differs from the so-called orally fixated character. In the psychopath, the tendency toward staticness is weaker than in the oral character, and in any case is considerably weaker than the tendency toward expansion, while in the oral character both tendencies are equal in strength. Oral erogeneity is not an essential characteristic of the psychopath. Congenital or secondary weakness (or absence) of anxiety accounts for an equal weakness of the tendency to repress instinctual demands or to satisfy them in a way which simul-

---

* On the other hand, it is precisely the impact of these frustrating experiences in the earliest period of life which accounts here for a delay in the postnatal development and crystallization of the congenitally given ego-nucleus into a final constitution.

† This is only another way of saying that inability to experience anxiety and inability to establish subject-object relationships are interdependent, are, in fact, two expressions of one and the same pathology.

taneously satisfies a striving for security. The psychopath does not depend on the object as an object of relationship because he has no feeling for otherness and lives without polarization. Incorporation, therefore, does not provoke in the psychopath fear of losing the incorporated object. Hence, the absence of conflict and of ambivalence in his development.

But the most important difference between the two is that of the time factor. Oral fixation takes place in a phase in which the object is already experienced as such (so that its loss can be feared); the psychopathic constitution is formed before that phase, that is, before the process of differentiation has led either to the normal polarity or to the pathologic separation between the ego and the non-ego.

The alleged constitutional erogeneity of the oral zone may perhaps explain a tendency toward oral fixation. A constitutional predominance of the tendency toward expansion, however, eliminates (in the congenital form of psychopathic developments) the infant's ability to experience anxiety: the ego, already in *statu nascendi*, does not feel threatened by processes of growth or by environmental influences, not even by objectively frustrating ones, if the tendency toward expansion is so strong that no need for systematization (involving self-restriction) arises; here, experience does not necessitate consistent reactions on the part of the individual, which in both, normal and neurotic developments, lead to the gradual crystallization of fixed attitudes and defense systems. In the noncongenital, the ontogenetic, forms of psychopathic development, on the other hand, reaction to the earliest (preconstitutional) disturbances in the child-mother relationship produce irreversible constitutional patterns; these, then, determine the child's subsequent development, not by way of defensive reaction-formations but (as every constitutional factor) by way of selecting experience.

This is what we mean by saying that in the psychopath frustrating experiences cease to be experienced as such because they only reinforce constitutionally given tendencies (p. 134).*

If we compare the above-described psychopathic types with the varieties of the instinct-ridden character described by Fenichel (24, pp. 373 ff.) or by Reich (84), it is clear that the clinical pictures are not identical. Idealization of antisocial behavior based on identification with negative images, or pseudo-moral fanaticism out of rationalization of

---

* Reinforcement of constitutional tendencies through experience, selected, as it were, by these very tendencies, is a process comparable to that of conditioning, as we find it, for instance, in waywardness. The essential difference between psychopathy and waywardness is one of reinforcement through selected control through recurring experience (see pp. 51 ff.).

one's own aggressiveness can usually be recognized as nonpsychopathic by the presence of unconscious motivations; such motivations indicate repression of aggressive impulses against parental images. To the extent that ego inflation characterizes these behavior patterns, it is considerably less natural and more defensive than in psychopathy. When we analyze the behavior pattern of the tense, resentful and never-satisfied hypersexual or of the egocentric rebel whose attempts to ingratiate himself with others strangely contradict his outward bravado, it is not too difficult to discover the underlying anxiety and the basically neurotic nature of these disorders. And the punishment-seeking juvenile delinquent undoubtedly is more of a neurotic than a psychopath. (There are other clinical pictures of dissocial behavior in children, waywardness or primary behavior disorders, which resemble psychopathic behavior much more than "punishment-seeking".)

By way of summing up the preceding comparisons we may say that, in spite of many similarities between the behavior patterns of the hysterical or the neurotic character, the pervert, the impulse neurotic or the instinct-ridden character, on the one hand, and those of the various psychopathic types, on the other, all of the former are essentially different from psychopathy : they are the outcome of unconscious forces; psychopathic behavior results from a constitutional predominance of the tendency toward expansion, from constitutional absence or weakness of anxiety and from ego inflation.

(h) *The epileptic character*

In contrast to the character disorders which have been compared so far with psychopathy, the so-called "epileptic character" presents an entirely different problem : not only is it *prima facie* an organically rather than an emotionally caused behavior disorder, many tend to consider psychopathy to be an epiphenomenon only of overt or covert epileptic disturbances. The violent crimes committed by certain epileptics have given rise to the hypothesis that at least the more severely aggressive types of psychopathy—the congenitally given moral indolence, the aggressive and the explosive varieties—may have an organic basis comparable to that of epileptic conditions. Certain electroencephalographic studies seem to have strengthened Hill's hypothesis that cerebral dysrhythmia, so apparent in epilepsy, is equally present in many non-organic aggressive psychopaths (54).

But to conclude from the similarity of the EEG that a structural similarity or even affinity exists between the behavior patterns accompanying the respective clinical pictures would seem to be unjustified.

Heterogeneous syndromes could in this way be brought together, particularly from the field of psychiatric conditions, in which the electroencephalographic patterns are not yet recognized clearly enough to allow for unequivocal differential diagnosis.

Those who claim that certain behavior disorders are significantly linked with EEG abnormalities have not yet been able to suggest a satisfactory answer to the crucial question of whether and to what extent an abnormal behavior pattern (particularly of the irritated, hyperkinetic and acting-out types) is a *direct result* or an *indirect cause* of a cerebral dysfunction as reflected in an abnormal EEG. Transient changes in the EEG (including passing intensifications of existing abnormalities) can be produced by minor traumatizations, pharmacotherapeutic interventions, temporary excitements or confusing experiences. This fact would seem to support the psychosomatic hypothesis according to which cerebral function and dysfunction can be influenced by certain types of behavior.

If so, however, it would not seem warranted to construct an unequivocal causal link between psychopathic behavior of the aggressive type and cerebral dysrhythmia. The most we can say in the light of present electroencephalographic studies is: (a) that certain psychopaths show an EEG similar to that of certain epileptics; and (b) that in certain epileptics a quasi-psychopathic behavior pattern is more in evidence than the typical seizure pictures.

In connection with the second claim, we want to mention the criticism leveled against the misuse of the clinical concept of "epileptic equivalents" (see, for instance, A. N. Foxe, 54) as well as the growing skepticism as to the justification of the term "epileptic personality". It would, of course, be begging the question to call "epileptic" every behavior pattern which is characterized by moodiness, uncontrollable outbursts, coexistence of cruelty and egocentric craving for affection, oversensitiveness in the face of environmental interferences and pedantic tendencies. To the extent that this pattern is found in true epileptics, it should be understood, as Piotrowski (54) has said, as the result of their adjustment struggles and not as a personality pattern preceding epilepsy (and it may even be a secondary or tertiary result only of environmental discrimination, of the effect of sedative drugs used for treatment purposes or of the mental deterioration which sometimes follows epileptic conditions).

Where the behavior pattern appears without epileptic seizure symptoms, it should not be diagnosed as an epileptic equivalent, although the EEG may show certain "epileptic" characteristics indicating cortical dysrhythmia. Comparative studies of epileptics and their nonepileptic relatives have shown that this dysrhythmia which may be present in both is in no way correlated to the behavior patterns of the epileptic (which is usually absent in the relatives). These patterns should therefore be interpreted as a result of the epileptic seizures rather than of their organic basis. If so, however, similarities between the EEG of epileptics and of certain antisocial (nonepileptic) individuals, though perhaps indicative of a similar dysrhythmia, do not justify calling the latter "epileptic personalities" or diagnosing their behavior as an epileptic "equivalent",* but should be regarded as a behavior pathology in its own right, maybe of the character-neurotic, maybe of the psychopathic type.

We are then faced again with the question of clinical differentiation. Egocentricity, aggressive intolerance of environmental interferences, self-magnifying tendencies and boastfulness, often evident in the behavior of epileptics, are certainly reminiscent of psychopathic ego inflation. Their emotional shallowness, lack of empathy and lack of concern for the interests of others indicate a relational inability very similar to that of the psychopath. Their strong existential fear of being overcome in the moment of attack, however, is typical of the epileptic behavior pattern only. Mittelman (54) has tried to show how expressions of aggressive and self-inflational egocentricity in the epileptic should be interpreted as attempts to escape that fear, and how in the attack itself the same fear and fantasy of destruction manifests itself organically. (Similarly, Clark [quoted in 69] suggests that the attack represents an effort to return to the maternal womb in an individual with an abnormal predominance of the death instinct.)

The reactive nature of the epileptic's oversensitiveness, stubbornness, jealousy and all-pervading resentfulness, on the one hand, of his occasional tendencies toward depression or moodiness on the other, and the organic nature of his restlessness, inattentiveness and excitability can serve as additional criteria of differentiation between the so-called epileptic and the various psychopathic behavior patterns.

Irrespective of whether these "epileptic" behavior traits are reactive to what might be called "holes in the psychosomatic personality structure" or to the anxiety-provoking experience and expectation of the attack or to environmental discrimination and isolation, there can be no doubt that certain symptoms of defensive egocentricity and self-magnification are

---

* We are speaking here of persistent behavior patterns only and not of bad behavior. Lennox (69, p. 959) claims that the latter may be diagnosed not as epileptic equivalents but as signs of true epilepsy provided they are accompanied "by a prolonged sequence of slow high voltage cortical waves". In these cases, he says, "the bad behavior *is* a seizure" (69, p. 962). It goes without saying that without the accompanying signs of cortical disturbance, the same fits of bad behavior have a different clinical meaning.

liable to emerge unless strongly protective counterforces operate in the epileptic individual's environment. Conceit, falsity and resentment are his armor against the inner threat and injury which he experiences as part of the non-ego. It is as if the threatening character of the *organic* non-ego were infecting the *human* non-ego, which the epileptic then is liable to reject, attack and destroy, while at the same time craving for its protection. In his cruelty he tries to destroy a depersonalized destroyer; in his often painfully sentimental and false craving for attachment and affection he tries to construct a pseudo-reality in which he can feel safe without forming an integral (relational) part of it. When he fails, as he is bound to, in his irrealistic quest for reality, he will again attack and destroy. But often enough destruction will be found to be a direct expression of his (depersonalized) needs for attachment rather than a reaction to disappointment.

In this respect he essentially differs from the psychopath for whom the non-ego is, as we have said, a (potential) possession and property of his inflated ego but not something to cling to. Psychopathic aggressiveness is characterized, in its extravert form, by incorporative intentions, in its introvert form by illusions of being master over a rejecting and rejected reality. Aggressiveness as observed in the development of epileptic individuals is automatic rather than intentional, resentful rather than inflational, and fear of destruction prevails over any illusion of mastery.

9. Psychopathy and Juvenile Delinquency

(a) Antisocial character formation

We shall now proceed to a comparison of the concept of psychopathy with a number of clinical concepts which are being used by different psychiatrists and psychologists in their analysis of juvenile delinquency. We refer to K. Friedlander's "antisocial character formation" (38), J. Bowlby's "affectionless thief" (9), F. Redl's "children who hate" (83) and to the concept of "waywardness" as used by the present writer in the second chapter as well as in other studies (26, 35; see also A. Aichhorn—2).*

K. Friedlander, whose method of classification was critically examined in the first chapter, claims that the *antisocial character* is characterized

---

* A separate chapter is devoted to a discussion of the different forms in which adolescent delinquency manifests itself in our culture. This discussion, we hope, will help clarify the interdependence of sociologic and psychological levels of interpretation. Reference is made also to the first and to the fifth chapters in which the two forms of what Ophuijsen calls "primary behaviour disorders of the oedipal and the pre-oedipal types" are being analyzed (79).

by ego weakness, faultiness in superego development and lack of instinct modification. The latter would seem to be the essential trait, as it is hard to conceive of an individual with unmodified instincts in whom the development of ego and superego proceeds normally. The symptoms mentioned in her case analyses are those of extreme delinquent behavior : truancy and chronic thievery starting from an early age and "supported" by calculated efforts to avoid being caught, exhibitionistic and sadistic fantasies and activities, verbal aggressiveness, cheekiness, intolerance of environmental restrictions, often strangely contrasted with ingratiating behavior), lack of insight or guilt feelings which are replaced by a completely externalized pseudo-conscience (38, pp. 78 f.).

Etiologically, extreme anxiety due to lack of parental love and dis-orientation due to bad relationships between the parents (irrespective of whether the faulty parental attitudes are rooted in their personality or caused by adverse economic conditions) are said to be responsible for antisocial character formation (38, p. 97); negative environmental factors operating at a later stage of development are considered auxiliary or precipitating causes only (38, pp. 106 ff.). But elsewhere (38, p. 117) we read that "the specific factor in the causation of the antisocial character formation is probably the constant *alternation* of too much frustration and too much gratification of primitive instinctive drives". The latter hypothesis is supported, for instance, by the case history of the "imposter type" (38, 140 ff.) to which we shall refer later on.

Friedlander considers the different forms of delinquency to be varieties of neurotic development rather than essentially different units. This monistic tendency, which is typical of the psychoanalytic approach to juvenile delinquency, seems unjustified both from a therapeutic and from a theoretical point of view. The time factor in the history of frustrating experiences, differences in the level of fixation, the relative causal function of economic stress versus personality disorders and conflicts in the parents, which Ophuijsen (49, 77) rightly stresses as differential factors in his interpretation of primary behavior disorders versus neuroses, differences in the formation of essential symptoms which serve as foci of the various clinical pictures, and, most important of all, the differential role of (congenital or secondary) constitutional factors as co-determinants of pathologic developments—all these prove the fallacy of any monistic system of clinical interpretation and classification.

We have already tried to show that (and why) the psychopath is not identical with the instinct-ridden or the neurotic character. We shall now try to show in which respects he differs from the child who hates, the aggressive offender or the wayward child. All of them are re-educable if exposed to methods such as those used by Aichhorn (2), Redl (83) and other psychoanalytically oriented educators, or to a combination of such methods with an integrated program of intensive environmental treatment (33). Not so the psychopathic youth who, as Friedlander rightly points out, may, after a period of irreproachable behavior in an institution, "go out into life entirely unchanged" (38, p. 139).* But this difference of reaction to therapeutic methods is only symptomatic of the essential, the structural, difference between the psychopath and all other juvenile delinquents, although different (externalizing or neuroticizing) factors may operate in the development and the behavior of the latter. This essential difference becomes evident when we relate the behavioral symptoms to the causal factors which produce the various outcomes.

Fixation on the so-called anal-sadistic level of development is said to be the decisive causal factor in the antisocial character formation of the *first* type in Friedlander's classification (38, pp. 113 ff.). Here, aggressiveness is basically directed against the parents who failed the child in that early phase of development in which he should have learned the rules of give-and-take (22) and of emotional polarity, that is, of the possible coexistence of contradictory feelings. Predominance of experiences which are liable to provoke aggressive reactions following a period of relative security and satisfaction of the elementary love needs, that is, disappointment in the parents, and particularly in the mother, may produce this type of developmental fixation. Its outstanding behavior symptom will then be heteronomous uniformity of hate reactions against the frustrating parents which will gradually become generalized by way of a kind of "inductive spread of effect". Later conflicts and frustrations may reinforce the early established reaction and behavior patterns but should not be considered primary factors of causation.

In this respect differ the offenders of Friedlander's *second* type, in whom frustrations occurring in various developmental phases have an accumulative effect on the process of identity formation. While in the first group alternation of satisfying and frustrating experiences appears as (disappointing) change, we find in the life history of the puberty offender (the second type) contradictory experiences at one and the same time, leading to inner conflicts and neurotic solutions which may be replaced, during puberty, by antisocial acts, particularly under the influence of

---

* From the very fact that Aichhorn succeeded in re-educating aggressive offenders by withholding punishment and thus helping them to develop guilt feelings, we can conclude that he did not deal with true psychopaths, contrary to what is often said by psychoanalysts when they question the justification of the concept of psychopathy by referring to Aichhorn's success.

added environmental stresses. These offenses can be explained as unconscious attempts to escape the ambiguity of disturbed identity formation by assuming the negative role of independence on social norms.

The compulsive character of the offenses in Friedlander's *third* group indicates extreme fear of ego-loss caused by the experience of severe threats to the child's elementary security needs. Earliest (oral) traumata, reinforced by subsequent limitation of the child's autonomy and initiative, to use Erikson's terms (21), lead to suppression or repression of aggressive tendencies and to their transformation into neurotic symptoms. A compulsive need to create, always anew, situations of danger and threat to the ego explains the choice of outwardly aggressive (allotropic, antisocial) rather than truly neurotic (autotropic, self-restricting) symptoms. In these cases, ego feeling seems to be dependent on the ever-recurring experience that the ego is not destroyable by the non-ego, but, on the contrary, is able to overcome by force the non-ego's resistance. The thus demonstrated (provocative) "mastery of fate", however, contrasts with, rather than indicates, an underlying belief in the omnipotence of the ego; it betrays the deep anxiety of an ego which knows neither autonomy nor initiative. Moreover, it is this constant tension between anxiety and fate-provocation which explains the compulsive discharge character of the antisocial acts. The latter are not only and not always, as Fenichel claims, substitutes of masturbatory acts, but should be understood primarily as expressions of pseudo-autonomy, that is, of the child's compulsive need to prove to himself his ego's organizational power and integrity.

In the light of the strong feelings of anxiety and the intense conflicts which underlie the hitherto discussed forms of juvenile delinquency and which explain the absence of ego inflation in each of them, their non-psychopathic nature is evident. In order to show that the *fourth* type mentioned by Friedlander is not a psychopath either, we shall refer to the case quoted by her under the heading of "impostor type" (38, pp. 140 ff.).

This is the case of a boy of 16 who, from the age of seven on, had committed innumerable thefts and who had been unable to adjust to any educational setting. He had become effeminate, apparently as the result of his overindulgent mother's prohibition of all masculine associations and activities and complete nonparticipation of the father in his upbringing. The acts of stealing were for the boy a never-failing source of excitement and satisfaction (comparable to masturbatory fantasies and activities). But still more important than the actual offenses, for him, were the arguments he had with everyone, particularly with his mother, over his guilt or innocence. He used his highly developed intelligence not so much for the planning of his offenses as for provoking his environment into proving his guilt; in other words, his main concern was how to remain undetected. He felt no guilt over his acts, and neither failure nor punishment caused him discomfort.

Friedlander's interpretation of the boy's demonstrated lack of anxiety and his efforts to remain undetected as actually referring to his excessive masturbation rather than to his thefts does not seem to be corroborated by the reported facts. We suggest the following alternative interpretation : The boy maintained that an offense was no reality as long as the adult representatives of reality were not able to prove beyond doubt that he had committed it. Thus, he deprived reality of its objective character and transformed it, as it were, into a system of concepts to be "managed" by his intellect. This behavior pattern indeed resembles that of the psychopathic *Hochstapler* (cf. pp. 108 ff.) or that of the "owner of absolute truth" (pp. 115 ff.). However, the compulsiveness of his acts and his constant anxious relatedness to the opinion of his environment betray a strong admixture of neurotic patterns.

This would mean that the here-described clinical picture occupies an intermediary position between psychopathy and compulsive antisociality. Etiologically, the overindulgence on the part of the boy's mother would account for his later inability to recognize objective ego-boundaries; her effeminating prohibitions may have been responsible for the emergence of strong inner tensions and anxieties over his identity, that is, for the neurotic admixtures to his psychopathic behavior patterns. The main symptoms, lack of guilt feelings and inability to learn from punishment, indicate psychopathy; his compulsiveness, the excitement and satisfaction derived from each act of stealing and the tendency to prove his untouchability, particularly in relation to his mother, indicate again neurotic involvement.

Whether the boy's ego inflation is genuinely psychopathic or not, will become evident only in the course of his further development. Friedlander is of the opinion that he, too, could have been brought to experience discomfort (and thus have been prepared for psychoanalytic treatment) had he been placed in an environment which would have refused to give in to his attempts to provoke arguments over his guilt or innocence (38, p. 214). In this way, it could have been proven that he was able to experience anxiety and that his feeling for otherness could be developed; in other words, that he was *not* a psychopath. If, on the other hand, such a response did not come forth, a diagnosis of psychopathy would have been justified in this instance, in spite of the etiologic and symptomatologic counterindicators which could be discovered in his previous history.

This raises an important question : Is it possible that psychopathic

behavior types crystallize only in the course of the individual's development and that the childhood history of every psychopath shows signs of
non-psychopathic behavior patterns due to the impact of the very process
of growth? Obviously, this question could be answered through the
analysis of case histories only.

(b) "Children who hate"

Redl describes the patterns of aggressiveness in children whose ego
formation was severely disturbed as the result of parental and environmental rejection. He calls them "children who hate" (83).

1) They are unable to live as individuals but are in constant need of
group contacts, particularly for the purpose of perpetrating acts of
delinquency or aggression, so much so that they may be called group-
intoxicated.

2) They do not learn from either success or failure, neither from their
own nor those of others.

3) They "do not care" and are utterly unable to evaluate correctly
their own causal role in the processes and the events that occur.

4) In strange contrast to their lack of objectivity, we often find an
extraordinary diagnostic acuity in these children, which helps them
manipulate adults for their own purposes, and particularly avoid change
of attitudes.

5) Every situation is likely to seduce them. They cannot wait but need
immediate satisfaction, and they will never be satisfied with partial
satisfactions.

6) An unknown situation, on the other hand, which does not appeal
to their drives and needs, is likely to bewilder them and to put them into
a state of panic. This also explains the fact that the delinquent children
tend to stick to their aggressive life style.

7) They experience every restriction as attack and react to it by
counter-attack. Destroying is their central mode of ego expression,
although they may submit temporarily to "controls from without".

8) The "children who hate" always try to justify their acts and demand
proof of their guilt. They will never confess, even if they know that they
are not in danger of being punished, but will put the *onus probandi* on
the adult representatives of values.

9) Following the lead of others, dependence on group patterns or retaliation are considered legitimate reasons for aggression.

10) Even the experience of a good adult will not lead to identification, although they may still remember him well years later—when they may be in prison. They are unable to commit themselves even when they feel attachment to someone good.

11) More frequently, however, they will do all in their power to provoke the good adult into badness, that is, into aggressive reactions, or they will avoid positive feelings toward him by making him look faulty or ridiculous in the eyes of their group mates. It is here that their diagnostic acuity helps them find the most suitable methods aimed at preserving their negative world conception.

12) A characteristic trait in the behavior pattern of the "children who hate" is their disregard for the possibility or even the likelihood of being caught and found out, that is, their conviction that they are "smarter than the other fellow" who, they know, has been caught and punished.

13) "Children who hate" often identify with a delinquent group code, "rebel for someone else's cause", vindicate their attacks with quasi-moral arguments or try to divide guilt by drawing others into the commission of their offenses.

This analysis proves that the clinical picture of the child who hates resembles that of the primary behavior disorder. Some of the characteristics are equally symptomatic of waywardness, for instance: the tendency to act in groups, passiveness and seducibility within a world in which everything, including the offenses, occurs, as it were, or the absence of internalized values.

Some of the here-mentioned behavioral traits clearly exclude a diagnosis of psychopathy, while others are common to both units but have a different clinical meaning in each of them.

To the first group of symptoms belong: the strong tendency to act in group contacts only and the corresponding inability to live and act as an independent individual; the tendency to identify with antisocial group codes; the externalized manifestations of an infantile pseudo-conscience (*post factum*); the "moral realism" and the readiness to submit to outside coercion; the panic reaction to new and unknown situations; the defensive avoidance of relationships with its marked, conscious or unconscious, intentionality. All these symptoms indicate anxiety and are definite counter-indications of ego inflation.

To the second group belong the child's inability to learn from past experience, his own or that of others, his lack of concern for objective facts, his inability correctly to evaluate his own causal role, the ego-syntonic nature of his offenses when the impulse arises, the diagnostic acuity and the legalistic demand to be proven guilty, the quasi-moral vindication of offenses and the occasional tendency to play the role of the virtuous. Such traits in the behavior of a psychopath result from his ego-inflational conception of everything non-ego as his potential or actual property; in the "child who hates", they are symptomatic of his attempts aggressively to deprive the hated adult world of its restricting powers and to make himself invulnerable, as it were. Moreover, we find these attitudes, here more frequently than in the psychopath, simultaneously with, and often resulting from, a low (or developmentally lowered) level of intellectual functioning. Another element of discrimination is the higher degree of compulsiveness in the behavior of the "child who hates" as compared with that of the psychopath.

But here we must add again what we have already said at the end of our discussion of Friedlander's "antisocial character formation" : it is conceivable that some of the described behavior traits will be found in the childhood history of true psychopaths and that only their post-adolescent development will retrospectively prove these traits to have been early symptoms of psychopathy.

(c) The affectionless thief

A few remarks should be added on Bowlby's "affectionless thief" (9). He considers persistent stealing in a child an illness caused by early deprivations and disappointments in his relationship with his mother. While the majority of the 44 cases studied are classified as normal, depressed, circular, schizoid or hyperthymic, 14 of the juvenile thieves are diagnosed as *affectionless*. They show symptoms similar to those found in the type described by Friedlander, Ophuijsen and Redl : stealing, lying, truancy, lack of responsiveness to treatment or to punishment, lack of attachment or loyalty feelings—though sometimes concealed behind seeming sociability —shamelessness, cruelty or apathy, particularly in the lower grades of intelligence. The aggressive and to some extent also the hysterical and the cheerful subgroups of Bowlby's hyperthymic type show certain similarities with the affectionless type, although their hyperactivity, their boastfulness and their accentuated defiance of authority, which indicate strong affectivity, justify the distinction between the two groups. Some of the affectionless thieves show also signs of withdrawal and suspiciousness resembling the behavior patterns of the schizoid type with his bizarre obsessions, his dreaminess and his nondirected, almost aimless destructiveness.

Invariably an experience of early separation from the mother after a period of relative (though insufficient) experience of contact with the mother is found to be an essential cause in the development of these children.*

Bowlby prefers the terms "affectionless", "schizoid" and "hyperthymic" to the concept of psychopathy which he apparently considers not specific and not dynamic enough for the purposes of differential analysis. He seems to believe that by borrowing his terms from other areas of psychopathology he has made possible a comparison of certain forms of antisocial behavior in children with their nondelinquent counterparts (without, however, going into a detailed phenomenological analysis of these other clinical units in order to prove the justification of his semantic analogies!). But the psychological interpretation which he offers along the lines of psychoanalytic theories is far from convincing. He contents himself with explaining the lack of inhibition and the lack of affection, the two main characteristics of the children described by him, as resulting from lack of opportunities for the establishment of one-to-one (give-and-take) relationships in the early, formative period of life and from the all-pervading feelings of rage, unmodified by feelings of love. This, however, is not much more than a tautologic statement and certainly does not help us understand the *varieties* of antisocial behavior.

We have tried to show that the clinical unit of psychopathy includes a number of sub-units which should be submitted to a comparative analysis (both etiologically and symptomatologically), if we want to use the general concept for the purposes of differential diagnosis. Only by defining and discovering the essential discriminating elements of a certain clinical unit in each of its sub-units can we justify the use of a concept connoting this unit. In this respect, Bowlby's attempt does not seem to have been successful. If early separation from the mother is said to be responsible for the development of the affectionless, the schizoid or the hyperthymic types (which resemble certain forms of what we have called psychopathic behavior), we are entitled to ask and to know what specific causal constellations account for the differences between these three forms of antisocial behavior. Should we look for such differentiating factors in the area of constitutional determination or in that of

---

* Bowlby's etiologic reasoning is not very accurate. He speaks of early separation from the mother without distinguishing properly between the life conditions under which such separation has taken place. In this later work (10) he has much more carefully studied the differential meanings of this causal factor.

the child's experience with his parents, with his environment and with his organism?

The material adduced by Bowlby seems to indicate that his group of "affectionless thieves" included a few who, at a later stage of their development, would probably be diagnosed correctly as psychopaths of the aggressive type, while the majority are cases of primary behavior disorders of the oedipal type.

Bowlby's affectionless thief should not be considered identical with Bender's *affectionless child* (7). Affectionlessness in children is a psychopathic or psychopathoid condition resulting from insufficiency of personal relationships in the early phases of life. Its manifestations are not necessarily aggressive (as are those of the affectionless thief). Indolence, apathy, withdrawal and infantilism are no less in evidence than lack of guilt and of anxiety feelings. But we do not agree either with Kanner (63) who compares (and almost identifies) it with the syndrome of his "early infantile autism". It is much more dependent on the quality of the child's environment than autism.

The picture of affectlessness in an adult has been drawn convincingly by A. Camus in his novel *The Stranger* (14). It is, of course, the author's existentialist philosophy rather than the hero's affectlessness which accounts for the latter's death-intoxication and his nihilistic drivenness. Contrary to N. Leites (44) who tries to explain the "stranger's" affectlessness as a *defense* against the intense feelings of rage he had felt as a young child against his indifferent mother, that is, as a distorted behavior pattern resembling that of primary behavior disorders, we believe that we have before us a description of psychopathic behavior with its characteristic absence of anxiety and relational inability (irrespective of whether its object is an idea, a task, or a person).

But in spite of his outbursts of violence (which could be explained as the result of organic tension and discharge processes rather than the heteronomous return of repressed anger), we should not call him aggressive or impulsive. Nor does any one of the other type descriptions which we have suggested exactly fit the hero's behavior. We think of his unwillingness to face changes which here stems from a deep-rooted and all-pervading feeling of emptiness and of futility; of his uncontrolled, associative way of speaking out what he considers the truth without regard for the foreseeable reactions of his environment; of his strong dependence on nonpersonal, sensory stimuli which almost takes the place of affectivity in normal persons. Such an utterly heteronomous dependence on a depersonalized non-ego, experienced as absolute outerness and otherness is not typical of psychopathic ego inflation.

On the other hand, the very closure of all communication channels and the extreme egocentricity of his monologic reactions, that is, his relational indifference, together with the above-mentioned absence of anxiety, is reminiscent of the morally indolent psychopath; and his feeling of emptiness reminds us of what we have said about the drifting type of psychopathy with his structuralized illusion of egoity derived from what we have suggested should be called a permanently ego-syntonic submission to drives and impulses.

This would mean that the affectlessness as described by Camus is the result of congenital weakness of anxiety modified by an introvert's reaction to an early experience of maternal indifference. The first accounts for the almost automatic, nonintentional character of the aggressive outbursts, the latter for the feeling of emptiness and futility; the first for the complete lack of feeling with the other (or better for the naive egoization of all otherness), the latter for the relative weakness of aggressiveness.

We have mentioned this picture of affectlessness mainly in order to show that it differs essentially from the affectionless offender as described by Bowlby. Of all syndromes so far analyzed, affectlessness is the only one that may be identified with psychopathy.

(d) The wayward child

Finally, we shall try to show the essential differences that exist between various psychopathic behavior patterns and what we call "waywardness" (26, 28). From the description of waywardness in children (see pp. 69 ff.) it would seem that this behavior pattern resembles that of psychopathy. Weakness or absence of superego inhibitions, of guilt feelings, of neurotic symbolism, of tension-creating identity feelings seem to be common characteristics, particularly when we compare the wayward child with the oscillating, the drifting or the unstable psychopathic types. And categories of (conscious or unconscious) intentionality are inapplicable to both of these clinical pictures. But such partial similarities should not make us overlook the essential differences.

The naive participation of the wayward child in the external world in which everything happens, his immediate, though unstructured, reactivity and his ability to enjoy his actions are clearly contrasted by the psychopath's ego-inflational tendencies. The latter are characteristic, as we have tried to show, of the oscillating psychopath with his constantly changing identities or the shallow-attachment type with his incorporative pseudo-contacts no less than of the drifting and the unstable varieties. They manifest themselves in the egocentric and egotropic conception of the non-ego as actual or potential property of the ego. The wayward child's ego, on the other hand, in its organizational weakness, feels itself contained in, and acted upon, by a non-ego which obeys its own strange and unalterable laws, a non-ego of which the child tries to take a part, whenever it happens to offer itself, but which will forever remain outside the orbit of his ego. He may be called passive but not apathetic, acted upon but not driven or unstable, like the psychopath who builds up his illusion of egoity with the help of this very drivenness or instability. His frequent and passing changes of mood and conduct are but unreflected reactions to chance changes in his environment; his weak ego naively accepts the fact that life is "outside", ego and non-ego alike.

His conscious orientation toward the haveable, too, essentially differs from the psychopath's incorporative tendencies; the psychopath *is* what he *has*, the wayward *has* it, though perhaps for a short moment only and only by way of passive participation in the non-ego. The psychopath tends to destroy, to eliminate the barriers and boundaries between the ego and the non-ego; the wayward overlooks and transgresses them. The psychopath is protected against fear of ego loss by ego inflation, the wayward by what might be called, ambiguously, his non-egoity. Thus, both are spared inner conflict, though for opposite reasons.

Waywardness seldom persists into adulthood. The wayward child may undergo a process of "delayed maturation" (44) under the influence of re-educational measures aimed at bringing into operation internalizing factors, or under the influence of life events which may have a similar effect. In this respect he again differs essentially from the psychopath, who is *not* responsive to such factors. But he may also glide into a criminal career, in which case it is always doubtful whether the earlier diagnosis of waywardness was correct. To this group belong those cases of primary behavior disorders whose neurotically defensive symptoms could not be recognized properly because of the marked polymorphousness of asocial and antisocial symptoms; or certain cases of neurotic delinquency which remained untreated and had thus been allowed to degenerate, as it were, into waywardness; or certain cases of psychopathy, particularly of the drifting or unstable variety, on the lower levels of intellectual development where ego inflation tends to give way to passiveness, automatism and perserveration, so typical of the feebleminded person's behavior (see also the fourth chapter). In all these cases the later criminal developments are continuations of the earlier behavior which was wrongly diagnosed as waywardness.

On the other hand, adult waywardness often emerges as a later stage of development only, though, of course, prepared by earlier personality disorders. Ego weakness in configuration with disappointing or isolating experiences may produce this clinical picture. The wayward adult, in contrast to the child, is characterized by a lesser degree of dissocial polymorphousness, an equal degree of passivity and a higher degree of personality disorganization.

We have already mentioned that the drifting psychopath is very rare and that most cases of vagabondage, addiction or perversion are due to neurotic involvements of a compulsive type (p. 114); they reflect either an unconscious search for the lost mother, or a deep-lying oral dissatisfaction and dependence, or a nonintegration or disintegration of sexual identity. Where similar pathologies are due to psychopathic conditions, lack of suffering, of depression, of compulsiveness and naive egocentricity allow for differential diagnosis.

Truly wayward adults, on the other hand, whom we not infrequently meet among vagabonds or prostitutes, differ from both the neurotic (or character neurotic) and the psychopathic varieties; from the first one by their absence of inner tensions, from the second one by their almost complete ego-extinction and their extreme passivity.

This leads us to our next chapter in which the behavioral pattern called "drifting" will be discussed briefly.

CHAPTER FOUR

Drifting and Drivenness

1. ASOCIAL BEHAVIOR IN THE FEEBLEMINDED

FEEBLEMINDEDNESS IS essentially characterized by lack of structure. It finds its expression in rigidity as well as in easy distractibility, in perserverative tendencies as well as in lack of perseverance. Non-cognitive factors, such as a relative inability to resist the interference of emotions or impulses with thought-processes, are intrinsic and yet not essential elements of defining feeblemindedness: their causal weight depends on differential type factors. Elsewhere (36) we have suggested a distinction between the apathetic and submissive types, on the one hand, and the paranoid and aggressive types, on the other.

Indicative of the first two, those that concern us in our present context, are a relatively weak affectivity and relatively strong tendencies toward staticness. Furthermore, associations rather than strong impulses here determine faulty thought processes and the often inadequate behavior. True enough: the submissive and the apathetic differ from each other in many other respects, and particularly in their conception of the non-ego which, for the one, is an all-determining subject, for the other an object, something that is "just there". But it is the common denominator of affective weakness that justifies their subsumption in one group when we study asocial behavior varieties. Both are equally liable to drift into asocial behavior of one kind or another, in which they may then remain caught, as it were.

The almost complete absence of selective and organizing ego-power may cause the submissive feebleminded, whether he be a child or an adult, to serve someone in whom he sees a hero figure. The objective social value of his service-actions is, of course, irrelevant to him. It does not even enter his consciousness, as a problem arousing doubt, or as a challenge to compare a present with a previous situation, in which he may have found himself.

In this way, he may, of course, be drawn into committing an offense, even a serious one, and yet it would be a mistake to classify him as a criminal. His lack of structure will make it difficult, if not impossible, for

153

him to continue in the "career", to "learn the trade", to develop any pattern of behavior that would require consistent activeness. On the other hand, what characterizes the feebleminded of the submissive type is the easiness with which any form of imitating the behavior, or serving the intentions of socially undesirable individuals may support *asocial* pattern-formation. This process, and not merely the often quoted fact that he is easily seduced or exploited, requires explanation. What prepares him for asocial rather than antisocial developments (and this in spite of the fact that his non-selective submissiveness may cause him, as said, to commit serious offenses)?

The answer has almost been given in our preceding remarks. When we say that the social (or dissocial) value of his acts is irrelevant for the feebleminded, the implication is twofold : he is unable to select his behavior according to objective criteria, let us say, to refuse committing a serious offense because of its seriousness; but the submissive feebleminded is equally unable to grade his self-evaluation according to the objective character of what he may have done while obeying the orders, or imitating the behavior, of his hero.*

Needless to add that he will frequently "find himself" in socially objectable behavior without experiencing any need for it or deriving satisfaction from it. What he *does* need and what *does* give him satisfaction, is the very act of imitating his hero figures. This causes him a feeling of value, of being important, a feeling, however, which is then likely to act as a force of determination and selection. It may induce him to commit other offenses *without* being "motivated" even by the image of a hero figure worthy, in his eyes, of being imitated. In other words : the more frequently he remembers having once felt important, the more easily will he repeat his offenses, no longer "in the service" of a leader but in the service of bolstering his self-esteem.

He does not wait for any affect to emerge, he needs no strong drives to incite him; all that must happen is a chance situation, reminiscent of another one in which he may have played what seems to him an important role—and again he will find himself drawn into dissocial behavior. But, paradoxically, neither his type conditions nor society allow him to become a criminal, truly antisocial individual : his aggressive capacities are much too limited, his ego emphasis is much too weak for any destructive patterns to crystallize; nor does society take his isolated, though often violent, acts of aggression as proof of character-deviations : their utter

---

* In this respect, incidentally, not all the feebleminded types resemble each other : aggressiveness, for instance, often accounts for the naive pride of a feebleminded delinquent in the extreme character of his offenses.

lack of inner logic or consistency is in itself evidence that we should see in them chance-outbursts rather than symptomatic character traits.

On the other hand, the more frequently a feebleminded of this type will glide into some socially rejected behavior (whether by way of imitating some "hero" or in order to bolster his weak ego), the more likely is he to become accustomed to an asocial life-style. Here, then, is the place to explain the essence of "drifting" as it appears in certain passive types of affectively weak feebleminded and of psychopathic individuals of low intelligence, as distinguished from what we have described as the typically wayward behavior of children (see the second chapter).

When we claim that the feebleminded of the submissive and the apathetic types are liable to drift into asocial behavior, we should not overlook the differences that exist between the two types, not only in their cognitive essentials but also, and primarily, in their social behavior. "Drifting" has one meaning when we speak of the good-hearted follower, the feebleminded who gives in and says yes to find grace in the eyes of anyone he may meet by chance; it has another meaning, when we speak of the indolent, whose mind is not reached by anyone or anything. The first will not drift into asocial behavior unless it is represented, as it were, by some seducing image; the second does not need such stimulation or support, but may by chance, that is, through the impact of some (accidental, non-directed, impersonal) combination of circumstances, one day find himself in such asocial behavior.

Both may, with equal ease, remain within the bounds of socially acceptable behavior, when the environment is conducive to it. In this case, again, the first one needs an example to follow, someone to emulate, while the indolent may remain socially adequate without knowing why he behaves as he does.

Drifting into asocial behavior, then, means: being drawn into it either by imitative drives or by the force of circumstances, mechanically, as it were. The difference between the two cases is, however, not as essential as it would seem : imitative drives, in the case of the submissive feebleminded, also operate as a chance factor rather than as a conscious motive.

It would therefore seem that in both cases of "drifting", the essential elements of waywardness are absent, as we have defined them in the chapter dealing with that form of asocial behavior : when the passive feebleminded, of the submissive or the apathetic variety, drifts into asocial behavior, he does not show that vitality that characterizes the intellectually normal wayward child. He does not enjoy himself in his street-life, nor are the manifestations of his asocial behavior as multicolored as they are in a typically wayward child of normal intelligence. He does not react, more or less consciously, to the ever changing stimulations of his environment, nor does he make more or less conscious efforts to avoid societal obligations.

We have already mentioned above (see p. 44) : the asocial behavior of the drifting feebleminded is the result of, rather than a series of reactions to, changing stimuli. When its manifestations change, it is not because reacting to different stimulations in different ways gives satisfaction, but because changes do take place. Hence the many contradictions that can be observed in the behavior of such an unstructured feebleminded child : it should not surprise us to find, in the midst of a long series of offenses, expressions of seemingly positive social feelings and attitudes, particularly in the submissive type; but it would be unjustified to conclude from such manifestations that a genuine change has taken place in the child's personality : they, too, are as automatic as are the symptoms of delinquency.

While contrariness (rather than diversity) of behavior is characteristic of the submissive more than of the apathetic type, it is in the latter more than in the former that we find a general mood of malcontent instead of the typically wayward child's readiness to enjoy his street-life. But, on closer scrutiny, we find this mood to be typical of drifting as such : the lower the degree of ego-participation and of ego-involvement, the weaker become the chances for the child to find satisfaction of *any* kind, even in a situation in which he would seem to have every reason to be satisfied with himself. Thus, there may be an undertone of helplessness even in that value-feeling that accompanies the feebleminded delinquent's achievements.

But even this feeling of helplessness is not articulate enough to act as a motivating factor in the "history" of his asocial behavior. He does not feel that he must defend himself against the world's superiority by playing the tough one; nor does he feel that he must avoid society's demands and expectations to safeguard a self-feeling, illusory as it may be. In this respect, too, he differs from a truly wayward child of normal intelligence. It is his feeblemindedness that limits his ability properly to apperceive society's demands and expectations. He misunderstands the world around, hence feels no need for avoiding it.

2. ASOCIAL BEHAVIOR OF CERTAIN PSYCHOPATHS

This type of drifting into asocial behavior, however, which must be distinguished from what we have described as waywardness, has much in common with the passive forms of psychopathic behavior, as they are known to emerge under the impact of maternal indolence, or of institutional care. The third chapter was devoted to an analysis of psychopathy in its extravert and introvert varieties. It will be remembered that we have described there, among others, those psychopathic individuals who are characterized by indiscriminate intake or imitation of the most contradictory forms of behavior, or by a tendency to attach themselves superficially and indiscriminately to whoever happens to cross their way. These, we have claimed, are extraverts. Their introvert counterparts were described as the drifting and the unstable psychopaths, among them certain types of vagabonds, addicts or sex-perverts.

We have mentioned already in the first chapter (p. 32) that there exists a certain resemblance between their asociality and that of the passive types of feeblemindedness. Although the former are characterized by ego-inflation even in their drifting, they can nevertheless be grouped together with the mentally retarded representatives of asocial behavior. Absence of inner determinants of action is common to all forms of drifting, although inexplicable impulses are strongly in evidence at least in the introvert types of psychopathic asociality. Absence of inner tensions, of irrational cravings for dependence, of compulsiveness, of depressive moods, of fears, not only makes a clear distinction between the psychopathic and the neurotic varieties of addictions and perversions possible but also helps us to understand the meaning of the concept here under discussion, that of "drifting".

In our analysis of psychopathy we tried to show how even the drifting and the unstable types reveal, in their behavior, signs of ego-inflation, inability to feel anxiety, predominance of the life-tendency towards expansion, signs that justify their inclusion in the clinical unit called "psychopathy". The comparison with other behavior patterns and other concepts which we added was meant as an attempt at clinical semantics rather than as an analysis of delinquent varieties.

In the present context emphasis is on different issues: to what extent, we ask, combine elements of passive psychopathy with elements of passive feeblemindedness to form a specific form of asocial (delinquent) behavior in children and youths, on the one hand, and in adults, on the other? To what extent are these forms different or identical, both etiologically and symptomatologically? What is the relationship between drifting and drivenness, as it finds its expression in the behavior of brain-injured children and adolescents?

Submissiveness in the feebleminded has much in common with the oscillating and the shallow-attachment types of psychopathy, while their

introvert counterparts, the drifting and the unstable psychopaths somehow resemble the apathetic feebleminded. The main difference lies on
the level of structural dispositions : neither the extravert nor the introvert
types of psychopathy are as such of low intelligence; every degree of
mental development, low as well as high, is represented among them.
Neither the submissive nor the apathetic types of feeblemindedness as
such are ego-inflated, and the life-tendency towards staticness rather than
that towards expansion prevails in both. Hence, we find these passive
types of feeblemindedness less than others among psychopaths of low
intelligence. On the other hand, absence of anxiety is common to both,
since in both, communication between the ego and the inner non-ego,
the unconscious, is interrupted, in the psychopath as a structural condition, in the feebleminded as a result of his lack of differentiation.

But it is precisely this last point that makes the two groups comparable
with each other : Maternal indolence or diffusion of the maternal image
in an institution account for the passive types of psychopathy, where an
infant of certain structural dispositions is exposed to the impact of these
traumatic experiences at the beginning of his life. The same experiences,
however, are liable to produce feeblemindedness of the passive types,
where the life-tendency towards staticness rather than that towards
expansion prevails.

It is difficult, if not impossible, to state in every case with certainty,
to what extent congenitally given factors, to what extent earliest
traumatization through maternal indolence or institutional care are
responsible for the emergence of feeblemindedness of the submissive or
the apathetic types. But it certainly seems legitimate to compare their
asocial behavior manifestations, and particularly those of the apathetic
feebleminded with those of the drifting or the unstable psychopath.

The similarities are obvious when we analyze cases of asocial *adults*.
We have already mentioned the expressions of low vitality (inconsistency,
automaticness, malcontent and non-perception of social meaning). What
has been said about the difference between waywardness in children and
in adults (see p. 33 and pp. 151 f.) supports the idea of the passive
feebleminded and the passive psychopath merging into one behavioral
unit, that of "drifting asociality". So far, we have defined their common
traits in negative terms only : *absence* of communication with the unconscious, of inner tension, of anxiety, of compulsiveness. But in order to
justify their inclusion in one unit, we must try to translate these negative
into "positive" terms. What characteristics must be *present* to diagnose a
certain form of asocial behavior as "drifting"?

Indiscriminate response to chance occurrences indicates in this case replacement of ego-participation and of intentionality by ego-diffusion in the universe of external givens. Even a *sexual reaction* is not necessarily indicative of strong impulses or urges but of something going on between two objects, one of which happens to be the reactor. It does not leave any trace of feelings, good or bad. He *wanders* not because he seeks newness or is driven by inner unrest, but because it does not make any difference to him where he is. His wanderings are associative, as it were, one place leading to another. He does not *drink* because he wishes to escape into a heaven of nothingness but because there is nothing that occupies his mind, and alcohol may have become a need of his body.

He is much too indolent to be *aggressive*. But when something or someone resists him in the execution of an act, he may with equal ease eliminate that resistance in a manner that resembles aggressiveness, as he may give up his action. The seriousness of his aggressions is, again, the result of chance constellations and not of deep personality disorders. (Similarly, it would be wrong to conclude from isolated acts of friendliness, which may occur from time to time in his unstructured life, that he is less asocial than he seems to be : such seemingly positive acts, too, are but signs of chance-constellations.)

He may *steal*, but will do so only when he is hungry or when something appeals to him, and be it for a fleeting moment only. "Having" has no meaning for him, and, if anything, it is this indolence towards the haveable that makes clear the difference between him and the truly wayward individual.

But here we are back at our initial questions : Is this form of asocial behavior which we call "drifting" typical of adults only? Is it identical with waywardness in its adult variety? Is true waywardness typical of children only? Or do we find drifting as distinct from waywardness in children as well?

As regards the first part of our questions, it is obvious that it requires a fairly continuous process of becoming accustomed to a certain style of life to produce this form of asocial behavior. Low intelligence facilitates a life without differentiation between subject and object, a life without contact with an inner or an outer non-ego; so does psychopathic absence of anxiety and of staticness. But in both cases the life-pattern which we have briefly described is the outcome of a long process of self-conditioning. Hence, we find this variety of asocial behavior in adults only. Those few truly wayward children who continue in their "career", are liable to glide into the "drifting" variety of asocial behavior to the extent that they lose their intellectual capacities and their vitality.

On the other hand, it would be wrong to identify this pattern with waywardness in adults; it is a well-known fact that there exists at least one other form of asociality—of vagabondage, sex promiscuity, alcoholism —one with strong neurotic admixtures and manifestations, one in which the eternal quest for the "unknown parental images" produces tension and dependence needs, fear and rejection. We shall have an opportunity to come back to this type of asocial behavior when discussing the neurotic varieties of delinquency in children as well as in adults. It may be sufficient here to mention that the drifting type is not identical with waywardness in adults.

To the second part of our questions our answer has already been given : there can be no doubt that the form of waywardness which we have described and analyzed in the second chapter, is typical of children only. And those few in whom waywardness persists into adulthood no longer show its essential characteristics which we have defined as diversity of symptoms, ability to enjoy them, reactivity, avoidance of social contacts. But on the other hand, we said, drifting into asocial behavior, as distinct from waywardness, characterizes at least the feebleminded children of the submissive or the apathetic types. The latter resemble certain psychopathic varieties. But since psychopathy as such, in whatever form it may appear, crystallizes at a later stage of development only (usually not before adolescence), the psychopathic elements and components of "drifting" will never be as clearly in evidence in children as will be those of feeblemindedness.

In other words : we conclude from an analysis of the *adult* representatives of this form of asocial behavior, in whom mental retardation as well as psychopathy can be shown to be present, on its child representatives as well. The ego-inflational element in the drifting variety of asocial behavior is almost identical with playing the role of an ego where, in fact, no clear differentiation between subject-object poles of relationship exists.

3. Drivenness and Drifting

L. Bender (7) describes the behavioral syndrome of what she calls "organic drivenness of brain-stem origin". It is most clearly recognizable after encephalitic affections : destructiveness without inhibitions or fears; polymorphous delinquency without attempts to avoid punishment; defective motor control, restlessness, insomnia, sleep-reversals and other signs of organic disorder such as respiratory difficulties together with anxiety dreams; depressions alternating with elations, hypochondriacal states as well as run-away tendencies—these are the symptoms of encephalic involvement and, through it, of organizational disability. Absence of compensatory mechanisms is perhaps the most comprehensive expression of this deficiency.

Bender continues to describe the behavior disorder which, she says, is characterized by hyperkinesis. The latter "leads the child continually to contact the environment by touching, taking and destroying . . . As the personality becomes integrated, there is a tendency for asocial behavior in every field . . . Although the child has some awareness that he cannot control his behavior, he does not show guilt or anxiety but rather fear and apprehension over the results of his actions. There are no neurotic mechanisms. The fantasy life may be rich, but it concerns itself with aggressive material in which the individual sees himself the leader or the innocent victim but never receiving punishment."

Bender adds that this pattern in some respects resembles non-organic psychopathy, which differs mainly by the absence of motor disturbances. But she does *not* try to answer the question of how the essentially different causes of the two clinical units account for their similar, yet essentially different, symptoms. Their comparison presents still another difficulty : psychopathic conditions, which, as a rule, tend to crystallize after the end of adolescence only, may by that time have been reinforced by a child-hood period of post-encephalitic disorders (irrespective of whether they had been diagnosed as such or not); the latter may degenerate into a pseudo-psychopathic state, with the behavior symptoms more in evidence than the organic manifestations. And yet, the two are essentially different units of behavior.

Reality threatens to "escape" under the impact of the organic dis-equilibration, and the subject feels that he has no control over his "escape". Since in most cases (with the exception of congenital disorders) the child had experienced normal differentiation between the ego and the non-ego and normal relationship-ability based on it, he now *feels* the threat and desperately clings to a vanishing reality. He attempts thus to regain staticness within and without, to eliminate the threat of dis-integration, which is so real for him. His basic mode of experience is one of "being destroyed". Hence, perhaps, his frequently recurring fantasies of being a leader or a victim of aggressive actions.

But it would be wrong to interpret his destructive clinging as proof of aggressiveness. His basic attitude is devoid of all intentionality : he does not relate his actions to his own ego, nor does he experience the non-ego as an independent subject. Both, ego and non-ego, are for him parts of an existential process of drivenness, the non-ego, the world of objects, being driven into nothingness, the ego—into destroying what should be kept extant, into clinging to what threatens to vanish.

It is against the background of this drivenness that we must understand the organic anxiety which is in the center of the syndrome : sleep disorders and respiratory difficulties resulting from the cerebral impairment and at the same time reinforcing anxiety feelings; fearful dreams; moodiness and particularly depressive episodes; run-away impulses and attacks—all indicate uncontrollable fears of threats from within, of organic tensions. They should not be interpreted as *reactions* to the organic disequilibration process but rather as its *concomitant*, its equivalent, as it were. Destructive actions here are not defensive or compensatory, they are but side-effects of drivenness and clinging.

In brief : when the polar relationship between ego and non-ego is interrupted, independence is threatening : the independence of objects because they may then "decide" not to be available, to "go away", to "evaporate"; and the independence of the subject, the ego, because such independence may end in isolation, in separatedness beyond all hope of contact with the non-ego. Hence the clinging so typical of the brain-stem-driven person; hence the destructive (rather than aggressive) manifestations of this clinging; hence his sex-offenses simulating contact; hence his stealing (which is "taking" rather than "taking away"); hence his indifference to punishment and his lack of guilt-feelings.

In contrast to the psychopath, even of passive varieties, with his illusion of being the master of his actions, neither the neurotic nor the brain-injured can ever indulge in such illusions of mastery; they are aware of, and they suffer from, the absolute superiority of what frightens them, the complexes rooted in the unconscious or the organically disequilibrated stimulations. Both represent the unknown and unknowable to which the neurotic as well as the brain-injured, each in his specific way, react with anxiety.

But the behavior *following* this anxiety reaction is essentially different in the two cases. And here we come back to our problem, that of drivenness : no one would ever speak of drivenness in a neurotic, since every manifestation of his behavior becomes understandable only when we interpret it as "reactive". Neurotic reaction may be stereotyped, even compulsive, but it nevertheless remains intentional. Although the motives of this intentionality may be hidden away from the eyes of consciousness, may be distorted by repression and its "offsprings", it is still there and accounts for the numerous secondary elaborations and rationalizations, so typical of every neurosis.

Drivenness, on the other hand, presupposes the absence of a reacting ego. Behavior, then, becomes the expression of processes occurring in a field of organic excitations. Not only cerebral injuries following encephalitis but other pathologies as well (f.i. meningitis, chorea, brain-tumors, head injuries) produce that mixture of asocial and seemingly antisocial behavior symptoms which can be brought on the common denominator of lack of polar relationships and drivenness (48, 62). Such manifestations as violent outbursts, viciousness, lack of consideration must not deceive the observer: they do *not* indicate the existence and operation of an ego as the center of consciousness.

4. Drifting and Drivenness

Although organically caused drivenness may express itself in symptoms of asocial *as well as* antisocial behavior, it is in almost every respect the opposite of the drifting variety of asociality. Affective tension, aiming at discharge but quickly accumulating again, is clearly contrasted by the weak effectivity of the "drifter" and his associative behavior. The latter is aware of the absolute superiority of his environment, although he does not understand its demands. The individual who suffers from brain-stem-drivenness, on the other hand, is *not* aware of what determines his reactions, although he feels strong anxiety in the face of his incomprehensible disequilibration, his being overflooded by inner irritations.

Imitating others, causes the drifting delinquent satisfaction, much more than the very asociality of his behavior. In drivenness the sole source of satisfaction is: tension resolved (and be it for a short period only!). There is little ego-participation and little ego-emphasis in the first, there is what might be called "playing with ego-participation" in the second: man's entire behavior in drivenness is ego-emphasis, although there is no really independent ego to be emphasized. Neither the one nor the other enjoy their asocial or antisocial life-patterns. But while the drifter is unable to enjoy his drifting mode of behavior because of the extreme weakness of his ego, it is the inner tension and tenseness of the brain-injured that excludes any positive reaction to asociality. Of the first we said that he does not crave for dependence, as does the neurotic representative of asociality; of the second—that he craves for independence, though he is intrinsically incapable of ever being really independent.

Contradictory behavior manifestations are characteristic of both. But while they reflect the rule of chance in the life of the feebleminded or the passive psychopath whom we find among the drifting types of delinquents, it is the ambiguity inherent in the very act of "clinging" that accounts for the seeming contradictions in the behavior of many brain-stem-driven individuals. While the former may by chance remain within the fold of socially accepted behavior, while they may by chance "drift" into conformity, the latter cannot be called "socially acceptable" even when they do *not* violate the laws or the customs of society (even their seemingly positive behavior betrays its negative and unstructured character by its exaggeration and its clearly felt falsity).

Some children drift into asocial behavior which may *differ* from waywardness by the absence of signs of vitality. In other cases, however, it is precisely the passiveness of drifting that produces *truly wayward* forms of behavior. It happens in children whose feeblemindedness is of a secondary rather than of a congenital variety, and who show relatively strong tendencies towards hypermotility, usually under the impact of certain organic factors. This combination of factors is not at all infrequent, and it accounts for those cases of waywardness that seem to differ from the ideal type, as described and analyzed in the second chapter.

But "drifting" also accounts for certain types of asociality in *adults* that can be clearly distinguished from the neurotic varieties of drifting into asocial conduct. In other words: when we come to analyze adults, we find drifting both as a unit of behavior in its own rights and as a symptom of neurotic complications. In the first case it may be the outcome of a prolonged career of child waywardness or of later failure to cope with society's demands, owing to feeblemindedness or apathy. In the second case, character-neurotic limitations may have prepared an individual without any childhood history of asociality for a later life as a "social drifter". Absence of inner tension as against a kind of negativistic, sometimes even hostile, self-abandonment, are the differential characteristics of these two forms of "drifting" in adults.

Finally, a few words about the diagnostic difficulties resulting from the fact that minor brain injuries, not infrequent in the child and adult representatives of drifting, are often responsible for a mixture of drifting and drivenness, which makes differentiation problematic. In another study (36) we have mentioned that a similar diagnostic ambiguity exists in the field of feeblemindedness: there, it is the slight cerebral impairment and its ensuing hyperkinesis that accounts for the modification of secondary by primary characteristics; here, it is the organically caused tension that modifies the symptoms of drifting.

CHAPTER FIVE

Varieties of Aggressive Delinquency

1. INTRODUCTION

THE FOLLOWING chapters will be devoted to an analysis of the various forms of aggressiveness as they appear in the delinquent behavior of children and adolescents. What are these forms?

We have mentioned, in Chapter 1, that in children neurotic delinquency takes the form of *substitutive* or of *guilt* offenses, among them not a few of an aggressive character (true perversions and compulsive offenses are more frequent in adult and to some extent also in adolescent addicts or maniacs).

We also analyzed there the essential differences between the so-called pre-oedipal and oedipal forms of primary behavior disorders, and we tried to show that these are two different clinical pictures: the first, we said, should be called *primary aggressiveness*; it is characterized by an early generalization of aggressiveness as against the specific directedness of hate against the parents (with secondary extensions to other parts of the environment) in the *primary behavior disorder of the oedipal type*; the former is less defensive, since the negative world conception is much more an integral part of the growing ego than it is reactive to later disappointment; doubt is not so much a source of suffering as it is part of an early established pattern.

We then mentioned two other forms of aggressiveness, as they can be found in feebleminded and psychopathic delinquents, and we suggested they should be called *the expansive and the paranoid types of aggressiveness*. Each of these, we claimed, appears in the mentally retarded as well as in the psychopath. In both, aggressiveness is non-directed, both lack the ability to establish and to maintain personal relationships, the psychopath because of his ego-inflation and his absence of anxiety, the feebleminded because of his lack of structuredness in all areas of his mental life.

Expansive aggressiveness finds its expression in complete rejection and negation of the non-ego as a restricting subject. It is essentially linked with extravert tendencies which are evident in constant and exclusive

165

concern with the world around. It is contrasted by the paranoid aggressiveness, in which introvert tendencies manifest themselves in constant attacks on a threatening world. But neither the one nor the other can be said to be directed by—conscious or unconscious—intentions as are aggressive acts in primary aggressiveness or in primary behavior disorders.

In psychodynamically oriented interpretations of dissocial behavior we find little if any reference to the constitutional forms of delinquency. The feebleminded is of as little interest to the psychoanalyst as is the brain-injured.* As regards psychopathy, we have mentioned in Chapter 3 the various attempts made by psychoanalytically oriented students of behavior disorders to reduce "psychopathy" to such psychogenetic concepts as the "neurotic character", the "impulsive neurotic", the "instinct-ridden character", "antisocial character formation", "the affectionless thief", "children who hate", etc.

But it would not only be a mistake to disregard the essential differences that exist between aggressiveness in neurotic delinquency and in primary behavior disorders or between what psychoanalysts calls the pre-oedipal and the oedipal forms of the latter. We should not lose sight either of the differences that exist between any form of aggressiveness as the result of traumatization and development and those forms that remain unintelligible, unless we take into consideration the factors of structural deficiency (we may be faced with cases of genuine feeblemindedness, of brain injury or of constitutional psychopathy). Even if it could be proven that more cases in clinics and courts lend themselves to psychogenetic interpretation than to reduction to structural deficiency, a phenomenological analysis of aggressiveness in the latter varieties does not thereby lose of its importance: it helps recognize even in cases of clearly neurotic delinquency or primary behavior disorders *elements* of varieties that we may describe as "feebleminded and psychopathic aggressiveness of the expansive or the paranoid type" (see pp. 34 ff.).

This is one of the reasons why we have devoted so much space to an analysis of psychopathy (Chapter 3), in spite of the fact that—as we have said—clear cases of psychopathy are very rare, particularly in children who did not yet reach the end of adolescence. Another reason is the comparability of the concept with those used in psychoanalytical interpretation, or, in other words: the chance to clarify the latter concepts through confrontation with the former. What traits, essentially present in

---

* See Chapter 4, in which certain forms of brain injuries have been mentioned as being responsible for delinquency of the "drivenness" type. Cf. also the remarks at the end of Chapter 3, on the so-called "epileptic character" as compared with psychopathy.

psychopathy, must be absent to make the child's aggressiveness comprehensible with the aid of concepts of experience and development?

Finally, we hope that the analysis of psychopathy in its varieties has helped us prepare the way to an understanding of adolescent aggressiveness which we shall try to analyze in the following chapter, and what seems to us the most important problem of delinquency in our times. The same purpose should be served by the present analysis of aggressive acts of delinquency in children, including neurotic, "primary" or constitutional varieties.

The fallacy of a purely psychoanalytical or a purely sociological orientation to the problems of adolescent delinquency is twofold.

a) They exclude certain varieties that do not lend themselves to their basic principles of interpretation; *psychoanalysts* exclude all constitutionally conditioned cases as well as those of true waywardness and psychopathy (unless they reduce the latter to the same psychic "mechanisms" that are held responsible for all disorders, neurotic as well as delinquent); *sociologists* exclude all cases of what they call personal distortions or deviations, in order to uphold their thesis, according to which delinquency, f.i. in adolescents, is primarily a group phenomenon and serves primarily the purposes of their compensatory status-seeking (19) or reflects their membership in a certain subculture (17, 18).

b) But it would be a mistake to draw from this first fallacy the conclusion that the psychoanalytical orientation is unable to account only for few culture-conditioned forms of delinquency (see f.i. our analysis of the "New Type of Delinquency" on pp. 199 ff.), or that the sociological orientation is unable to account only for the personal development of a child delinquent into later forms of dissocial behavior. Both are equally deficient in accounting for the interaction of personal and cultural pathologies.

Neurotic guilt-feelings of an oedipal type, for instance, have a different meaning in a period of culture-condition stability of moral values and in a period of uncertainty and ambiguity. Substitutive offenses may have less significance in a family order in which personal intimacy is unessential and oedipal involvement less pronounced. Where the culture facilitates personal disappointments in the parents' reliability, the child's readiness to feel insecure and suspicious and to refuse the establishment of relationships with a personally relevant environment will be much more "patterned" than in a cultural situation of relative economic and personal stability.

On the other hand, what sociologists call the subculture of delinquency, is *not* the result of an interplay of social factors only; the adolescent members of such a subculture have had each a different "pre-history" of childhood deviation : some may have suffered from an early phobic, hysteric or compulsive neurosis, others—from psycho-somatic complications; some may have overcome their handicaps, at least seemingly, others may not; some may have gone through a more or less prolonged period of waywardness or of more or less severe primary behavior disorders, others may be mentally retarded or psychopathic individuals either of a predominantly aggressive or of a predominantly submissive type; some may *have been* guilt-offenders, others may *continue* to be.

We shall later come back to the problem here mentioned, the problem of individual differences between members of certain culture-conditioned types of adolescent delinquency according to their personal "pre-history" of waywardness, drifting, neurosis or aggressiveness. Here we shall try to compare with each other the essential characteristics of aggressive behavior in neurotic delinquency, primary aggressiveness, primary behavior disorders, constitutional deviation of the expansive and the paranoid varieties. Certain repetitions will be unavoidable, since, in Chapter 1, we have compared with each other the varieties of juvenile delinquency for the purposes of classification. It will be remembered that "aggressiveness" had been one of the twelve criteria of comparison. We have also analyzed the meaning of aggressive behavior in waywardness (see Chapter 2) and in certain types of psychopathy (see Chapter 3).

It is the main purpose of the present discussion to show to what extent and in which respect a number of otherwise clearly distinguishable varieties of delinquency can be subsumed under the heading of "aggressive delinquency". Not every manifestation of aggressiveness is relevant in this context; it must be more than a character trait, more than a general *attitude*; there must be an illegal, destructive *act* to justify the term of "aggressive delinquency" (an act, we should add, that is not motivated by some transpersonal consideration).

2. Aggressiveness

In another place (29, quoted and summarized in 34) the present author has defined the essential elements of negative aggressiveness; it always manifests itself in some kind of dissolving wholes into unrelated parts and of rejecting change and otherness to protect the ego's narrow frontiers. These are the elements of negative aggressiveness which we suggested :

a) A feeling of being exposed, as an object, to the danger of destroyability, by forces from within or without, over which man has no control; accompanied by

b) inability or refusal to change, that is, a compulsive clinging to a given pattern or situation;

c) under certain cerebral conditions conducive to simultaneous emergence of strong tendencies towards staticness and externalization;

d) a strong need for heightening a feeling of potency against that of destroyability (not to be identified with phantasied transformation of being attacked into being the attacker);

e) a relatively high degree of ego-participation co-existent with a low degree of mobility;

f) coexistence of conscious attack on an external object with unconscious referral to some archetypical elements which may be "represented" by that external object.

When the first element (the feeling of destroyability) is excessive, aggressiveness is replaced by helplessness in the face of overwhelming danger; the same may be the result of an excessive increase of the second element (rigidity). "These are the cases", we said, "in which the ego shrinks to a point where it completely ceases to be a subject relating itself to reality without and within. Although we may sometimes be able to trace back such behavior to childhood repression of allotropic aggressiveness, we can no longer speak here of autotropic *aggressiveness*, because, and to the extent that, the ego has ceased to *participate* in the acts of self-denial. In other words : lack of ego-mobility (condition b) operates as a condition of negative aggressiveness only within the limits set by ego-participation (condition e); only then can negative aggressiveness fulfill its function of heightening the feeling of ego-potency (condition d)" (quoted from 29, pp. 266 ff.).

These, then, are the structural conditions of destructive (as against constructive) aggressiveness. There exists yet another, socio-cultural condition which may, or may not, be present and which can be said to facilitate and modify the emergence of aggressiveness. We quote again from the already-mentioned essay (29, pp. 267–268) :

"What is the meaning of aggressiveness in social or cultural groups which are characterized by what might be called a 'climate of hate'? We find such climate and its concomitant patterns of aggressiveness produced, maintained, developed and transmitted not only in certain cultures but also in sub-cultures of any society, and in certain historical situations more than in others. The hate-climate is due to the prevalence of conditions favorable to the emergence of a generalized feeling of destroyability and supported by isolationist tendencies towards collective self-identification and group-closure. In such groups the individual is brought up in the 'spirit of projection' (irrespective of the degree to which group-identification is *consciously* emphasized in the process of education); the individual not only does not learn how to relativize, on the contrary, he learns how to absolutize himself, by a kind of 'participation mystique' in the collective totum which is conceived of as the only and absolutely valid reality. Hence the extreme vulnerability of each individual belonging to this group as well as of the group as such; hence the universality of aggressiveness in the conduct of both, the individual and the group.

"There exists, however, one basic difference in the structural elements and patterns of aggressiveness between individuals belonging to 'hate climate' groups and those belonging to other groups: ego-participation means there much more participation in, and following the lead of, the collective pattern of hate than self-investment in the attempt to eliminate the threatening 'attackers'—for, the ego is, under those conditions, threatened as a group-member rather than as an ego. Even if it has already reached the stage where it is able to experience itself as an individual unit, not totally identical with the group, the feeling of destroyability is still likely to be channelled, as it were, through the experience of belonging to a certain group, characterized by a common fate; to act-out aggressively requires less courage under such conditions than under conditions of education aimed at individual autonomy. We are faced here with a variation of unconscious aggressiveness which is not the result of repression but of dissolution of the ego in the collective. Functionally, this aggressiveness does not aim at restituting or heightening the feeling of ego-potency directly, but at maintaining a quasi-magical group-potency (resulting necessarily in group-inflation) through which the ego unconsciously expects to reach a feeling of potency.

"It can be concluded, from what has been said about hate-climate groups, that aggressiveness as a collective phenomenon not only *depends* on the prevalence of conditions conducive to the emergence of a general feeling of insecurity, but also tends to *increase* such a feeling by way of strengthening projective relations. But it would be wrong to conclude that patterns of apparent *non*-aggressiveness indicate the prevalence of opposite conditions: there are societal institutions which 'tend to keep overt aggressiveness in face-to-face relations at a minimum but provide means for projecting, displacing, and rationalizing aggression' " (21).

3.   COMPARISONS

We now return to the question from which we set out: What is the meaning of the general term of "aggressive delinquency", as it finds its expressions in *primary aggressiveness*, in *primary behavior disorders*, in neurotic offences of the *guilt-* or the *substitution*-type, in *expansive* and in *paranoid aggressiveness* (of the feebleminded and/or the psychopathic varieties)?

(a) Primary aggressiveness and primary behavior disorders

We do not want to repeat what we have said in Chapter 1 about the essential differences between the pre-oedipal form of primary aggressiveness and the oedipal type of primary behavior disorder. Obviously, the *feeling of destroyability* by outside forces (our first element of aggressiveness) is more in evidence when the individual is not only able consciously to experience the world as bad, or, more correctly, badness as the governing principle of life, but also consciously feels the need to prove it through his provocative acts of aggressiveness.

This, however, is much more the case in primary behavior disorders than in primary aggressiveness: the earlier in life a disappointing event occurs, which comes to confirm the child's basic doubts concerning his parents' reliability, the easier is it for doubt to be replaced by negative certainty. Hence, we see in this case aggressive acts indiscriminately directed toward all adult representatives of values and ego-transcending demands, and reflecting an earliest identification with a negative world conception rather than intended to strengthen a threatened ego-feeling.

To what extent should we speak in this case of *intentionality?* When the world is conceived of as being negative and rejectable, the individual must attack not only in order to protect himself against the constant danger of being injured or destroyed but also, and mainly, by way of identification, which is part of the only realistic life-pattern. These acts can, of course, also be defined as attempts to maintain at least the illusion of mastery over this world (by being equally bad); but the fact remains that "destroyability" is here experienced as a quality of existence as such more than as a personal danger and threat.

We may construct a similarity between this variety of aggressive behavior and waywardness, on the one hand, and psychopathy, on the other: earliest conditioning (in waywardness) helps establish a non-defensive life-style; earliest structurization (in psychopathy) helps establish a certain, type-conditioned, behavior-pattern which cannot be reduced to defense-mechanisms either. It is the time-factor that explains this similarity. But whereas waywardness does *not* require structural pre-conditions in addition to environmental influences (see Chapter 2), psychopathy *does* (see Chapter 3). Primary aggressiveness differs from both; the traumatic experience does not belong to the *earliest* period of life, nor is it *continuous* (as in waywardness), and the structural pre-conditions (of doubt and vulnerability) are much less severe and decisive than in psychopathy.

Lack of ego-mobility, we said, must combine with a fairly high degree of *ego-participation* to produce aggressiveness. This holds good for both, primary aggressiveness and primary behavior disorders of the oedipal type. But a primarily aggressive child does not "learn" ambivalence at all (due to the fact that the disappointing experience takes place already in the second phase of his development); his limited mobility is therefore much more of a structural than of a reactive variety; in primary behavior disorders, on the other hand, the tendency rigidly to cling to the conception of a given state as being unchangeable, results from a defensive intention. Ego-participation, however, is equally high in both units of behavior, irrespective of whether it stems from unambiguously negative identification or from defensive intentions.

The very fact that in primary aggressiveness a "negative certainty" is present from early childhood on (so that experiences of disappointment play a secondary role only), would seem to indicate strong extravert tendencies: although negative certainty operates as a selective principle, the human and the material environment, nevertheless, remains the main object of relationships. In primary behavior disorders, on the other hand, the ego rather than the environment represents that main object of relationships. Could it not, then, be, we must ask, that it is the type-factor which determines in these cases the "choice of pathology"? More: could it not be that the *organic preconditions of aggressiveness* (which we have defined as cerebral dispositions for a simultaneous emergence of exter-nalization *and* staticness) form an integral part of this differential criterion?

Congenital tendencies of extravert object-cathexis (in primary aggres-siveness) may support a conception of the ego as part of an externalized non-ego, which at the same time is experienced as static, as unchangeable. (If one of the two parts of this condition is absent, externalization or staticness, other forms of abnormal behavior may appear, for instance rigidity and indolence or extreme distractability, but not aggressiveness.) Introvert ego-cathexis—whether congenitally given or resulting from reactions to experiences—may lead to aggressive behavior (in primary behavior disorders) under the following conditions: The individual must bring with him a cerebral structure in which, to use Rothschild's terms (87), the normative connection between the *Weltpol* and the *Ichpol* is disrupted; as a result, the non-ego is experienced as threatening, and the function of the ego—as one of maintaining the separation between the world and the ego.*

We should, however, remember what we have already mentioned: that we do not deal here with varieties of aggressiveness but with varieties of delinquency. Not every aggressive act, even if we exclude autotropic aggressiveness, constitutes an offense. Many children are known to be hostile, against their parents or siblings, against their class-mates or strangers, without ever coming into open conflict with the law. And an occasional conflict with the law does not yet constitute delinquency. What bridges between aggressiveness and delinquency is a more or less conscious rejection of society as symbol and representative of ego-transcendence. (We shall later see to what extent this definition excludes not only certain types of organically caused and uncontrollable eruptions of violence in brain-injured, intoxicated or psychotic individuals, but also most cases of compulsive delinquency.)

But the *way* in which society is being rejected differs from one variety of delinquency to the other. In our present context, "rejection" means, paradoxically, "imitation" in the case of primary aggressiveness, and "anticipation" in the case of primary behavior disorders.

In the first case, the child feels that society by *definition* is against the individual. Hence, attacking it, trying to destroy it, at least in part, taking from it, challenging its authority, competence or validity—actually means "being in" this hostile world, being part of it, being adjusted (to put it again paradoxically). The very fact that society has established a network of laws and institutions for their implementation is proof of its badness. There is no one to rely upon, no one to be trusted, since "trust" *presupposes*—accepting dependence, and this child has had no chance to learn such acceptance.

In primary behavior disorder, we encounter a different type of rejecting society. Here, society is defined not only as bad but also as "traitor", as "deceiver". The child may have learned in his early years to put his faith in adults, though never without reservations. Both, predisposition and experiences, failed to let his sense of trust take deep roots in his growing ego. Hence his vulnerability when unavoidable disappointments occur. Hence his constant readiness to prove to himself and to others that establishing relationships is not only "counterindicated", "not worthwhile", but is actually a danger to be avoided. Society here represents

---

* This is an attempt to introduce into the causal equation of primary aggressiveness and primary behavior disorders type-tendencies and type-preferences, in addition to the ordinarily emphasized environmental causes, such as faulty parental attitudes due to economic stress, frustrating experiences, and the time factor.

a source of threat. Hence, assailing it, "hitting out first" (to quote Ophuijsen—77), limiting its hostile power, means—increased security for the individual, increased and strengthened feeling of potency.

Two questions remain to be answered:

a) What impact have the socio-cultural factors which we have defined as "climate of hate", on the relative frequency of primary aggressiveness and of primary behavior disorders in certain historical periods?

b) What is the essential difference between the aggressive manifestations of feeblemindedness and psychopathy of the "expansive" or the "paranoid" type and the two forms of delinquent behavior that are here under discussion?

In spite of all we have said about the structural preconditions of the two last-mentioned varieties of aggressive delinquency, the fact remains that they occur much more frequently in times of value-disorientation than in periods of relative stability of social norms. This is due to the fact that ambiguity of cultural values and economic uncertainty are liable to make doubtful the parents' meaning as objects of trust and identification, particularly when their primary functions within the family become questionable and when everyone's mind is preoccupied with fear of total destruction.

This leads us to our second question. Primary aggressiveness and primary behavior disorders differ from psychopathy* in causes *as well as* in symptoms: needless to repeat what has been said in Chapter 3 about (a) the time factor in psychopathy (traumatization in the first months of life), (b) its constitutional predispositions (predominance of the life tendency toward expansion, the absence of anxiety, ego-inflation), (c) the absence of economic stress as factor of traumatization (against its causal weight in primary behavior disorders). The most important difference is that between ego inflation in psychopathy and the feeling of destroyability and aggressive reactions to this feeling in primary aggressiveness and in primary behavior disorders. This will be the subject of our discussion, in the next paragraph, of the "expansive" and the "paranoid" varieties of the psychopathic (and feebleminded) forms of aggressive delinquency.

But before we analyze these varieties, a few remarks may be added on the relationship between the primary aggressiveness or the primary behavior disorder, on the one hand, and Redl's "children who hate" (83), on the other. Reference is made to the short summary of Redl's

---

* We disregard for a moment the second structural cause, feeblemindedness.

description which we included in our discussion of clinical concepts comparable to that of psychopathy (see pp. 145 ff.).

There, we claimed that some characteristics of their behavior clearly indicate the non-psychopathic nature of this form of delinquency, while others have a different meaning in both behavioral units. Here, we add that a similar ambiguity of symptoms can be discovered when we ask whether the "children who hate" belong to the pre-oedipal or the oedipal variety of aggressive behavior.

Most characteristics seem to prove a deep-rooted identity with the world as hostile and bad, a feeling of being part of such a world. In this way, a kind of antisocial reality is being constructed to which the child belongs, in which he even submits to a specific code (point 13), and through which he excludes everything unknown that may arouse in him a feeling of bewilderment (point 6). What Redl calls "group-intoxication" (point 1) is actually a symptom of that same illusion of belonging to the constructed reality of badness to which the child then sticks : its selectiveness excludes and prevents individual confrontation with its social facts and demands. Hence the absence of norms of general validity with the exception of one : aggressiveness and delinquency. Such behavior is justified and does not indicate punishable deviation or guilt; guilt must be proven to be a fact and can be eliminated through argumentation (point 8).

No need to add, then, that logical considerations are superseded by reality distortions, when it comes to drawing a conclusion from success or failure (point 2). Such social learning presupposes polar relationships between an independent ego and a generally recognized human environment. It is replaced by two seemingly contradictory traits : a stubborn tendency to use, often highly sophisticated, argumentations, indicating what Redl calls psychological acuity (point 4), and a general attitude of "don't care" (point 3). But the contradiction is only a seeming one; both traits reflect a strong need for independence, for denying, rather than fighting against, destroyability, for raising the ego to the level of absolute mastery over the hostile world, from within, as it were, by way of identifying with the universe of hostility. Its most "convincing" expression is the child's conviction that he is "smarter" than everyone else (point 12), so that nothing untoward can happen to him which may have been the unfortunate lot of others. This feeling of being protected by his superiority must not be interpreted as a defense mechanism, as a *rationalization* of his inability to delay satisfaction (point 5); on the contrary : the latter inability is but one of the *expressions* of his naive feeling of superiority.

All the traits mentioned so far indicate that the "children who hate" fall into the category of primary aggressiveness. There are, however, other traits which belong to the syndrome described as primary behavior disorder of the oedipal type : the unwillingness to identify with a "good" adult (point 10), the tendency to "provoke" him into badness (point 11), the readiness to reject every limitation of his freedom through the environment as proof of destructive intentions (point 7), and the vindication of offenses as acts of retaliation (point 9).*

Not every aggressive child shows all the traits mentioned here : some belong to the first, others to the second variety. But most are "mixed types"; hence the coexistence of traits that are characteristic of both, even in one and the same individual. It is the great merit of Redl's analysis that, through his empirically found concept of "children who hate", he has brought on a common denominator the pre-oedipal and the oedipal types of behavior disorders. This allows us to return, as it were, from the area of typological abstraction to that of clinical reality in which these types appear on a continuum scale only.

(b) Expansive and paranoid forms of aggressive delinquency

The clinician and the educator, both, know of those exasperating cases in which a child or a juvenile aggressively violates the law, time and again, and fails to react to all efforts made by the environment or within an institution to re-educate him. If examinations which may be carried out at school or in a clinic reveal that he is of inferior intelligence, the educator will feel relieved : he certainly cannot be supposed to know how to fight against nature . . . The most he may then try to do is : to protect society against the feebleminded child's aggressive delinquency, to try and decrease the tension that is bound to accumulate in the family through the child's unbearable behavior, to isolate the focus of what seems to be an incurable disease.

Much more frustrating, for the educator as well as for the family, are those children beyond control in whom psychological examinations do *not* reveal low intelligence or severe deficiencies in the parents' attitudes. Their number may not be large, but their social weight is increased by the vicious character of their delinquent activities and their utter lack of response to educational or therapeutic interventions. These are the cases diagnosed as "psychopathic disorders".

We have tried in Chapter 3 to show the *structural* causes that are

---

* Redl mentions in this context that following the lead of someone or acting according to group patterns also serve as vindications of delinquency. These tendencies, it would seem to us, belong to the aggressive child's identification with the world as symbol and reality of badness.

responsible for them. We have also asked in which respect they differ from those disturbances which psychoanalysts have in mind when they speak of the neurotic or the instinct-ridden character or use similar terms. We have maintained that it is difficult, if not impossible, clearly to diagnose psychopathy before a child reaches the end of adolescence. Among the varieties of this behavior disorder are some that have no relevance for an understanding of juvenile delinquency; others have been mentioned in Chapter 4 when we discussed the drifting-type of delinquency. Only those types of which destructive and aggressive behavior is the main symptom are relevant in the present context.

They differ from primary aggression and primary behavior disorder not only causally (reflecting as they do constitutional defects) but also in manifestations, as we shall try to show immediately. They differ from each other in so far as the *feebleminded* representatives of both, aggressive and paranoid delinquency, reveal their basic deficiency in the *automatic character* of their antisocial behavior, whereas the *psychopathic* representatives are recognized by the *ego-inflational* character of their offenses. But in spite of these differences, the feebleminded *and* the psychopathic varieties of aggressiveness, on the one hand, and of suspiciousness, on the other, have so much in common that their classification as *expansive versus paranoid* forms of delinquency seems justified.

The term "expansive" designates, as we said in Chapter 1, the tendency in the *extravert* types of the feebleminded or the psychopath to expand the boundaries of his ego, while denying the non-ego's right to impose on him any limitation.

The term "paranoid", in the present context, designates the tendency in the *introvert* representatives of feeblemindedness or of psychopathy to feel threatened and to react to such a feeling by attacking and destroying "the hostile" non-ego. His aggressions, however, are reactive only, not purpose-directed; he cannot act intentionally (to eliminate whatever threatens him), since he feels himself to be an object only,* and only his offenses produce at least the illusion of being a subject.

Thus we could compare the expansive variety with primary aggressiveness, the paranoid variety with primary behavior disorder. Constitutional predisposition of the expansive as well as the paranoid types of feebleminded and psychopathic aggressiveness and delinquency are : the child's inability (or earliest repression of the ability) to feel anxiety, strong ego-emphasis (coupled with a *low* degree of ego-participation in feeblemindedness, with a high degree in psychopathy), absence of inner tensions

---

* A truly paranoiac sees himself simultaneously as an object *and* a subject of destruction.

which ordinarily originate in conflicts between the ego and the unconscious. To the extent that similar tendencies are present in primary aggressiveness (PA) or in primary behaviour disorders of the oedipal types (PBD), they are the result of factors of experience and development, not of constitutional predispositions.

This causal difference accounts for the essential differences between seemingly similar behavior manifestations in the constitutional and the reactive types of aggressiveness. In PBD, acts of violence and destruction or obstinate refusal to accept any limitation reflect hate, in PA they reflect illusions of superiority. In the constitutional varieties, on the other hand, the place of hate and defensive aggressiveness (PBD) is taken by *reactions* to a hostile world, and the illusion of superiority (PA) is replaced by a feeling of *"being within"* a universe of violence.

Stealing is neither an act of provocation (as it is in PBD) nor an expression of mastery over a world held in contempt (as it is in PA); it is revenge in the paranoid variety of aggressiveness, it is an "act of right" in the expansive variety. Anxiety or guilt feelings are, of course, unknown in the constitutional as well as in the reactive varieties. But whereas in PBD and in PA the absence of anxiety and of guilt is compensated by loud assertion of independence, both the feebleminded and the psychopathic representatives of expansive or paranoid aggressiveness, with their complete absence of intentionality, are not in need of such or similar compensations.

Sex delinquency, too, has a different meaning in the reactive and in the constitutional varieties. There is much spite in the sexual offenses of youngsters who can be diagnosed as cases of PBD. Such offenses are, as a rule, less frequent than in PA. There they are often accompanied by a more or less conscious wish to conquer, and to rule over, the victim. In the constitutional varieties, on the other hand, thoughtless exploitation of "objects" as they happen to appear, is more in evidence than spite or tyranny, particularly in the expansive aggressiveness of feebleminded and psychopathic individuals.*

To what extent can the elements of aggressiveness, as we have tried to define them in the second paragraph, be found in the constitutional varieties? The *feeling of destroyability* here originates in some kind of identification with the aggressive character of the world; it is accompanied by an attitude of "being equal", of being *un*destroyable to the extent that man takes part in destructions and aggressions. Can we, then, speak of a need for *heightening a feeling of threatened ego-potency*? Do

---

* In this symptom-area, paranoid suspiciousness may produce delinquent behavior in which elements of spite are more frequent than elements of thoughtlessness.

not both, psychopathic ego-inflation and feebleminded automatism of reactions, indicate a naive absence of insecurity? *Rigid clinging* to a static self-definition and at least a fictitious kind of *ego-participation* may be present in these varieties of aggressiveness, and *cerebral conditions* may be found to be similar to those of aggressiveness in general. But the semblance of security that stems from this quasi-identity with a non-ego, conceived of as being hostile and destructive, raises the—seemingly paradoxical—question whether we could still speak here of aggressiveness.

The answer should be, that it is the constitutional nature of the factors responsible for the emergence of this type of aggressiveness which accounts for the different meaning of its elements. Both, the automatic reactivity of the feebleminded and the ego inflation of the psychopath, help make destroyability into a general quality of the non-ego with which the ego identifies. This attitude, however, like all constitutionally caused attitudes, qualities and processes, should be interpreted as a concomitant of a certain form of existence, of "So-being", rather than as a symptom of awareness of danger and as a means of defense. The absence of polarity in feeblemindedness and psychopathy does not allow for the emergence of a feeling of being endangered or of being in need of defense.

The other elements of aggressiveness, too, mean something different in its constitutional varieties: Ego-participation is here never as genuine as it is in PA or in PBD, and it is often superseded by ego-emphasis; the latter is easier compatible with the structural types of aggressiveness. Clinging to a given situation is here less in evidence than it is in the reactive varieties. It means, paradoxically, clinging to the illusion of being one with the hostile world. Externalization, then, means: defining the ego in terms of the non-ego, without any traces of projection.

In every form of aggressiveness, the object of attack unconsciously represents something *beyond* the level of objectivity, something structural or archetypical. This explains why aggressiveness always "comes back", always finds a different object, never leads to a feeling of being protected and secure. This holds good for the presently discussed variety of aggressiveness as well. It is the very identity of the "carrier" of aggressiveness (the ego) with his ever-changing objects of attack that could here be called its unconscious representation.

Thus we see how in these constitutional varieties of aggressiveness all its elements of definition, in a peculiar way, have one and the same meaning: the ego's hostility is part and expression of the non-ego's hostility. It is this identity which gives the delinquent acts a semblance of compulsiveness, in spite of the absence of all neurotic elements.

(c) Neurotic delinquency

There is little we could add here on the nature of neurotic delinquency to what we have said in the first chapter (see pp. 27 ff.) and in two previous studies (33, 34). In the chapter on classification we have tried to show what essential differences exist between guilt offenses, substitutive offenses and compulsive forms of delinquency. We suggest the following table as a summary of what we have said on the subject.

None of the three forms of neurotic delinquency is truly aggressive :

1) *In substitutive delinquency* the feeling of destroyability is replaced by a feeling of vulnerability and by a—partly conscious, partly unconscious—need for testing the adults, particularly the parents, of whose love the child is not certain. The offenses are not meant to heighten his feeling of ego-potency. Thus, the first two elements of aggressiveness (see p. 169) are absent. The others may be present, particularly a relatively high degree of ego participation in the delinquent act and coexistence of the external object of aggressiveness with its unconscious representatives. But in the light of the absence of the two first-mentioned elements, on the one hand, and in the light of all-pervading doubts, fears and tensions, on the other hand, it seems questionable whether even seemingly (phenotypically) aggressive acts are truly aggressive.

2) Aggressiveness may seem to characterize certain delinquent acts of the *guilt-offense type* as well. But we must not lose sight of their basically autotropic nature, resulting from the unconscious need for punishment. It is not so much a feeling of destroyability as it is a deep-rooted certainty of worthlessness that here motivates seemingly aggressive offenses. And it would not be justified in this case to interpret aggressive acts as attempts to heighten a basically weak or weakened feeling of ego potency : the sought-for punishment, whenever and however it is obtained, indicates opposite tendencies, that is, tendencies toward lowering, in a masochistic way, the ego's feeling of being "worthy" and "potent".

Hence, guilt offenses should not be characterized as truly aggressive any more than substitutive offenses. On the contrary : in this case, even the other elements of aggressiveness are absent : the degree of ego-participation is not high; the objects of aggression, though perhaps evoking unconscious images, do not represent archetypical elements, either of the parental reality or of the world's badness.

3) While substitutive and guilt-offenses are not infrequent in childhood, truly *compulsive delinquency* is an exception. We have in mind addictions, perversions, manias and unrestrained acting-out of impulses. These

	Substitutive Offenses	Compulsive Offenses	Guilt Offenses
1	Ever different isolated acts of delinquency.	Ever recurring offenses of the same type.	Some kind of "specialization".
2	Consciously or unconsciously referring to the parents.	"Generalized" and not related to the parents.	Unconsciously directed against own self.
3	Dependent on temporary increase of affects.	Dependent on deeply rooted unconscious defenses.	Dependent on permanent needs for punishment.
4	Oedipal involvements.	Anal conflicts.	Oedipal involvements.
5	Not systematized.	Structured.	Defensive.
6	Reality, more or less adequately perceived, supplies eliciting causes,	Reality remote, almost of hallucinatory character,	Reality contacts needed and found through receiving punishment,
7	but is being transformed into hostile environment through offenses.	so that the immediate environment is liable to be overlooked.	so that the environment is being "used".
8	(Causal interpretation.)	(Causal interpretation.)	(Finalistic interpretation.)
9	Own badness uncertain (doubt),	Own badness hidden (distortion).	Own badness certain (despair).
10	hence, no strong guilt feelings after the offense.	Guilt-feelings appearing only when offender "returns" to reality.	Guilt feelings are avoided through receiving punishment.
11	Relatively lenient superego.	Superego being "eliminated".	Strong (unconscious) superego.
12	Ego-participation stronger than ego-directedness towards offense.	Intensive ego-directedness toward offense is stronger than the relatively high degree of ego participation.	Ego directedness is stronger than the relatively low degree of ego participation.

forms of compulsive dissociality are, as we have said above (pp. 27 ff.) determined by unconscious forces, by a lower degree of ego-participation than the intensity of the mind's concentration on each delinquent act, and by rigid clinging to one specific mode of behavior. In the third chapter, we compared compulsion neurosis with compulsive dissociality. There, we said that the allotropic character of the latter requires a higher degree of ego-participation than compulsion neurosis and at the same time still more increases the ego directedness toward the delinquent act. This simultaneous increase, we said, may give the erroneous impression that compulsive dissociality is less ego-alien than compulsion-neurosis.

We added that the impulse neurotic and the pervert are liable to lose their identity when their impulses "rise" and they become mere "organs of execution". Their extreme dependence on uncontrollable drives appears in the disguise of extreme dependence on external stimuli which may "happen to them", by chance.

The third element of compulsiveness, rigid clinging to a certain mode of behavior, does not affect the total personality to the same extent as in the case of compulsion neurosis, where it is basically defensive and therefore tends to be felt in every manifestation of the personality.

Here, again, it would seem to be self-evident that the elements of aggressiveness are not present in compulsive dissociality: neither can we speak in this case of a feeling of destroyability, the place of which is taken by a feeling of "being filled" with impulses or drives; nor can we speak of conscious or unconscious wishes to heighten the ego's potency by destroying the sources of danger, the attacking enemy; tension release is not essentially connected with a feeling of strength or of being protected, it is an aim in itself. And to the extent that the object of attack and satisfaction represents something beyond the level of its objective appearance, it certainly is not some archetypical content but, rather, some organic process. Hence, it would be wrong to subsume the impulsive acting out, the pervert sex attacks, the often destructive acts of mania under the heading of aggressiveness: they are too much related to the ego and too little to the non-ego to be called aggressive acts.

There is, however, another way in which neurotic delinquents may become aggressive offenders. We should not only think of their delinquent acts which may have a symbolic meaning or may be meant to satisfy some irrational needs for punishment or some uncontrollable drives. We should bear in mind that at least certain acts of violence born of unconscious punishment needs or perversions may force the offender into a life-style in which he can no longer live without aggressiveness.

We are not concerned here with the problems of adult criminals: a sadist may be driven by irresistible impulses into perpetrating acts of cruelty; crimes of violence may be committed by hopeless guilt-offenders; a pyromaniac may set on fire irreplaceable art treasures. The elements of true aggressiveness, however, are unlikely to be found in their crimes: we will look in vain for feelings of destroyability, attempts to heighten ego potency or a high degree of ego-participation in acts of perversion, in manias or guilt offenses. Often, such signs of aggressiveness do not characterize even the non-delinquent part of their lives. But all this does not apply to delinquent children.

To the extent that a child or an adolescent are involved in guilt offenses or even in acts of compulsive delinquency, they may try to extend their dissocial activities to the areas of day-to-day life. It is as if they wanted to cover their irrational behavior by more rational, more accountable aggressions. The latter are then, indeed, attempts to bolster up an ego which feels threatened by the very irrationality of its delinquent impulses, attempts to provide a feeling of belonging. We therefore should not look for guilt- and punishment motives or for traces of compulsiveness in each offense that may be committed by such a child or adolescent. They may glide into an aggressive "career" without really belonging to one of the clinical units which we have analyzed in this chapter.

We also know of those unambiguously neurotic children who, upon reaching the age of pre-adolescence, feel ashamed of their phobic or hysteric handicaps and jump, as it were, into aggressive behavior. In this respect, they resemble the neurotic delinquents with their tendency to compensate for their irrationality by "generalized" aggressiveness. Both groups often offer considerable difficulties for the diagnostician (unless he uses depth-exploring methods such as dream-interpretation, word-association tests, etc.).*

---

* We are not including in our present analysis cases of therapy-induced aggressiveness, that is, cases in which repressed aggressiveness is brought to the surface in a permissive atmosphere. These are *not* cases of delinquency, the aggressive tendencies being controlled for the purposes of therapy. Neither do we include cases of wayward children whom the therapist tries to lead through a period of induced neurosis in order to cure and rehabilitate them (20).

CHAPTER SIX

Delinquency in Adolescents

1. INTRODUCTION

No DIAGNOSIS OF psychopathy, so we have said, can be made with any degree of certainty before the child has reached adolescence.* On the other hand, the adolescent, at least in certain cultures, behaves in a way strongly reminiscent of psychopathic conditions: weakness of relational ability and of the time concept, artificiality of feeling, quasi-oscillating change of roles, antisocial acts, all these symptoms seem to indicate that the adolescent *qua* adolescent passes, as it were, through a developmental phase of psychopathy. We shall try to show, on the following pages, the fallacy of this interpretation.

Are we allowed to diagnose as psychopathic those cruel and vicious manifestations of adolescent delinquency which today disturb the minds of educators and social workers all over the world? We tend to believe with others, that this form of dissocial behavior, with its typical combination of complete disregard for all group norms and inclination toward group intoxication, reflects a value vacuum which, in turn, results from the paradoxic combination of technologic, social and psychological progress, with conscious and unconscious fear of total destruction through the atom bomb and totalitarian regimes. Can such a configuration of external factors account for a substantial increase in the number of psychopaths, that is, of constitutionally disordered individuals? Or, bearing in mind that, as we have maintained, most psychopathic constitutions crystallize after birth, under the impact of earliest frustrations in the area of child-mother relationships, can it be proven that the latter frustrations occur more frequently under the influence of the above-mentioned value vacuum?

---

* With the exception of the very few cases of congenital psychopathy.

2. Some Characteristics of Middle-class Adolescence

In another place (34), we have defined the essential elements of adolescence, typical of the middle class in Western culture, as follows:

a) As the result of the fact that society no longer allows the adolescent to be a child, yet does not agree to accept him as an adult, his time-perception tends to be unrealistic, and his awareness of continuity between his personal past, present and future is bound to be weakened.

b) As a result of tension between increasing sexual demands and a still weak ego, defense mechanisms are mobilized, particularly against the danger of oedipal revivals (37).

c) As a result of such defensive moves, which are primarily directed against family identifications, many previous internalizations are being canceled, including superego formations.

d) As a result, the adolescent tends to live "with principles" rather than realities, without feeling that he is under a moral or logical obligation to realize these principles.

e) As a result of such partial alienation to reality an experience of defeat becomes inevitable, particularly at the end of adolescence.

f) The adolescent lives a life in contradictions, not only between principles and reality, between arrogance and despair, but also between the non-committal character of his identifications and their emotional intensity and inherent illusion of finality, between the misinterpretation of his static "life with principles" as dynamic and his perception of the adult world as static, hence as a threat to his very existence.

g) Fear of adult staticness leads to a dethronement of the parents as value authorities and to a replacement of internalization by external imitation.

h) In this way, paradoxically, he protects himself against all "threats" of adaptation.

i) On the other hand, he likes to imitate the external signs of adult behavior, thus trying to live simultaneously on two planes, as someone who need not sacrifice his "life with principles" to the demands of adult adaptation.

j) The falsity and inconsistency of many of his imitations bears witness to this adolescent pathology, while, at the same time, preventing dangerous withdrawals.

k) This explains why most adolescents of the middle class end up in average-adaptation (after the experience of deadlock and despair at the end of adolescence) rather than in personality-disruption or suicide.

3. Adolescent Delinquency in the Middle Class

We now propose to discuss some forms of delinquent behavior in adolescence. We shall limit our discussion to allotropic behavior disorders only which appear in male adolescents of middle-class, lower-class and higher-class families within our (Western) society, and only to the extent that these disorders can be reduced to the age-factor. In other words, we shall not include in our discussion neurotic, psychotic or otherwise auto-tropic disturbances which may appear in adolescents, or those manifestations of delinquent behavior which may result from specific traumatizations or from preadolescent personality deviations. In this way, we may hope to be able, at a later stage, to compare adolescent behavior disorders with certain psychopathic conditions.

The discrepancy between the developmental increase in the intensity of id drives and the defensive flight into intellectualization is liable to further the emergence, in adolescence or later, of such negative qualities as emotional coldness, cynicism, lack of readiness for value identification. The same negative qualities, however, may result from another characteristic of adolescence, the moratory, unrealistic and non-committal way in which the adolescent plays a variety of changing roles. While coldness and cynicism will accompany nonidentification under the impact of adolescent drive increase, superficiality of feeling will be its concomitant under the impact of the adolescent moratorium. But in both instances the ground is laid for defective social behavior (the specific manifestations of which will, of course, be determined by additional factors, environmental and internal). We may, then, find passive drivenness and seducibility or lack of integration between mutually opposed personality traits; compulsive aggressiveness (which sometimes may take the place of a former phobia or obsessional neurosis) or limitation of moral behavior to the narrow area of certain conventions, that is, lifeless heteronomy.*

---

* As already mentioned, we are not including here such typically adolescent *auto*tropic symptoms as depressive moods, suicidal tendencies, psychotic disintegration, nor do we include those manifestations of emotional and moral coldness which result from repressed aggressiveness.

The psychological connection between these symptoms (cynicism, passivity, lack of integration, aggressiveness, moral limitation) and the essential characteristics of adolescence which we have mentioned in the first paragraph, on the one hand, and between both and delinquent acts, on the other, seems to be self-evident. Sudden impulse-eruptions in the wake of irrational attempts to avoid the parents and their introjected counterparts may lead to the commission of unplanned offenses which are sometimes described as *short-circuit actions*. Loss of value orientation after the "repeal" of internalized directives explains the adolescent's unwillingness to accept the parental command or to resist libidinal stimulations. The static conception of the present (a conception which ignores its function as a bridge between the personal past and the personal future) weakens the adolescent's identity feeling and thus helps obscure the individuality of his behavior.

Here lies one of the sources of those apparently senseless offenses which have been committed by not a few adolescents : they remain inexplicable, as long as we try to understand them against the background of personal development only; but when we interpret them as results of the adolescent's attempts to realize a principle by realizing himself at a given moment, we will be able to understand that only by completely disregarding the existence and the rights of the non-ego does the adolescent maintain the illusion of being master of *his* absolute, unchanging present. (Here again, a comparison with similar tendencies in certain psychopaths will be illuminating.)

The attitude is essentially connected with two other characteristics of this adolescent's delinquency, his lack of remorse even after a most serious crime and his tendency to idealize antisocial acts as realizations of a principle. The two attitudes are interrelated : lack of remorse reflects the adolescent's way of experiencing his offenses as experimentations with principles and himself as their representative and servant. His very refusal to accept the demands of society proves to him his value and justifies his existence : committing an offense or a crime means more than disregard for law and tradition; it proves his power objectively to abolish and eliminate law and tradition. The offender raises himself, in and through his offense, to the level of a fighter for freedom, a fighter against dependence on adult staticness which would be liable to limit and weaken his potentialities. It is this idealization of his role as an offender which explains two facts : his unwillingness to admit that what he really seeks is but a momentary pleasure, and his failure to show remorse after his offenses. But, paradoxically, it is this same idealization which accounts for the appalling radicalness of some of his offenses.

Fighting against adult-represented staticness means, at least partial, loss of contact with the generally accepted areas of social communication. But like every form of social isolation, this one, too, has its specific compensations : the adolescent delinquent either associates with one or more friends in an esoteric group, or he joins a gang and submits to the dominance of a leader. In both instances a fictitious social reality emerges which is not subject to the laws of adult behavior. The illusion of intimacy in the esoteric group, whose members share identical drives and views, supports the adolescent's tendency to live *in principiis*, and membership in a gang not only exempts him from his duties toward the traditionally accepted social institutions but also protects him against the danger of isolation inherent in any form of living with principles. Some adolescent delinquents prefer esoteric, other gang groups; still others present the strange picture of extreme individualism and passive collectivism coexistent without conflict : they may define themselves as alone in the responsibility for the realization of principles, while at the same time tending to efface themselves in group intoxication.

But not every offense committed by an adolescent can be reduced to the age factor. We have already mentioned that not a few offenses committed by adolescents are the outcome of environmental, constitutional and developmental factors which operate long before the individual has reached adolescence, and which continue to operate afterwards. These factors are present in every adolescent offense (while, on the other hand, the age factor modifies the causal equation of *every* case of delinquency).

And yet, although the division between age-conditioned and other adolescent offenses is somewhat artificial, we may still contend that the age factor produces certain characteristics of delinquent behavior in adolescence. In other words, the foregoing analysis should not be regarded as a generally applicable description but, rather, as an attempt to construct the ideal type of adolescent delinquency in the middle-class stratum of Western society. Every case participates, as it were, in a different way and to a different extent in the ideal type.

4. ADOLESCENT DELINQUENCY IN THE LOWER-CLASS FAMILY

We agree with those sociologists who maintain that adolescence in a child who grows up under conditions of poverty in the lower-class family*

---

* We do not intend to consider here those forms of poverty which may prevail in the rural family with its different economically, nationally and historically conditioned patterns, nor the problems of socialization under the impact of poverty and religion (see 34).

is essentially different from what it is under conditions prevailing in the middle-class family. Where the conditions of education include neither emotional intimacy in the family circle, oedipal tensions, ambivalence feelings nor that moratory form of adolescence which is characteristic of the end of childhood in the middle-class family, there will be no need for the adolescent to escape into a life with principles and, consequently, his delinquent behavior as well will be different.

Under conditions of extreme poverty, man's conscious orientation is liable to be focused on his external needs and their satisfaction. Externalization is likely to pervade his entire existence. This externalization will find its expression, as we have tried to show elsewhere (35), in the identity of feelings with their precipitating causes, in the way man relates to his fellow men as if they were part of a world of things-to-be-manipulated, in his fixatedness to the area of the known (or of what he believes he knows), in the relative weakness of his ability to think in abstract terms, in the impersonal nature of his relationships in general and of his relationships to his child in particular. Hence, the relative weakness, in the child, of ambivalence feelings toward his parents, of oedipal conflicts and their repression; hence, the relative weakness of that moral agency which directs man's decisions and judgments from within and which, under different conditions of education (that is, under the impact of a more intimate and emotionally charged family atmosphere), is likely to emanate from repression and introjection; hence, the relative weakness of emotional conflicts in adolescence and the absence of the need for such defensive reactions as have been described by A. Freud (37).

On the other hand, it is precisely the pattern of externalization that prevents the double prohibition in which we see one of the main societal causes of adolescent conflicts in the middle-class family (35). Under conditions of poverty a child learns already during the latency period, and certainly as an adolescent, realistically to take part in the life of the adults. They, on their part, do not deny him his rights as an adult, provided he fulfills the role of an adult. Moreover, there is ample opportunity in his life for truly adult experiences.

Under such conditions adolescence will never be a non-committal period between childhood and adulthood where the adolescent is free to try himself out in all sorts of changing roles and to live on a level of principles. On the contrary, it is now that he becomes more and more adult-oriented, that he wants to belong to the world of adults whose external status symbols he imitates. Because society does not allow him a moratory existence, he lives in anticipation of adulthood; it is precisely the fact that his conscious orientation, too, is almost entirely focused on what he has not, on his external needs and their satisfaction, which provides the identification bridges between the generations. Externality of values, feelings and relationships, the concomitant and result of this orientation, prevents the emergence of serious internal conflicts between parents and children; to the extent that conflicts do emerge, usually about some external problem, they are as a rule solved without delay and on the level of open, direct, conscious confrontation.

But the adult-orientation of this adolescent—tied as he is to the area of the known, weak in his abstractive abilities, externalized in his values —does not mean adjustment to the exigencies of law and social order. On the contrary, both by way of imitating asocial or antisocial behavior manifestations in his adult environment and by way of accepting the pattern of externalization, with its emphasis on immediate satisfaction, is he likely to become a delinquent.

However, if we want to understand the specific nature of adolescent delinquency under conditions of poverty, we must add to the factors mentioned so far (adult-orientation, tiedness to the known, interpretation of reality as the area of the haveable, inability to postpone satisfaction) another one : the adolescent's strongly aggressive resentment. It is this element which explains the difference between adolescent and childhood delinquency under conditions of extreme poverty : all the other elements can be found already in the life of the lower-class *child*; as a result, waywardness is his typical form of social maladjustment; but it is this aggressive resentment which, under the impact of *adolescent intensification of id drives*, becomes now the decisive factor in the patterns of delinquent behavior.

Aggressiveness fulfills here the function which the existence *in principiis* fulfills under conditions of middle-class family-life; it is a kind of pseudo-abstraction from the multitude of possible forms of relationship.* Negating the non-ego because it does not belong to the ego, delineating the areas of the ego and the non-ego, that is, of the negator and the negated, on the basis of chance associations and of chance affects, attacking, damaging, taking possession of, or destroying the (human or material) non-ego and thus restricting its extent and its power—these are the elements of adolescent delinquency in the slum quarters of our cities. Its manifestations are well known: gang-fights, destructions often devoid of all meaning and inner logic, organized thefts, organized or unorganized sex offenses,

---

* Similarly, the reduction of all reality to the common denominator of "that-which-I-have-not" could be called a kind of pseudo-abstraction from the multitude of possible manifestations of reality.

and all these against a background of passive impulsivity, lack of integration and lack of planning for a personal future.

Just as the middle-class adolescent's life with principles allows for coexistence of idealism and egoism, so the realism of the adolescent who grows up under conditions of extreme poverty allows for coexistence of an adult life-pattern and aggressive negation of everything non-ego.

It would seem that this form of delinquent behavior resembles the clinical picture of the so-called *primary behavior disorder of the oedipal type* (49, 77). The question then arises how the latter, which emerges at a much earlier stage of development, differs from that form of adolescent delinquency which we have briefly analyzed here.

We refer the reader to our discussion of PBD in Chapters 1 and 5 where we emphasized its reactive and defensive character. We said that the child's hostility makes it possible for him to maintain his conception of the world as hostile, and that the maintenance of this conception serves as a means of protecting him against the danger of renewed disappointment by the adults who have already deceived him. Under conditions of extreme poverty, on the other hand, no such defense is needed as the child experiences his parents not as disappointing but as an integral part of his world of want, in which *all possible satisfaction is expected from things and happenings, none from persons and feelings.*

The similarity of symptoms, therefore, should not deceive us: generalized hostility in an adolescent delinquent means something essentially different from what it means in a child who suffers from PBD. It betrays resignation rather than fear, impersonal drivenness rather than conscious or unconscious intentionality, resentment of the "have-not" rather than revenge of the injured.

5.   ADOLESCENT DELINQUENCY IN THE HIGHER-CLASS FAMILY

Asocial and antisocial behavior in the adolescent who grows up under conditions of poverty is determined by those patterns of externalization that characterize present-day life-in-want. Similar patterns, however, crystallize under opposite conditions as well, when the one experience that is absent in the child's development is that of wanting-things-not-attainable. When the environment satisfies every single material need the child may feel, when none of his demands remains unfulfilled, feelings of emptiness and want are liable to emerge in his interpersonal relationships, and the child may indulge in pseudo-feelings, in false emotions, which are bound to lead to neurotic involvements. When he reaches adolescence, he may try to find a way out of these involvements by committing delinquent acts, as if he hoped he could thus fill the void of his existence and become real. The adolescent quest for self-definition accounts for this illusion.*

But there exists yet another aspect of delinquency among the adolescent sons of wealthy parents. When the environment hastens to fulfill every wish the child may express (and often enough even before he may have expressed it), without expecting or demanding a personal effort from him, an adolescent is bound to emerge who will expect reality to be always and everywhere at his disposal. "Taking" whatever he wants, material goods and persons alike, will seem to him his right. Reality will lose its character as subject-object of relationships and will become a mere object at the mercy of his omnipotent ego.

And yet, it would not be correct to call him a psychopath (though he may be no less egocentric) : as a rule, he is not aggressive enough to act out incorporative tendencies; his expectations are rather naive and devoid of aggressive intentionality. So are his antisocial acts : he may attack, injure or even destroy another person simply because he is unaware of this person's existential rights as an independent individual, not out of any feeling of hatred; simply because he may experience that person as an irritating or disturbing part of his world of objects in which he moves at will, not as the result of any interpersonal conflicts. Not only the other person, but he himself, as well, exists not as a subject but only as a receptacle of happenings and objects. In this respect, too, his self-conception differs essentially from psychopathic ego inflation and approximates again the patterns of externalization, as we know them from the study of child development under conditions of poverty.

Under conditions of poverty and of plenty, it is the external world of the *haveable* which provides the illusion of being the source of all satisfaction; but in the first case, the individual experiences the haveable as that which is always part of the non-ego, while, in the second case, he experiences it as part of the ego, hence as always available. This dialectic emergence of externalization under opposite conditions, of poverty and of plenty, reflects the operation of a common factor in the development of children from lower- and from higher-class families : because of their orientation toward the haveable, not only their oedipal involvement and conflicts but also the incentive for the introjection of parental images will

---

* Psychoanalysts tend to interpret such cases in the context of the individual's development rather than as direct results of specifically adolescent processes (for instance, 38). Social psychologists and sociologists, on the other hand, try to explain both the neurotic involvements and the delinquent behavior of middle- and higher-class adolescents as results and expressions of the patterns of family education (see refs. 39 and 46).

be weak. The parents, under both conditions, are liable to remain so remote that the child experiences them as strangers who do not evoke strong personal feelings. Thus, the vicious circle of impersonality and defective relationality is being closed.

The outcome, however, will be different according to the different conception of the haveable. Lack of internalized directives in configuration with the experience that the non-ego is always outside, always *not-mine*, may produce that type of offense which we know from the many studies of the so-called delinquency areas : there, offenses, often extremely serious ones, "occur" in an almost impersonal way, though they may be accompanied, at least in adolescents, by strong resentments against the frustrating non-ego.

Lack of internalized directives in configuration with the experience that the non-ego is always available, always mine, is liable to produce a different type of delinquent behavior : here, we find those acts of wanton destruction, those cruel aggressions, seductions or perversions that impress us with their seeming absence of all ego involvement. Although they may be planned meticulously and often enough in a rather sophisticated way, the adolescent delinquent's ego is not present in the feeling tones accompanying the delinquent acts. They indicate neither imitation of adult behavior nor anticipation of the future, neither defensive flight from parental values nor substitutive transformation of neurotic symptoms.

Here again, we may ask whether this adolescent's behavior should not be diagnosed as psychopathic. His inability to accept any kind of limitation from without, his rejection of whoever and whatever represents law and authority, his readiness coldly to destroy any obstacle—would seem to indicate the presence of psychopathic conditions. But we shall try to show in which respects this pattern of adolescent delinquency, too, essentially differs from psychopathy.

Before doing so, however, we shall supplement what we have said about the dialectic similarity between adolescence in lower- and higher-class families by a few remarks on the differences between the essential characteristics of adolescence in higher- and middle-class families.

Not merely adolescence but life in general is a *moratorium* when the means of satisfying every material need are available and no personal effort is required for their attainment. Under such conditions, non-committal experimentation with changing roles takes the place of genuine confrontation with the tasks of reality not only in the life of adolescents but of many adults as well. The adolescent, therefore, does not feel that he must realize his identity in opposition to that of the adults in his environment, and he will not come to experience that deadlock which, as a rule, marks the end of adolescence and the beginning of adult realism in middle-class families.

But in spite of the similarity, under such conditions, between the adult's and the adolescent's moratory mode of existence, they are strangers to each other, since their whole life is one of separateness, devoid of polarity. The roots of this separateness lie in the child's earliest mother-experience (though later experiences act as reinforcing factors and determine the processes of structurization): both a poverty-stricken mother's orientation toward what she has not, toward want and its (temporary) elimination, and a wealthy mother's excessive orientation toward her personal problems, her lack of genuine contact with reality, may support the emergence in the child of overdependence on external stimuli, weakness of ambivalence of feelings, inability to grow through identification. But it is this very similarity between the mother's and the child's externalized orientation which separates them from each other and thus prevents polarization, interrelation and introjection. Hence, we will not find in the adolescent son of wealthy parents that escape into a life with principles, into intellectualizations or into asceticism, which is characteristic of the middle-class adolescent. (And again we see a greater proximity of higher- to lower-class, than of higher- to middle-class adolescents!)

6. SUMMARY

We shall now sum up briefly our discussion by way of comparing with each other the patterns of adolescent delinquency as they crystallize in lower-, middle- and higher-class families.

In *middle-class adolescent delinquency* (MAD) we find short-circuit or explosive actions resulting from the coexistence of contradictory and mutually incompatible attitudes and the concomitant inner tensions. Such tensions are absent in the two other forms of delinquency. But the result of this absence of contradictions is different in each: in *higher-class adolescent delinquency* (HAD) it is responsible for the adolescent's ability coldly to plan his offenses in all details, while it accounts in the *lower-class delinquency* (LAD) for passive drivenness and the occurrence-character of all actions.

In MAD, offenses are often committed in protest against the adults' expectation that the adolescent learn how to postpone or suppress the satisfaction of his (maturationally intensified) instinctual demands, without rewarding him with the benefits of adult status. In this respect, MAD again differs essentially from the two other forms. The basic similarity between the parental and the adolescent life-patterns explains why, in HAD and in LAD, aggressiveness is not specifically directed against the parents (as it is in MAD). But the naively egocentric interpretation of everything non-ego as belonging to the ego accounts in HAD for the utter lack of feeling, of considerateness, of concern for the other person; and the ever-repeated experience that nothing belongs to the ego accounts for the strongly aggressive resentment in LAD. Each of these forms of aggressiveness characterizes in particular the adolescent in the higher- and the lower-class stratum respectively, whereas the corresponding attitudes in the adults have either become attenuated in the process of adaptation-through-compromise or have grown into openly criminal tendencies.

In MAD, many delinquent acts can be interpreted as attempts to translate into reality a value or a principle, or as expressions of self-realization. In HAD, on the other hand, the delinquent act serves one purpose only, that of satisfying a personal need, and this purpose sufficiently justifies the act to prevent the emergence of guilt feelings or of remorse even after the commission of a very serious and vicious offense. In this respect, again, LAD is similar : here, too, the offense is, as a rule, the result of a direct, immediate response to an external stimulus and serves the sole purpose of eliminating the momentary tension created by that stimulus. It differs from the HAD offense by its lower degree of self-reflection and of egocentricity.

Finally, a word on the place of the group in each of the three forms of adolescent delinquency. We have said that MAD is characterized by the adolescent's tendency either to form an esoteric small group or to join a gang and thus to create his individual illusion of contact with social reality. In HAD, this quest for contact-illusion is absent and in its place we find open libidinal strivings, mostly of the homosexual or the sado-masochistic varieties (which, in MAD, are admitted, if at all, on a level of principles only). In LAD, joining a variety of chance groups is the most important form of group-life, while small friendship unions are almost unknown. Membership in organized street gangs is found in each of the three forms of delinquency, but it has a different meaning in each : in MAD it may indicate a neurotic escape or the realization of a principle; in HAD it may provide some adolescents, though usually for a short while only, with a kind of extra-thrill through the illusion of power; in LAD, finally, it may emerge almost automatically from chance associa-tions or from external contacts with gang-forces that operate in the adolescent's neighborhood and, at the same time, it makes possible the acting out of aggressive impulses.

7. COMPARISON OF PSYCHOPATHY WITH ADOLESCENT BEHAVIOR

It now remains for us to compare in some detail adolescent behavior and, more particularly, its delinquent manifestations, with the corresponding symptoms of psychopathy. We hope we shall be able to show in which respects the two groups of behavior pathologies differ from each other essentially, and why it is a fallacy to interpret adolescence as a kind of developmental psychopathy.

The inner contradictions in the middle-class adolescent's behavior and his intrapsychic tensions indicate (according to the psychoanalytic interpretation) flight and defense. In terms of psychological vector-analysis, we could add that this adolescent is characterized by absence of direct intentionality toward a given, clearly defineable goal. Not only his need for defense but also the staticness of his life with principles can be adduced as proof of his structurally weak goal-orientation.

In this respect he may be said to differ from the psychopath who, in his orientation toward incorporating the non-ego, is indeed goal-directed, while, on the other hand, he is devoid of inner tensions, even when he adopts the most self-contradictory identities. And he certainly needs no defense against oedipal reinvolvement, as his relational inability and the weakness of introjection in the earlier stages of his development as a rule prevent deep oedipal involvements and conflicts in the first instance.

The adolescent's ability to experience anxiety and despair pervades most of his role-playings and even his ordinary day-to-day behavior. It certainly tinges the pathologic outcome of adolescent identification with images, ideas and principles with that dangerous superficiality of feelings which is liable to result from too many identifications, or that emotional coldness which may follow a period of an overly intensive life with principles, particularly where such adolescent overintensity is symptomatic of a constitutional or developmental impairment of the ego's integrative abilities. Emotional superficiality and coldness in a psychopath have a different meaning altogether : they are essential symptoms of that absence of polar relationships which we call psychopathy; and they are never tinged with contrasting feelings such as fear or despair. Neither the character neurotic nor the middle-class adolescent can be as genuinely cold and unattached emotionally or as shallow in his relationships as only a psychopath can be, for he alone needs no defense against himself, he alone is able to relate to nobody but himself.

When we compare the delinquent manifestations of adolescent behavior with psychopathic conditions, we obviously find many similarities between the two. This may account for the fact that a diagnosis of psychopathy is more frequently made in cases of adolescent than of child delinquency (the other reason being, of course, as already mentioned, that during the earlier stages of the child's development, psychopathic behavior has a better chance of remaining disguised behind a mask of neurotic disorders than in adolescence).

The tendency of certain middle-class adolescent delinquents to yield to sudden impulses, the apparent senselessness of some of their offenses and the extreme nature of these offenses, non-recognition of the law and absence of remorse after the act are equally characteristic of psychopathic behavior. But the psychopath, particularly of the introvert (driven or unstable) variety, who yields to a sudden impulse differs from the adolescent by the absence of behavioral ambiguity : his drivenness does not produce one of those short-circuit actions that are so typical of the adolescent. And to the extent that seducibility is one of the characteristics of psychopathic behavior, it is not the result of too many changes of roles and identifications (as it may be in the adolescent delinquent) but of a constitutional tendency to play identity by mirroring the behavior of others (see p. 115). The senselessness and radicalness of offenses committed by a psychopath (particularly of the explosive or the aggressive types) are but expressions of the fact that the non-ego in its own right does not exist for him; they do not, as in adolescents, indicate a tendency toward the realization of a principle but are symptoms of his tendency to master reality by negating everything non-ego. Laws do not exist for him; hence, he does not have to abolish them in the way the adolescent tries to liberate his existence from the shackles of adult limitation. Egocentricity and lack of remorse after the offense are common to both, the adolescent delinquent and the psychopath, but for different reasons : the adolescent because he feels his life to be a realization of the potentials of existence *per se*, the psychopath because existence is identical with his ego.

Although symptomatically the adolescent's egocentricity closely resembles psychopathic ego inflation, we can distinguish between them by considering the role which group-belonging plays in their behavior : the contradictory coexistence of isolationist tendencies with group-intoxication* which is characteristic of many adolescent delinquents will never be found in a genuine psychopath. The introvert psychopath will show a more marked tendency toward isolating himself, the extravert toward seeking group contacts, but neither one will indulge in one of those

---

* Cf. Redl's description of the "child who hates" (83); see above, p. 145 ff.

illusions of finality and truth, of individual responsibility or collectivism, which are characteristic of the adolescent. We may find, particularly in the *Hochstapler* type of psychopathy, a conscious manipulation of individualistic and collectivistic attitudes, according to the role he wishes to play at a given moment, but this is clearly not to be confused with the adolescent's coexistence of contradictory attitudes (such as the assumption of aloneness and group-intoxication).

Thus far, we have compared only the middle-class type of adolescent delinquency with psychopathic disorders. We shall now add a few remarks on the similarities and differences that exist between these disorders and the lower- and higher-class types of delinquency.

We should remember that lack of truly polar relationships between the ego and the non-ego is symptomatic not only of psychopathic conditions but also of externalization, as it emerges under conditions of extreme poverty and educational impersonality (35). Absence of anxiety, sometimes coupled with aggressiveness, sometimes with passive subjectedness to all chance occurrences, unawareness of the non-ego as a partner of the ego and impulsiveness are common to both forms of behavior. But in contrast to the type of adolescent delinquency which appears under externalizing conditions, psychopathic aggressiveness is much more matter-of-fact and much less tinged by resentment, much more anchored in the ego structure and much less reactive.

The adolescent who has grown up under conditions of plenty, without adequately experiencing object-resistances and limitations, often tends to assume, in an almost nonaggressive way, that everything non-ego is at his disposal. His delinquency may then be interpreted as the naive conclusion he draws from this egocentric assumption. But it would be wrong to speak of ego inflation or of incorporative tendencies. Why should he incorporate what is already part of his ego? Although his ability to plan offenses meticulously without getting himself affectively involved or his readiness coldly to eliminate every obstacle are strongly reminiscent of psychopathic brutality, he differs from the latter essentially in two respects: (a) he remains aware of his existential emptiness and of his parents' responsibility for its emergence; (b) socio-cultural conditions equally affect juveniles of different structural dispositions, those in whom the life-tendency towards expansion as well as those in whom the opposite life-tendency predominates. As a result, we may find many more tension factors in the personality structure of the adolescent son of wealthy parents than in the psychopath.

We have tried to show how each of the three sociologically defined forms of delinquency differs from psychopathy. It might perhaps not be superfluous to emphasize that by analyzing these patterns we did not intend to add new clinical units to those already known and accepted in psychopathology (such as neurotic dissociality, mania, perversion, psychopathy, primary behavior disorders, waywardness). Each of these units may be found in any adolescent irrespective of the social class to which he belongs (though we may also find certain class-conditioned preferences). On the other hand, we believe that every clinical picture appearing in an adolescent is partly determined and specifically modified by the class patterns which we have tried to analyze. The latter may, in certain individual cases, be much less decisive than constitutional and developmental factors, but no case analysis would be complete without taking them into account.

8. A Modern Variety of Juvenile Delinquency

Since the end of World War Two a new type of adolescent delinquents has made its appearance, all over the world. They are known as Teddy Boys in England, as Blousons Noirs in France, as the Halbstarken in Germany or Vienna, as Hooligans in Moscow. Their acts of senseless and destructive cruelty, their specific form of group-life, their nihilism, their exhibitionist style of dressing, have been described often, by writers like Finc (25) or Fyvel (40), by social scientists like Barbara Wootton (94) or Muchov (75). To some extent a shift can be observed from the Teddy Boy type of group delinquency to that of asocial drifting and withdrawal, whose well-known representatives for the last ten years have been the Beatniks and the Hippies. They, too, have been the subject of many studies, mostly descriptive (12, 56).

Little efforts have been made to compare these manifestations of asocial or antisocial behavior with those of the children and adolescents in the Europe after the First World War, when many symptoms of reckless aggressiveness and moral laxity appeared under conditions of want that today appear under conditions of affluence. This similarity should be sufficient to set us on guard against the danger that is inherent in sociological oversimplifications. No theory of delinquency based on an analysis of cultural and socio-economic factors alone would seem to be adequate. Such factors undoubtedly explain the higher incidence of certain types of asocial or antisocial behavior or, better, of "delinquency-proneness"; but the finding of correlations between a certain set of cultural conditions and the appearance of a certain type of misbehavior becomes causally relevant only when it is preceded by a differential analysis of the different forms of juvenile delinquency. Their representatives constitute the "population" of these very groups of contemporary delinquents that we are going to analyze.

In other words : the terms "Teddy Boys" and "Beatniks" designate and emphasize certain traits of behavior that appear differently in each individual and should be seen in each juvenile against the background of his specific pathology : some who join the gang may be genuine psychopaths or feebleminded of the aggressive or paranoid types, others may be —psychopathic or feebleminded—drifters; some may have had behind them a long history of waywardness, others—of neurotic delinquency of the compulsive, the substitutive or the guilt-offense types, again others— of primary aggressiveness or of oedipal behavior disorders; some may be drawn into the gang without having passed through any kind of pathology, others may be driven into it by a temporary resentment or disappointment.

We have analyzed each of these varieties, in its own rights, as an individual pathology. We are now going to describe the workings of Teddy Boy and Beatnik groups, composed as they are of the different types and unities of delinquency. These descriptions will, we hope, supplement the previous analyses. At the same time we shall try to keep in mind what we have said in the preceding paragraphs about the class-conditions of delinquent behavior in adolescents. However, before entering into case descriptions we propose briefly to analyze the socio-cultural conditions that characterize "Modern Time" and form the *collective* background against which the "New Type" has to be seen : conditions that favor, as we shall try to show, both the emergence of certain individual varieties and the formation of heterogeneous groups of adolescent delinquents.

9. The Conditions of "Modern Time" and Adolescent Delinquency

Since we have analyzed these conditions in greater detail in two places (33, 35), we shall content ourselves here with a summary of what has been said there, elaborating some of the points made to emphasize their relevance for the problems of juvenile delinquency.

a) We speak of adolescents who grow up under conditions of *parental insecurity*. Parents who had made possible the victory of totalitarian regimes, the destruction of millions, the rule of falsity and force—how could they be trusted as value-guides, *how could they be accepted as images-to-be-internalized* and to be transformed into agents of inner direction, into "controls from within"? Was it not inevitable that intercourse with such parents injured the growing child's ability to differentiate between good and bad? That it increased his insecurity, his disorientation, his dependence on chance-factors of determination? More : could it not happen that internalization of such parental images, to the extent it *was* brought about in the socialization process, became in itself a source of doubt and discomfort?

b) Neither should we forget that the years following the end of World War Two saw an unprecedented *rise of welfare services* and opportunities for consuming ever new goods. It has been said often that the relative security provided and guaranteed by the State necessarily *deprived the individual to a large extent of his initiative*. But we tend to forget that fear of uncertainty in the personal future is *not* only conducive to inner tension but also to ego-transcendence. The latter may take the form of escape into fatalistic indolence but may also help develop and strengthen an orientation towards overindividual values. *External security*, on the other hand, sets free mental energy that can be invested in one value only : *"having"*.

c) The latter becomes increasingly relevant (and exclusive) in an era in which society considers the production and distribution of more and more variegated consumer goods its main duty. Galbraith (41) brilliantly exposed this *ideology of consumption*, without, however, analyzing the disastrous effect it may—and almost must—have on the socialization process. It is bad enough when it produces that utterly *externalized attitude towards work* that we know to be characteristic today of adults and juveniles alike; but much worse than that is the *immediacy orientation* (85) it produces in the mind of the growing child. If work is no longer associated with learning, with ego-investment and ego-development, with tension that makes possible a fuller future, but is there to satisfy immediate needs, as quickly as possible, work is bound to lose even its instrumental function. Anything that brings with it the means to satisfy such needs, is welcome : gambling, stealing and, if necessary, doing something, as briefly as possible, that "they" (the adults) call "working".

d) We must not forget that we have in mind a juvenile who had not been able to internalize a meaningful father-figure and therefore tends to become dependent on external stimulations. This dependence is increased by another socio-cultural factor: *the father often fails to fulfill his culturally ascribed functions as provider*, when, by the whims of a technological economy, he finds himself outside the productive process, for a short or long-continued period of time. His failure does not reflect personal weakness but dependence on anonymous, incomprehensible and uncontrollable forces of market and policy. When a father's failure is due to personal insufficiency—disappointment, resentment, revolt or rejection may be the child's and particularly the juvenile's reactions—always accompanied by inner tensions and conflicts. But when his failure is due to transpersonal factors, the father figure's *structural* meaning (his "archetypic function") changes: he no longer represents, or supports, the son's orientation toward the future. The dimension of the *future as such becomes questionable.**

e) Here is the place to mention modern man's existential fear of total *destruction through nuclear weapons or through totalitarian domination. Prima facie* this fear is in contradiction to the feeling of security through the Welfare State's promise and intervention that we have mentioned. But *de facto* the one affects the individual exactly as does the other : both paralyze his initiative. Following without delay upon the experience of senseless destructiveness and brutality (during the Nazi regime and the war), the new and even more radical threat of extinction accounted and continues to account for the unwillingness of many juveniles, all over the world, to accept adults as representatives of values, or to take learning seriously beyond its defineable, practical results. *Nihilism and cynicism* are inevitable, the latter particularly in the light of the falsity that is inherent in the contradiction between welfare ideals and war preparations : what is good for man as an individual—security, progress, peace —does not commit mankind; ideals are but phrases, and the difference between allowed and forbidden is man-made and arbitrary.

f) Through his destructive acts the juvenile may express his identification with the fate of the world, with the future and its inherent logic : since he does not live "from within", guided by internalized values, *acceptance of the world's aggressiveness by way of imitation* is his way of being true and genuine. Such an interpretation would seem to account for the—seeming or real—absence of ego-involvement, for the affectlessness (6, 68) in his senseless destructions. (See also pp. 149 f.)

g) In this respect he resembles the aggressive psychopath, as we have described him in the third chapter, though it would be wrong to call the adolescent ego-inflated : the very fact that manifestations of *withdrawal and escape coexist with destructiveness* in the delinquent behavior of many juveniles of our time, comes to prove that their needs are *not* identical with those of the psychopath. He is not as far away from

---

* This condition should not be identified with lack of differentiation as it may result from poverty and neglect (35): neither an all-pervading orientation towards the "haveable" nor imitation of paternal behavior characterize the here-discussed cultural pathology; in their stead we find conscious disregard for the future, expressed in the escape symptoms of the "modern delinquent" as well as in his ruthless destructiveness (see later).

anxiety as is the psychopath. Inner tension, resulting from uncertainty, we said (see b) may be conducive to ego-transcendence, and one of its manifestations may be escape into indolence and fatalism. Absence of inner tension, resulting from external security, may make ego-transcendence impossible, without, however, excluding the possibilities of escape. *Awareness of the falsity* inherent in the adult value system and behavior clearly distinguishes between the adolescent delinquent of our time and the psychopath, on the one hand, and the lower- and the higher-class types of dissocial behavior of juveniles, on the other.

h) It would seem that *escape, for instance, into drugs*, becomes a pre-dominant symptom of "the modern variety of juvenile delinquency", at the expense of destructive behavior, whenever an individual becomes more acutely aware of the contradiction between ideals of security and technological progress, on the one hand, and planning total destruction, on the other. In other words: escape as a predominant symptom of juvenile delinquency, which is more typical, we said at the beginning, of the Beatnik than of the Teddy Boy, indicates the emergence of a *new type of tension*.

i) We have become accustomed, under the influence of psychoanalytic interpretations of individual cases, to conceive of inner tension as of a dynamic process going on between what Freud calls the structural agents of the psyche (id, ego, superego). But we should not forget that inner tensions also indicate dynamic processes going on between conflicting structural tendencies or between self-contradictory identifications or internalizations. These inner tensions become evident in certain historical situations and under certain socio-cultural conditions which are con-ducive to a *disintegration of parental images*. We claim that the modern variety of juvenile delinquency cannot be understood without an adequate analysis of this disintegration process.

j) At the beginning of our present analysis we have spoken of "parental insecurity" resulting from the role they played in the cruel history of the past decades (see a). We have also mentioned the fact that fathers often fail to live up to their structural functions (see d). Here we add another element of the same constellation: the frequently observed *rejection of masculinity by the mother*, who no longer feels that she can rely on her husband as provider or as symbol and representative of unambiguous value-differentiation. She is often being forced into the execution of paternal roles, not only as a provider but also as an agent of value differentiation and determination. This, however, causes the emergence of inner tension in her psyche, particularly when *she fails to give her children that feeling of nearness* without which a normal development of their cognitive, relational and emotional functions is imperilled. (We do not speak here of a class-conditioned pathology but of a general trend.)

k) The results are not only basic insecurity and value-disorientation in the child but also in the parents : the mother may react to her own failure with bad conscience which, in turn, may lead her to *overprotecting her sons*. We are not concerned here with the individual aspects of over-protection which have been analyzed by many students of psychopathology (see, f.i., D. Levy's study, 70), but with its meaning as a social pathology in modern times. Its twofold function, as aggressive revenge and atone-ment, explains the resulting ambiguity of the educational climate in which the overprotected boys grow up (even under conditions of poverty, where overprotection and irritated rejection do not exclude each other). The adolescent is then liable to react to the threat that is implied in his overprotecting mother's "antimasculinity" *by showing off his masculinity*. Aggressions, destructions, rejection of social norms and prohibitions, all these are irrational attempts to prove to the mother that she was wrong and to the father—that she was right!

l) But he is incapable of living or acting alone. Not only has he failed to learn initiative (for reasons analyzed above), he is forced into a protect-ing, though non-committal group existence by his *need for parental substitutes* : the mother who failed to supply him with an experience of nearness and its resulting "sense of trust" (21), the father who failed to supply him with an experience of reliable value direction—both are now replaced by *the group*. Its leader is the external substitute for the normally internalized *father figure and the directives*, which a structured ego is capable of giving and receiving from within. There is no identification with the leader but self-submission only, blind obedience; on one condi-tion, however : that the individual is never ordered to act alone, as he would be in an ordinary delinquent gang (see, f.i., the description and analysis of such a gang in Thrasher's still classical study (91)). The *maternal experience of nearness* is replaced by the illusion of contact and connectedness. There is more in such an experience than a feeling of being protected : all differences are eliminated, the member ceases to be an individual. One could almost say that it is through his submergence in the de-individualizing group that the adolescent serves his mother's anti-masculinity. The "maternal" group eliminates "paternal" individuality, while it serves, at the same time, both infantile dependence needs and illusions of masculinity and toughness.

m) Acting within his de-individualizing groups allows the adolescent to live egocentrically without ego-emphasis, to *remain isolated and alone within the groups*, attached to no one, using no one, and yet being ready to collapse as soon as he is forced to leave his groups. We could call this the basic paradox inherent in this adolescent delinquent's "groupism". One of its external symptoms is the *exhibitionist tendency* of each member to dress in a way likely to offend society, and yet without employing in any way individual imagination; he wants to "look different", provided others look like him.

n) One of the characteristics of this delinquent group is its *indifference to the social class of its members* : the "ideology of dirtiness", the addiction to indolence (not to mention again the addiction to drugs or to violence), the utter inability to live individually, to maintain differences, nihilism and cynicism coexistent with fear and tension—these symptoms of the "modern variety of juvenile delinquency" are capable of eliminating all class-conditioned patterns that may have distinguished between the individual members of the group before they joined it.

10. COMPARISONS

(a) With adolescence in general

Transformation of lawlessness into the law of human existence is evidently one of the core symptoms of the "new type". The adolescent who is left in a vacuum of values and relationships may use his maturationally increasing drive-energies for the purpose of filling this vacuum, as it were, by playing the role of determining the laws of existence and of belonging to a community. To dispose of human beings as if they were dead objects is, for him, a means of *proving* the non-existence of a human non-ego; to demonstrate rejection of law and authority is another way of proving, and at the same time of filling, the void. He, too, tends to replace reality by principles, like any other adolescent : he raises his relational inability to the level of a law of behavior.

In the light of this analysis it might be asked whether lack, or weakness, of inner tension is really an essential characteristic of the "new type" of adolescent delinquency : both, the contrast between his demonstrated pseudo-masculinity and infantile dependence needs and that between his relational inability and his tendency to establish, through lawlessness, a new set of laws, can constitute, so it may be argued, a tension field no less strong in intensity than one resulting, under conditions of internalization, from the contrast between suppressed instincts and moral demands, or from repression and defense against the unconscious. In the case under discussion, however, toughness and infantility, as well as destructiveness and its transformation into a universal law are rooted in the same primitive layers of immediate drive satisfaction and indicate the same vacuum of values and relations. Etiologically, this characteristic is paralleled by, or rooted in, the absence of feelings of security *as well* as of anxiety; taking the future for granted (in the double meaning of achievable status and of unavoidable perdition) prevents the emergence of either one of these feelings.

(b) With middle-class adolescent delinquency (MAD)

The middle class seems to be particularly sensitive to those socio-cultural factors that we have analyzed in the preceding paragraph. Would it not, then, be more appropriate to include the here-analyzed new variety of adolescent delinquency in what we have described in the second paragraph as MAD?

Neither coexistence of contradictory attitudes and the resulting short-circuit actions of the MAD nor his fight against the adult representatives of staticness, neither his way of experimenting with principles nor his tendency to idealize his aggressions, neither his escape from the introjected parental images nor the compensatory character of his group associations are characteristic of the "new type" of adolescent delinquency. And yet, there is in both the same senseless brutality of offenses; the same lack of remorse, the same combination of emotional coldness with aggressiveness.

These common symptoms, however, have a different structural meaning in each of the two entities. In MAD, they, like the first-mentioned (specific) symptoms, indicate avoidance and secondary externalization and therefore bear the stamp of irrational, quasi-neurotic symptoms of inner tension. *In the "new type" of delinquency, on the other hand, they indicate an almost psychopathic absence of fear, of relational ability, of inner tension.* The latter indeed closely resembles certain psychopathic conditions.

(c) With lower-class adolescent delinquency (LAD)

Still more essential are the differences between the here-discussed form of dissocial behavior and LAD : neither the latter's extreme dependence on his "area of the known" nor his inability to think in abstract terms, neither his tendency to imitate the adults in his environment nor the chance character of his actions or of his group associations, neither his strong resentments nor the naive way in which he enjoys his destructions are typical of the "new type" of adolescent delinquency. And even such (seemingly similar) symptoms as absence of true intentionality, of fear, of personal involvement and relatedness, again mean something different in each of the two behavioral entities: while in LAD, they indicate an externalized mode of existence, they have, in the "new type" of delinquency, the psychopathic qualities of a matter-of-fact egoism.

(d) With higher-class adolescent delinquency (HAD)

When we compare the "new type" of adolescent delinquency with the higher-class variety, with what we have called HAD, we find relatively more similarities than in the preceding examples. Both are able coldly to plan and perpetrate the most cruel crimes, without ego-involvement. Although they reject any attempt on the part of their adult environment (including the parents) to restrain and restrict them, they are so radically separated from them that they do not feel any need to protest against them or to fight them *as* adults. Both consider the non-ego their property, which they, therefore, dispose of at will. Both use their delinquent acts to fill the existential vacuum in which they grow up owing to what we have called "parental disintegration". Both know no inner tension in their hedonistic orientation toward the present. Both resemble the psychopath, although at least the HAD cannot be called "ego-inflated" in the same sense and to the same extent as the former.

And yet, it would be wrong to identify the "new type" with HAD. Not only can it be proven empirically that the majority of adolescents in this type do not stem from higher-class families and that the etiologic equation of their delinquent development contains fewer personal than cultural elements of causation; it can also be shown that most delinquent sons of wealthy parents do not indulge in the typically adolescent illusion that, through their delinquency, they establish a new pattern and a new law of behavior. Furthermore, they are much less group-addicted than those adolescents whom we consider to belong to the "new type" of delinquency.

(e) With psychoanalytic concepts

Is the "new type" the form which, under certain cultural conditions, the hysterical or the neurotic, the instinct-ridden or the oral character, perversion or impulse neurosis, primary behavior disorder or waywardness tend to take (see pp. 120 ff.), whereas, in another cultural constellation, these pathologies would manifest themselves differently?

Oversexualized behavior and histrionics, two main characteristics of the hysterical character, are indeed not infrequently noted today in adolescent delinquents. Should they therefore be called hysterical characters? Their demonstrated (pseudo) masculinity is reminiscent of the pervert's attempt to prove that he is not castrated (according to Fenichel (24) the core trait of every perversion). Should they for this reason be diagnosed as perverts? The tension-intolerance of Reich's (84) instinct-ridden character may be considered almost identical with what Riesman (86) described as the "immediacy cult" of modern youth. Short-circuit actions are a frequent symptom of the neurotic character. Emotional coldness and lack of ego-involvement characterize Bowlby's (9) affectionless thief. Group-intoxication is found in many cases of primary behavior disorder, in Redl's (83) "children who hate", in some of Friedlander's (38) antisocial character types. And we could go on enumerating additional similarities between the "new type" of adolescent delinquency and those syndromes of dissociality analyzed in the preceding chapters.

But what is the meaning of these similarities? Do they indicate that the "new type" is, after all, not a unit in itself, but a variety of individually different syndromes of behavior? Are all represented in any chance group of adolescent delinquents whom we may meet anywhere in modern society? Should we perhaps speak of a kind of inductive process in the course of which each member accepts at least some behavioral characteristics of the others? Or are all these similarities external only, while the basic symptoms nevertheless indicate a specific syndromatic unit of delinquent behavior?

It would seem to us that the answer to *both* alternatives should be in the affirmative : the "new type" of adolescent delinquency is indeed a behavioral unit in its own right, as regards its symptoms as well as its causes; at the same time, many adolescents come to "belong" to this type by way of chance association only, while, according to their individual pathology, they "belong" to another clinical group. This associative, inductive, contagious effect is, indeed, one of the essential characteristics of the "new type" of delinquency.

Moreover, the cultural conditions responsible for its emergence are *less* conducive to the crystallization of behavioral pathologies that pre-suppose introjection of parental images, ambivalence conflicts and inner tensions. Hence, most of the clinical pictures which we have analyzed in the preceding chapters, and in which this or that similarity with our "new type" of delinquency may be discovered, are found less frequently today than in other, more repression-oriented, periods. And to the extent that they do emerge, owing to individual configurations of constitutional, experiential and developmental factors, they tend indeed to be tinged with such characteristics of the (culture-conditioned) "new type" as emotional coldness and absence of inner tension, sadistic tendencies and group-intoxication.

We have in mind here primarily the "child who hates", the oedipal type of PBD, the antisocial character, the affectionless thief. When these children reach adolescence, their pathologies are liable to merge in the "new type" of delinquency. The defensive character of their aggressions, which are essentially directed against their disappointing parents, and the always present undertone of neurotic involvements will then gradually give way to a generalized disregard for all human existence outside the narrow area of their immediate personal concern. Their delinquent behavior tends to become patterned to such an extent that the individual ceases to be felt, as it were, in his actions.

The wayward child, on the other hand, who is characterized by his "non-egoity" and by his lack of neurotic involvements and defenses, may, under the influence of adolescent drive-increases, glide into a more active form of participation in delinquent activities; his waywardness will continue, at the same time, to account for his lack of inner tension and emotional involvement, for his group-intoxication and the extreme limitation of his time span. In other words, the wayward child, too, will find his place in the behavioral pattern of the "new type" of adolescent delinquency.

(f) With psychopathy

Should the "new type" perhaps be considered a specific form of dissocial behavior, closely related to, though not identical with, psychopathic conditions? We indeed find in both the same relational inability, the same deficiency in polarization (though not in differentiation), the same weakness of anxiety and inner tensions, of superego directions and guilt feelings, of neurotic defenses and symptoms, of time concepts and fantasy, the same emotional coldness and egocentricity. In both, parents (and adults in general) are not sufficiently meaningful representatives of the non-ego to become, as such, the object of either imitation or rejection, although in both any adult attempt to restrict them will be violently resisted. In both, we find absence of relatedness to the future, even of the adolescent form of playing with changing roles. In both, we find the same disruption of contact between consciousness and the unconscious. Affectionless sadism is equally characteristic of certain psychopaths and of those whom we include in the "new type" of adolescent delinquency. And yet, there exist also certain essential differences between the two patterns.

Whereas the psychopathic pattern of "fear-of-the-void-suppressed-through-aggressiveness" emerges already in the preconstitutional phase of the child's life, the adolescent patterns may be *prepared* during a long period of experiencing the parents as "remote", if not as absent, but are later nevertheless the result of pathogenic factors which operate in the post-oedipal periods of development.

While the adolescent delinquent tends, as we have said, to be group-intoxicated, the psychopath is not, though he may use a group, passively or actively, when it serves his incorporative tendencies. One hesitates to speak of such incorporative tendencies or of ego-inflation in the case of most adolescent delinquents who represent our "new type": it is precisely their dependence on the group which makes them appear *non*-inflated. Their specifically adolescent form of living with principles (that is, of transforming their own lawlessness into a universal law of human existence) also proves the *non*-inflational nature of their behavior pattern, in contrast to certain psychopaths who extend their ego by fanatically fighting for, or, better, by incorporating, a truth as their own personal property.

We would, of course, not be right, were we to conclude that the relative absence of ego-inflation in the "new type" of adolescent delinquency indicates an ability adequately to relate to each other experiences, that is, a normal life-tendency toward staticness. But it does prove, in any case, the absence of that basic condition of psychopathy which is predominance of expansion over staticness. *We believe that the delinquent pattern which we have discussed here is not identical with psychopathy.** But in the light of the many similarities between the two patterns it would seem justified to speak, in the case of the adolescent here discussed, of a *psychopathoid form of dissocial behavior.*

Not only when comparing the *symptoms* of each of the two patterns, but also when comparing the *causes* responsible for their emergence, we will find basic similarities between them (which justify the use of the related term "psychopathoid"). We have mentioned, in our analysis of psychopathic conditions, besides a constitutional predominance of the life tendency toward expansion (and a primary absence of anxiety in the rare cases of congenital psychopathy), a number of traumaticizing mother-child experiences in the earliest period of the child's development. These experiences lead to a secondary but nonetheless constitutional defectiveness in the growing child's ability to feel fear of ego loss (anxiety),

---

* The congenital type has the impersonal, almost machine-like moral indolence in common with many adolescent delinquents of our time, but he, too, knows no group-intoxication and is self-sufficient in the ego-inflational way of the psychopath. The second type, the brutally destructive psychopath, differs by the intentionality of his aggressions. The similarities between the adolescent delinquent and these, as well as the oscillating, the shallow-attachment or the *Hochstapler* types of psychopathy are even less essential than the similarities that exist between his dissociality and the egocentric type (see table after p. 101).

and the equivalent of this defectiveness is ego inflation. They account, in configuration with the type factor (extraversion-introversion), for the varieties of psychopathy which we have discussed in the first part of Chapter 3.

We maintain that the cultural factors which are characteristic of our technologic era* have a similar effect on the child's ability to feel anxiety as have the different forms of early experience of maternal deficiency. But while the latter will produce psychopathic reaction patterns only when operating on a child with a structural predominance of expansion over staticness, the former are likely to produce psychopathoid behavior patterns, at a later stage of development, *irrespective* of structural tendencies and dispositions. On the other hand, their pathogenic effect will always remain dependent on continued environmental support and reinforcement and will never become structurized to the same extent as earliest traumatization will be, when it leads to the emergence of psychopathic constitution. It is in the nature of those cultural factors* that they operate on the child in *later* stages of his development only. As a result, factual absence of anxiety rather than structural inability to feel anxiety is characteristic of the psychopathoid form of adolescent delinquency.

But even if the behavior pathology described here as a "new type" of adolescent delinquency is not identical with psychopathy, it may well be that there can be found among its representatives, everywhere, a number of genuine psychopaths of the second (the brutally aggressive), the third (the egocentrically incorporative) and the fourth (the oscillating) types (see pp. 104 ff.). We tend indeed to believe, although we must admit that we are not yet in a position to base our belief on proven facts and figures, that the number of true psychopaths in any group of adolescent delinquents today is relatively greater than it used to be in previous generations.

This would mean that the cultural factors which we have analyzed as being responsible for the emergence of our "new type" are conducive not only to a transformation of other abnormal behavior patterns into psychopathoid patterns, but also to the crystallization of psychopathic constitutions in the earliest years of not a few normally born individuals.

Feelings of being rejected, of being left alone or of being treated as a nonentity are liable to operate as pathogenic factors in the beginning of a child's development, when his parents' attitude toward life is determined by such (cultural) factors as : de-individualization of responsibility and of value-orientation, coexistence of weak intentionality toward their

---

* Deindividualization of responsibility, orientation toward the average and toward the group, decrease of inner tension, expectation of universal chaos, parental disintegration, contrast between family and societal ideals.

individual future and expectation of universal destruction, contradictions between the norms of family and of society. Under such conditions, many a child is likely to experience his mother as an impersonally dim image, unsuited to his primary needs for staticness. He will consequently remain in an existential vacuum, devoid of polar relationships, a vacuum which can be filled only if the emerging ego incorporates everything non-ego. Under different cultural conditions, that is, under conditions of strongly personal relationships between the child and his parental environment, he may grow up to become a normal or a disturbed child, according to the total configuration of causal determinants in his life, but not a psychopath.

11. Clinical Composition of the Adolescent Gang

Much has been said in defense of the adolescent delinquent of our times. Thus, Matza (73) objects to all those theories that fail to take cognizance of the fact that 60–85% of all juvenile delinquents do not become adult criminals. The delinquent, he says, operates on a delinquent and an adaptive level simultaneously. A negative social environment, the "subculture of delinquency", may be conducive to the emergence of asocial or antisocial behavior, but we should not overlook the non-delinquent aspects of this subculture. Nor should we seek purely deterministic answers to the question of what causes delinquency, since illegal behavior does not exclude conventional behavior, and radicality often co-exists with attempts at moral apology.* Gliding into delinquent activities, says Matza, is at least as important a cause of juvenile delinquency as are those many factors of individual or of social pathology which, as a rule, are held responsible for this kind of deviant behavior.

There is, however, yet another conclusion to be drawn from the "drift" theory. Matza refers to the so-called "ordinary" delinquent only. This means that he excludes all "compulsive" types, whether they are of an organic, a neurotic, a psychopathic variety. The same applies to all other sociological theories. But since these varieties *do* exist, they can be found in any chance group of delinquents, particularly in the adolescent age group.

We accept the claim that the socio-cultural factors analyzed in the present chapter or the individual factors analyzed before, are not in themselves sufficient to account for the emergence of delinquent behavior.

---

* Psychoanalysts could, of course, counter this argument as they do, for instance, with the help of a theory of periodical change between gratification of instinctual and of superego demands (see pp. 106).

In fact, such a claim is a logical consequence of the configurational approach to the problems of causation in any field of psychopathology (see the chapter on etiology in the author's study *The Roots of the Ego*). We have in mind first and foremost the law according to which every behavioral outcome of a causal equation operates as an additional cause of the behavior in question, in our case, the asocial or antisocial conduct of adolescent delinquents.

In the present context, the question should be formulated differently : What is the impact of the presence of different types of delinquents in any chance group of adolescents on the behavior of each of its members?

At the end of Chapter 1 (on classification) we summarized the asocial and antisocial varieties of juvenile delinquency as follows : Asocial behavior may be of the waywardness, the drifting or the organic drivenness types. Antisocial behavior may be the result of constitutionally expansive or paranoid aggressiveness, of primary aggressiveness or primary behavior disorder, of unconscious guilt feelings or other neurotic needs. Not all of these varieties are equally frequent in each social class. The latter also produces certain variations of the basic pathologies. But all varieties may be represented in any group of adolescent delinquents. What, then, is their psychodynamic interaction?

Another question that may be raised here refers to the non-delinquent, though asocial, elements in the behavior of present-day Beatniks or Hippies. Here, too, many observers claim that these adolescents should not be identified with delinquents. According to the Dutch writer Buikhuisen (12), this form of asocial behavior does not reflect deep-rooted conflicts or frustrations but simply reflects modern society's failure to give its adolescents meaningful interests. They are far from being delinquents, says Mulock Hower (56), and they easily respond to adequate helping programs. They may be critical of adult values, adds G. Mik (56); their pseudo-manliness combined with their loud exhibitionist rejection of all socially accepted norms may bring them near to truly delinquent activities. But what makes them into delinquents is invariably some early pathology and *not* their adolescent groupism : their loosely knit groups may or may not turn into truly organized gangs of violence.

The two questions we have raised here are closely connected with each other. It is, indeed, the pathological "pre-history" of each individual member of an adolescent gang that accounts for the specific psychodynamic interaction between their different needs and between their different patterns of behavior. At the same time, it is through this interaction, and *not* only on the basis of the individual's pathology, that the adolescent group receives its dangerously delinquent character. When we speak of the "new type" of adolescent delinquency, we must not identify it with the case history of each individual. This history reaches from early childhood experience to the present; it determines the individual's development with or without the causal "co-operation" of what might be but a passing episode of participation in the delinquent activities called the "new type".

In brief : what we have said in this paragraph of the present chapter about the "new type" of adolescent delinquency

a) is the outcome of those socio-cultural factors we have tried to analyze, modified by the interaction of individual pathologies;

b) is not identical with the deviant behavior of the much spoken about Teddy Boys, Beatniks, or Hippies (and their often changing variations); these may glide into truly delinquent patterns, under the influence of both, their own pathological "prehistory" and their mutual response to each other's needs and, more or less crystallized, behavior patterns.

There can be found in every adolescent group young people for whom it is more important to raise non-conformity to the level of a principle of human existence than to derive immediate satisfaction from their conduct. Their strange mixture of toughness and infantility loses its typically *adolescent tension* character under the impact of an all-pervading awareness of living in a value vacuum.

Many of them come from low socio-economic strata. But they do *not* display those signs of dependence on the area of the known or those tendencies to imitate (and radicalize) their elders' dissocial behavior, which usually characterize the lower-class adolescent's delinquency. It is probably due to the fact that the tensionless climate of emptiness not only offers equal chances of satisfaction to sons of all classes but also eliminates class-conditioned differences of behavior :

The *lower-class* adolescent loses his orientation toward adult behavior, so characteristic of growing up under conditions of externalization. The *middle-class* adolescent gives up his tendency to "experiment with principles". The *higher-class* adolescent—to the extent that he will join an adolescent gang—brings with him, strangely enough, a factor of disturbance : he is too cold, too remote from every form of group-addiction, to be acceptable, for any length of time. He remains an outsider, unless he succeeds in cutting all ties with his social past.

A wayward child may grow up under the influence of his unstructured life on the streets to become a member of an adolescent gang. It would seem that he will then be ideally suited for any role characterized by unruliness, passive drifting, responding to chance stimuli. But among more actively delinquent adolescents he rather runs the risk of becoming an easily exploited tool in their hands. In this respect, his role does not differ greatly from that of the *feebleminded* drifter with his automatic reactivity. Since we do *not* have in mind here "retreatists" of the Beatnik type, but, rather, the gang of aggressive adolescents, we understand why they have little use for the unstructured behavior of wayward, feeble-minded (and still less of brain-damaged) individuals. Their sole place in such gangs is that of victims, of tools or of easily managed followers who "do not count".

Neurotic delinquents, on the other hand, are liable to disturb the group through their irrational complexes, through their inability to account for unconsciously motivated actions. Though they may, for some reason, be capable of assuming leadership roles, particularly when it comes to the perpetration of viciously sadistic aggression, they use the group even when they lead it, and the others feel and resent it.

Not so the youngsters in whom *primary aggressiveness* or *primary behavior disorders* had been at the root of their delinquent career. When they join an adolescent gang they have no difficulty in translating their "hate" into a philosophy and practice of generalized destructiveness. Usually, they dislike the neurotic delinquents and compete with them—successfully—for leadership positions. Their aggressive behavior is in any case more convincing than that of guilt offenders or otherwise neurotically motivated delinquents.

A few words may be added on the interaction of the feebleminded and the psychopathic varieties of *expansive and of paranoid aggressiveness*, as described in Chapter 5, with all the pathologies mentioned before. It has often been said that many of the aggressive offences committed by adolescent gangs are so utterly incomprehensible in their viciousness that no psychodynamic interpretation could do justice to them. We have discussed here, in some detail, in which respect our "new type" of adolescent delinquency should nevertheless *not* be interpreted as psycho-pathic, and why it is best classified as "psychopathoid" (see pp. 206 ff.). However, this classification refers to the phenomenon in its generality only, it refers to those members of the adolescent gang only who are not clearly diagnosed differently, as wayward, as drifting, as driven, as neurotic, or as primarily aggressive.

How is the pathological behavior of each of these individual members of the adolescent gang affected by the psychopathoid pattern of the "new type" of delinquency?

It is the pattern of relative weakness of anxiety, guilt and inner tensions, relative absence of contact with the unconscious and absolute lack of concern for the human environment, combined with group intoxication, that is liable to modify the behavior of the individual gang member with a background and past of primary aggressiveness, of waywardness or of neurotic delinquency :

Aggressiveness will then be more radical, on the one hand, less intentional on the other, than in the "original version" of the oedipal type. When group-intoxication determines the adolescent's actions, in an almost compulsive way, *waywardness* can never be as naive as it is in its "original" form. And the lack of contact with the unconscious, the lack of guilt and inner tension transform the *neurotic delinquent* into a near-psychopath : guilt is then replaced by an almost conscious confrontation with oedipal resentments and with the aggressive feelings resulting from them, fears and fantasies then make room for loud demonstrations of independence—within groups.

CHAPTER SEVEN

Cases

CASE ONE (Expansive Aggressiveness of the Psychopathic Variety)

ABE WAS BORN shortly before the outbreak of World War Two. His mother was a very attractive young woman who had been spoiled all her life. At the age of 18, she had married a man of weak character, 8 years her senior, only son of an extremely wealthy old man whose wife had died shortly before. She despised her husband from the start and openly blamed him for the fact that his father did not die quickly enough to leave him, or rather her, his fortune.

Already while on their honeymoon journey, she had her first extra-marital affair and continued to have lovers one after the other. She not only did nothing to conceal these affairs from her husband but even forced him to know all about them and laughed at his infatuation with her which prevented him from divorcing her.

When she became pregnant after five years of marriage, she was furious. She tried abortion, but something went wrong, and she gave birth to a son who, she maintained, was not her husband's child. Complications necessitated surgical interventions shortly afterwards, as the result of which she remained physically handicapped.

She rejected the boy from the first day of his life on, although he was a beautiful baby, outgoing, friendly, intelligent. She entrusted him to nurses, one after the other, while she went to spas and divided her time from now on between her love affairs and her doctors.

At the age of four months, the baby developed intestinal disorders, owing to wrong food he was given. Whenever his mother came near him, he screamed violently, while he was quiet and friendly with his father. When he was slightly over one year of age, the family had to flee Paris, which was then about to be captured by the Germans. On route, the father was killed, and the mother moved with the infant to the United States.

By that time, it had already become obvious that the child's behavior was abnormal. With eight months he showed extreme obstinacy and demandingness. At ten months he once bit and injured a nurse who had dared to slap him when he screamed. He was strangely unconcerned

217

with his environment, but in a destructive rather than in an autistic way. The mother continued to hate him as the cause of her illness. One of her many perversions was to have sexual intercourse with one of her ever-changing companions when she knew that the child was about and could witness the act.

Bowel training was easy. He was at that time under the control of a very domineering nurse. But while he seemed to yield to her forcefulness, he remained demanding as before, exploited all in his entourage. He did not show any reaction to punishment whenever it was inflicted. His aloofness irritated and even frightened those who came in contact with him.

At the age of $3\frac{1}{2}$ years, he was placed in a kindergarten, but his behavior there was unbearable: he tyrannized the other children, led them into mischief, while he himself remained at the periphery, denied his guilt, even when it could be proven to him. It was therefore decided to expel him. A private nurse was engaged, a student at one of the progressive training institutes. In the end, it was he who, at the age of six, with the help of one of his mother's lovers, introduced the nurse into the perversions of the family.

He ran away frequently, and when he was found and arrested he told a story about his family which was not only consistent in all its details but could also be verified, and yet was one web of lies. His mother never went out of her way to bring him back. At school, he proved to be a highly intelligent though rather erratic student. Intelligence tests showed an IQ of 170 at the age of 7, of 175 at the age of 11, in spite of some partial failures (e.g. information). His teachers thought, or rather took it for granted, that he knew all the answers, although he did not always care, so they said, to give them. They were right: the boy himself admitted, later, that he enjoyed making "them" (the adults) believe that he was not what they thought he was. He did not care *appearing* as less intelligent, as long as he could prove to himself that "they" were stupid enough to accept what he offered them.

In his contact with other children he lacked every consistent interest. He would tyrannize or exploit them one day, only to show them complete indolence the next day. Sometimes he would astonish them by the loving interest he seemed to take in one of them and by the depth of his human understanding. But this, too, was for him a kind of role playing only, meant to satisfy his conscious attempts to evade identification, as it were.

The only area in which he was self-identical was that of his sex activities. From early childhood on through the latency period, into adolescence, he displayed an almost unsatiable desire for sexual contacts of an ever increasingly vicious character. Sadistic and exhibitionist tendencies were much in evidence. His objects included children, girls, women. At one time, he even used his own mother, while she was under the influence of a strong drug.

Whenever he was in need of a certain object he took it or the money needed for purchasing it, as if this was the most natural thing to do. He had always a convincing story ready to disentangle himself or understood how to draw suspicion on someone else, who was then blamed or even punished for what he had done.

At the age of 15, he was arrested for the first time, on charges of rape and theft. He was acquitted of the first charge after he had convinced the court that the young woman in question had actually seduced him. The theft, on the other hand, was so irrational and so inexplicable that the court decided to have him examined by a psychiatrist. The latter tried to construct a connection between the boy's antisocial behavior and his mother's hatred, but had to admit that there were no unconscious elements in his relationships with the mother; nor did he show any signs of anxiety or inner tension. Hence, the diagnosis suggested by the psychiatrist, somewhat reluctantly, was one of *psychopathy*.

The boy's entire life story seems to support such a diagnosis. His perversions and aggressions, his tendency to master and to tyrannize (or, at best, to exploit) his environment could perhaps also be interpreted as indication of primary aggressiveness. But the absence of all signs of anxiety, the extreme degree of ego-emphasis, the complete lack of concern for his human environment—to the exclusion of all defensive intentions— are counterindications of any diagnosis other than psychopathy.

Of the boy's subsequent development, it may be of interest to mention the following facts: the mother refused to pay for his maintenance in a private institution. The court therefore committed the boy to a reformatory school, from which he escaped very soon. He managed, with the help of adult friends (including a well-known actress with excellent "connections"), to leave the country and to settle elsewhere. There, already at the age of 16, he established himself as a successful entrepreneur of vice. He understood how to "catch" men and women of important social standing in the web of his affairs, until he was practically invulnerable and enjoyed almost complete police protection.

CASE TWO (Expansive Aggressiveness of the Feebleminded Variety)

BENY could be called the feebleminded counterpart of Abe. He was the third child of intellectual middle-class people, brother of an 8-year-old boy and a 4-year-old girl, both well developed intellectually and well adapted socially.

The birth process was easy. Soon afterwards, however, the infant showed signs of hypermotility which seemed unusual. The father, himself a physician, had the infant thoroughly examined, but all findings were inconclusive. There were, in any case, no signs of measurable cerebral disorders.

The years that followed were full of distress for the parents and the two older siblings. Beny's frequent screaming attacks and his fidgetiness understandably caused tension to all members of the family. He was slow in learning bowel control, was a great eater, generally destructive. The favored objects of his aggressiveness were his mother and his sister.

In the light of these facts, it seemed justified to have the child removed from the family as quickly as possible. The first attempt was made when he was 4 years of age. He was placed in an institution for brain-injured children (for lack of a more suitable place). But after a short time he was sent back, because the staff felt unable to cope with his vicious attacks. Every attempt, on the part of the environment, to limit him aroused immediate outbreaks of fury and destruction.

When he was returned, it was decided to subject him to pharmaco-therapeutic treatment, in spite of the inconclusive findings of repeated neurological examinations.

His reactions were not uniform: one day he would display signs of extreme apathy and drowsiness, would perhaps whimper for hours, like an abandoned kitten, without any obvious reason, and his "depression" would often be accompanied by temporary regressions into bowel incontinence. On the next following day he would behave as aggressively as ever before, the only difference being that he was now quickly and easily exhausted and would fall into a stupor-like sleep from which he awoke 12 to 15 hours later.

He did not react to the special school to which he was sent at the age of 6 years. His extreme unrest and hypermotility did not allow him to concentrate even on simple manual training activities. On the other hand, he reacted violently against any form of recognition which another child might be given. His primitive jealousy expressed itself again in aggressive disruptions of the class activities.

He played truant more often than he would attend school, and his parents were helpless. When on the street, he tried to ingratiate himself to other children, either by playing the clown or by taking orders from them.

Arrests led to the boy being placed in reformatory schools, from which he would invariably run away. At the age of 10 he was used sexually by an older boy, as feebleminded as he. When he tried to apply this newly acquired experience to a younger child, he was caught and brought before the court, for the tenth time. The police reported that he was known to have committed innumerable thefts, but that he was no longer brought to trial, since no school or institution was capable of keeping him for any length of time. It was decided to have him declared "morally insane" so that he could be sent to a hospital for severely disturbed (psychotic, epileptic or otherwise brain-injured) children.

There he was kept for four years, during which period he did not run away even once. He liked being considered insane, regarded his new role of "patient" as one of higher status. He had contact with the most seriously disturbed patients only, whom he treated with a kind of absurd benevolence. When they did not react, it would make no difference to him. With the female nurses he was unable to get along : with them he was aggressive as ever and was caught several times in acts of stealing from them—in a rather clumsy way—or of damaging their clothes or property.

Once he attacked a nurse sexually, but was caught and overpowered. Since then, he did not cease to boast about his sexual prowess and his successes with the nurses. He was completely unaware of the fact that no one took him seriously. This typically feebleminded tendency to substitute an unrealistic, inflated self-perception for reality could also be interpreted as an indication of psychopathy. The fact comes to show that the inclusion of both, the psychopathic and the feebleminded representatives of aggressiveness in one clinical group, that of "expansiveness", is indeed justified.*

Contact with his parents and siblings was almost non-existent. When they visited him, he not only showed no signs of affection for them but hardly seemed to notice them. A psychoanalytically oriented psychiatrist who worked in the institution had tried to construe a psychodynamic connection between the boy's ever-recurring aggressions against the women in his environment and his early experience of maternal rejection. He knew, of course, that a feebleminded child's lack of structure was liable to express itself in the inconsistency of his relational reactions. But he nevertheless expected some kind of inner logic, as if to prove through it the universal validity of psychoanalytic laws of development. He

---

* Needless to add that the degree of delinquent efficiency obviously depends on the level of intelligence. Not every psychopath is intelligent, and it is not his psychopathy as such that guarantees his delinquent success, as we can see when we compare with each other psychopathic delinquents of different intelligence levels.

thought an encounter with the mother might evoke childhood patterns of negative feelings and reactions, and was somehow disappointed when he saw the boy's utter indolence towards her, as if she were a complete stranger. It was clear that he reserved his reactions to those he happened to know within the narrow boundaries of a present beyond which nothing human existed.

At the age of 16, he was transferred to a vocational training center for feebleminded boys, and pharmacotherapy was resumed. By that time he had grown into a stout fellow, bigger than his fellow mates, the strongest in his age group. He ran away frequently, but always returned on his own accord.

At the age of 17–18 he joined an adolescent gang in the neighboring city and became one of its most active members, although he was utterly undisciplined and uncontrollable. He was frequently exploited when the gang decided on an exceptionally audacious and dangerous "job", and he proved his usefulness particularly when the execution of his "assignment" offered a chance to satisfy his sadistic drives.

Once he took part in the destruction of a drugstore, after its Jewish owner had refused to admit some of the boys, who were known for their obscene antisemitic slogans. He was caught while he was submitting the man to vile tortures of a clearly sexual nature. He was sentenced to a prolonged prison sentence.

CASE THREE (Paranoid Aggressiveness of the Psychopathic Variety)

JERRY was born four years after his brother. He was sensitive and physically weak from birth on. While the older brother was the father's son, Jerry was being spoiled by the mother who somehow felt responsible for his weak constitution.

The parents did not get along well with each other : the husband who worked as a technician in a large factory was known there as reliable though devoid of initiative or imagination. He was a withdrawn man, showed little interest in his family and had one hobby only—to go away on long excursions, all by himself. He was twenty-five years older than his wife, whom he had married when he was 45. She was an artist and had been successful already at the art school. The husband did not take her ambitions seriously, and she felt starved with him both emotionally and intellectually.

Shortly after Jerry was born, the woman met a young artist who paid attention to her paintings, flattered her and evoked in her new dreams of a creative career. She fell in love with him and left the family abruptly

when the infant was in his fifth month. She did not care about the older
boy but wanted to take the baby with her. This was interdicted by the
court, although the father would not have objected too strongly. She then
left the country with her lover (whom she never married).

The father welcomed this development since he had discovered a long
time ago that he disliked his wife. He left the upbringing of his children
in the hands of an unmarried sister, not much younger than he, a strict,
compulsive, dried-up woman who looked older than her age. The interest
he took in his sons was from now on still more sporadic than before. Even
his first-born, whom he had always preferred and who was well-behaved
enough to be acceptable in the eyes of his aunt, did not elicit in him any
paternal feelings.

Jerry rejected the aunt from the first moment she had appeared in the
family. The more he grew up the more aggressive he became, against
the father's sister as well as against his brother. He used to mishandle and
destroy the brother's toys whenever he could lay hands on them. But there
was no personal envy or rivalry in his acts of aggression : the brother was
just a stranger to him and he behaved towards him as towards everyone
else. There was nothing provocative in his behavior, nothing meant to
"try out" his environment, nothing that could have been diagnosed as
indicative of "primary behavior disorders" : he was certain that no one
accepted him, and he accepted no one.

Bowel training was as quick as it was effective, apparently not only
because of the aunt's compulsive methods; the child brought with him
to this phase an aggressive tendency to refuse "giving away part of himself" (to use terms of a psychoanalytical interpretation contained in the
boy's later court-file). This led to the emergence of constipatory habits.
All sorts of radical treatment, in which the aunt was an expert, remained
to no avail, and typically anal handicaps accompanied from now on the
child in each of his phases of development.

When the boy was sent to a kindergarten he was destructive from the
first day on. At the beginning he used to complain, again and again,
about some injustice of which he claimed he had fallen victim. But he
never even waited for the teacher to "investigate"; his reactions were as
immediate as they were exaggerated and destructive. He was frequently
punished by being isolated or sent home. There, the aunt added punishment by refusing him food or by chaining and beating him.

His reactions to these cruel punishments clearly indicated the psychopathic nature of his behavior disorder; he never cried; he tried to enact
with younger children the punishment inflicted on him, as soon as he was
set free, and he told stories about cruel monsters, about man-eating

animals, about fires and floods that destroyed whole towns, and all without any apparent signs of either fear or rage : he spoke about it in a matter-of-fact tone of someone who reported a story, and he usually said that someone had told him what he repeated or, later, that he had read the story.

Serious acts of delinquency made their appearance when he was six years old. Many times neighbors complained about his cruelty or his acts of wanton destruction of property. When he was caught, he had always a story ready about how he had been injured or offended by someone whom he simply "had to punish".

In contrast to Abe whom we described in the first case story, Jerry never cared about leadership roles. It would be wrong to hold the intelligence factor responsible, since he was intelligent enough to obtain a verbal IQ of 125, but he was a typical introvert, too much involved in his fantasies about the world's cruelty and injustice or in his constant attempts to act on behalf of this aggressive world, as it were, and to translate his fantasies into imitative acts of cruelty.

Until he reached the age of 11, his aunt refused to have him sent to an institution for maladjusted children, as it was suggested to her several times. She felt it her duty, so she said, to deal with him alone, particularly since her brother, the boy's father, had died in the meantime. Her own sadistic needs apparently found satisfaction in the rigid methods of brutal punishment which she applied in order "to save the boy".

It was at that time that Jerry joined a street gang of considerably older boys. However, unlike the feebleminded Beny (see case story 2), who as an adolescent enjoyed being exploited by others, Jerry knew already at this young age how to imitate the most daring adolescents whose acts he had witnessed, and how to gain their respect. But even this success did not let him become a real gang member. His introvert paranoid tendencies made it impossible for him to accept orders. When he once noticed that some of the adolescents laughed at the "little devil" and made derogatory remarks about him, he took his revenge by informing the police, and the older boys were arrested.

Since then, however, he was no longer able to evade arrest himself, and he was sent to an institution by order of the court. His mother came to "rescue" him but he refused to go with her. He did not show any feeling towards her—much to the delight of the old aunt.

From now on, he stayed in institutions for most of his time. To the surprise of the teachers and the psychologists, he showed excellent progress in his class studies, particularly in natural sciences (though for a limited period of time only). He remained completely unattached to the boys and spent his free time on inventing tools of destruction. (Which were, of course, much too primitive to be taken seriously.)

At the age of 17 he became a Beatnik, but as a "lonely wolf", shunning the company of others, sharing no interest in sex or, for that matter, in any of the other activities of the gang. But once he was nevertheless drawn into a drug orgy during which two girls used him sexually. His reaction was out of all proportion to the seriousness of what the girls had done : he had them sold to a white slave dealer, and in addition, informed the police about the gangs' secret drug channels. He was arrested together with the white slave man and was brought to court.

Because of his relatively young age, a probation officer was asked to investigate the case and to make recommendations. It was through the skill of this probation officer that the details of the boy's story became intelligible, in spite of the seeming incomprehensibility of some factors of his manifest behavior.

His last act of "revenge" in fact threw light on the psychodynamics of this case : the boy defined life as negation of life, humanity as negation of humanity. Instead of reacting with anxiety to the threat of ego-loss, he transformed this threat into threatening others. This transformation sometimes would take the form of revenge but there was less compensatory intention in his acts of seeming revenge than identification with the aggressor (in a more realistic and less defensive meaning of the term than in Freud's metapsychology).

CASE FOUR (Paranoid Aggressiveness of the Feebleminded Variety)

DAVE, like Beny, was committed to an insane asylum, though only when he was 18 years of age. The diagnosis was "feeblemindedness with strong paranoid tendencies". His father owned a small grocery. He was known to be a quiet, shy and submissive person while the mother was domineering, loud and aggressive in her relationships with everyone in the family and in the neighborhood. The family was of Irish descent, Catholic, classifiable as "lower middle class". Apart from Dave, there were eight children in the family, of which four were born before and four later. When reaching the age of 15, each of the children started to work and to support the family, some continuing their studies through evening courses. The wife's mother, an ailing woman, had been living with the family almost from the beginning and had helped take care of the children when they were young.

Six of the boys and girls offered no difficulties. One boy, three years older than Dave, had left the family at the age of 15 to join a circus troupe, after a series of arrests for minor offenses, mostly thefts and homosexual escapades. One of the younger sisters was a severe cerebral palsy case and had to be placed in an institution when she was a few years old.

Dave had been violently jealous of a brother immediately preceding him, and of the two youngest children, twins who were born late, when he was already 12.

He was in the habit of accusing his brother, who was an exceptionally intelligent child, of taking things from him when the opposite was true. He would maintain that the brother had beaten him when, in fact, he, Dave, had received punishment for having attacked the brother. When the latter entered school, Dave was found more than once destroying his brother's notebooks or papers. Later he used to tell "dirty stories" about him, while it was obvious that he actually described his own fantasies or actions with neighborhood girls (among whom he was famous for his obscenities and perversions already as a child of 8).

But whereas the boy's hatred of his brother could still be considered rational and comprehensible, no rational element whatsoever could be discovered in his wild rejection of the youngest twins. Again and again he was caught in acts of dangerous aggressions, and disaster was prevented at least on three occasions, solely through the timely intervention of others. His reactions to being caught were, on each of these three occasions, rage and violent protest against the injustice done to him by his parents. This *leitmotif* of revenge recurred in every phase of his development.

Dave committed more or less serious offenses against outsiders as well, always in revenge, as it were, for some injustice he felt he had suffered at the hands of his victims. His attempts to answer factual questions were always very clumsy. And yet, psychologists and psychiatrists often were puzzled by the strange appearance in this definitely feebleminded boy, of elaborate persecution ideas, supported by obstinate rationalizations. The manner in which he tried to prove the injustice done to him by everyone and everything and in the way in which he tried to convince police or court representatives that his aggressions and destructions had been "his last choice", often deceived the observer, at least at superficial contact.

But an analysis of his offenses not only failed to reveal all traces of inner consistency and structure but also, strangely enough, all ego involvement. Although he seemed so very clever with words of vindication, his acts of aggression were never more than quasi-automatic reactions to stimuli coming from nowhere and ending nowhere.

He could not be said to suffer from his ideas of being the victim of persecution. On the contrary : they gave him a feeling of importance, of being in the center. The very fact that he reacted without delay to any such "idea", as if it were a well-proven fact, aroused in him a strange *joie de vivre*, a feeling of potency. This contradiction between a feeling of potency and a self-perception as a persecuted victim, as an object of the world's hostility—did not disturb him at all. Logic was not meant for him.

Once, at the age of 14, he was brought before the juvenile court on a charge of causing another boy serious bodily harm (by hitting him over the head with a piece of wood that happened to be "at hand"). He was concerned with two aspects of the case only : he accused with loud utterances of moral indignation the evil nature of his victim (who, in fact, had deserved death !); and he paid careful attention to the prosecutor's description of the offense, correcting him here and there, when he forgot a detail, or when he failed to report every atrocity in his acts. He took pride in what he had done, in defense of his assaulted "ego", and did not care that he harmed his cause with every word he said.

He, too, joined a gang when he was 16 years old. Although he never agreed to observe any rule of discipline, it was his paranoid aggressiveness that made him useful, whenever the gang decided on, or glided into, committing a particularly vicious offense. But what distinguished him from most of the other members was his always proclaimed wish to relate to himself every act of assault in which the gang may have been engaged, to see in it another opportunity for revenge. It was due to this irrational need of his that he was once caught on the spot after all the others had managed to escape. When interrogated he claimed, though in a rather clumsy and unconvincing manner, that he had committed the offense alone.

It was on this occasion that he was committed to an insane asylum (at the age of 18). Young children were the victims of this last offense, it was therefore understandable that the psychiatrist whom the court had asked to examine the boy tried to construct some rational ties between the offense and his particularly violent rejection of the twin siblings (at that time 6 years old). Although he was fully aware of the irrationality of the offender's behavior, due to his feeblemindedness, the psychiatrist wrote in his report, it seemed as if "Dave tried to express a denial of birth and of life *per se*, through his hatred for the youngest in the family, hence also through his aggressive rejection of young children as such." The very fact of life being continued through birth threatened his existence and called for revenge.

The interpretation may not seem acceptable in this case where the object of analysis is a feebleminded boy, and psychodynamic interpretations may seem misplaced here. But since it is his paranoid tendency that calls for an attempt to make it comprehensible, the explanation is of interest: it may perhaps throw light on the meaning of paranoid tendencies in general, irrespective of the individual's level of intelligence.

CASE FIVE (Drifting Feebleminded of the Submissive Type)

The social workers and the probation officers who tried to do something for him, and always failed, saw in RAMI a typically wayward child. And since he was a charming boy with a friendly warm look in his great eyes, looking at everyone as if loving him, they tried again and again, and then blamed his low intelligence for their lack of success. But he was *not* a wayward child, as we shall try to show.

As an infant he grew up carefully guarded by his parents, who were well-off financially. The nurses whom they employed kept him clean and spoiled him. When he was five, one of them introduced him into sex practices, about which he then spoke so frankly that the parents were deeply shocked. But the boy did not show any signs of being traumatized. On the contrary, he tried to share his newly acquired experience with other girls and women, much to their bewilderment. After a while, this sex storm subsided, until much later when he fell into the hands of his older sister who had developed serious behavior disorders and was definitely nymphomanic.

The special school to which he was sent did not do him any good, although it was an expensive modern school equipped with lots of tools and teachers. But there were no complaints about his conduct. He never displayed any signs of affect or involvement. On the other hand, he was always ready to imitate someone's behavior, mostly some other child to whom he liked to attach himself and who could do with him whatever he wanted. But since in that school only few were of the aggressive types, nothing very serious happened during the boy's childhood.

Then events occurred in the family that changed the course of his life. The father died when the boy was 12. In reaction to being left alone, the mother, a weak, dependent, anxious woman, withdrew into a depressive mood and ceased to give the boy that care and those signs of tenderness to which he had become accustomed. It was pathetic to see his dog-like attempts to draw her attention to him, but all to no avail.

The older sister, then 17 years of age, took over the mother's function, as it were, but in a rather peculiar way : she treated him as her "pet", using him for her never abating erotic and sexual needs, either alone or in the company of her many friends of both sexes. The boy quickly developed under her "care" and became an attractive young man even before he had reached the age of 14.

One day, however, she left the family to go abroad, and Rami was left to his own resources. It was then that his delinquent career started. He easily attached himself to everyone who happened to be nice to him. He could not understand why he was sometimes accused of being disloyal to one of his protectors only because the latter's interests and values were incompatible with those of another one. He was naively proud of his sexual attractiveness, was exploited by prostitutes or homosexuals, but also took part in numerous property offenses.

He never acted on his own initiative, although it happened that, after obeying orders received from one of his "friends", he would repeat the act without being told to do so, only to prove his usefulness. It was on such occasions that he was easily caught by the police because he had overlooked a risk implied.

He quickly lost his charm and his attractiveness and became more and more isolated, drifting without purpose from one place to another. The only persons that would now accept him as a follower were vagabonds like him. The sporadicness and the superficiality of their attachment usually had a different meaning for them and for him : while it often reflected apathy and absence of emotional ability in his partners, it was, in him, a symptom of his typically feebleminded distractability.

To sum up : as a boy, his behavior was obviously *not* that of a wayward street urchin : he did not enjoy the occurrence character of a life with others in chance groups; nor did he participate in their unstructured play activities. He was content only when he had found someone whose behavior he could imitate, and whom he could serve, though his temporary master was often exchanged for another one, without any logic and without any signs of inner conflict or tension.

In adult life his tendency to follow the lead of others persisted even after he had lost his "usefulness" for them. We would, however, fail to understand the essentials of his behavior if we were to interpret his submissiveness as indication of masochistic tendencies : he never showed any proof that he enjoyed maltreatment or being a victim; on the contrary : by obeying or by what he meant to be imitating his "hero"—he felt strong and important.

CASE SIX (Drifting Feebleminded of the Apathetic Type)

In contrast to the foregoing case, lack of initiative was the central characteristic of JACK's personality. His mother died, as the result of a post-pueral infection, two days after his birth, while still in hospital. The infant was sent to a babies' home, pending arrangements to be made by the father. The two older children, aged 2 and 4, were taken care of by the mother's younger sister, whom the father intended to marry. In the end, however, this sister-in-law left the family for reasons of her own, the father married another woman, and the infant was returned home.

By that time, more than a year had passed during which Jack had developed into a typical "institution child". The fact that he had "chosen" apathy rather than shallow attachment as his pattern of reaction and behavior, was probably due to constitutional type conditions (introvert tendencies) rather than to his low level of intelligence (since other equally feebleminded children in institutions show different patterns of reaction).

His development, too, was determined by this type-conditioned apathy: he was slow in the acquisition of social habits and appeared much more retarded in his learning tasks than was to be expected in the light of his measurable intelligence quotient. On the other hand, however, it was his indolence that protected him, as it were, for a fairly long time, against the danger of becoming involved in serious mischief.

At the age of 11, he went through a period of rapid physical development and premature sexual maturation. It was probably due to the accompanying somatic tension process that he now started to react to negative environmental stimulations. But, again in contrast to the behavior of the previously mentioned feebleminded boy (Rami), there was something almost mechanical in his reactions: he would see an object that attracted him and would take it, but would almost immediately lose interest in it. Once, he was accused of indecent behavior with a girl of his age: he had lifted her skirt and tried to look at her genitals while, at the same time, masturbating. The girl seemed to be an unessential addition to the act.

It was decided to send him to a foster family in a village. Kind elderly people who had already successfully taken care of similar cases. There, in the quiet, primitive environment, he behaved very well indeed, doing what he was told to do in an impersonal, often absentminded way. He had never looked for people to get attached to them, to imitate them or to quarrel with them. He therefore did not miss the absence of such opportunities in his new surroundings. His face never showed any expression, neither of tender feelings nor of rage. He was empty.

When he was 16, the foster parents decided to join one of their grown-up children in another part of the country, and Jack had to be transferred to another family, since his father and stepmother refused to take him back. There ensued a period of unrest for the boy, filled with examinations, temporary placements and neglect. One day, he was forced into a fight with a group of boys who had for some time nagged him and were irritated by his initial lack of reaction. During that fight he seriously injured two of his opponents, one of whom died of the wounds received. When Jack was brought before the court he was unable to defend himself and was sentenced to prison. Only much later, one of the attackers who had quarreled with the gang revealed the truth.

When dismissed from prison Jack took to the streets and became a lonely vagabond. At the age of 25, looking much older than his age, he was detained for a while at a treatment and observation center for asocial delinquents (in one of the European countries). At that time, a comparative study was being conducted there, in which his case record was included. Of special interest in the present context are a number of cases diagnosed as psychopaths and neurotics.

We find there, among many others, three case summaries which are likely to throw light on the psychodynamics of drifting.

CASE SEVEN (Drifting Psychopath)

There is the story of a man aged 45 with an extensive court record. GEORGE had seen many lands, was a restless vagabond; but he never recalled anything essential, never more than some peripheral detail in which he had been involved. Distortion of facts came to him quite naturally, and he was not aware of the often absurd discrepancy between the facts and his own presentation of them.

He had spent time in many prisons, for drunkenness, disturbing the peace, molesting young girls and women, petty thefts. Whenever he was arrested, he felt the need of giving his onlookers a performance : he resisted the police, violently and obstinately, although he did not really mean it. Already in the police van, with his exhausted captors, he was quiet and seemingly affectless. But whenever he had an audience, he simply had to show off.

He was in many respects Jack's opposite : his face was seldom empty, on the contrary, it usually showed feeling, either of naive pride in his performance or of being offended. He preferred not to be alone, always looked for company but only to brag about his cleverness, without the slightest interest in his temporary companions. In fact, he could easily continue with his boastful monologues long after the other fellow had fallen asleep. Drifting from one place to another, into one offense after the other, was for him, strangely enough, proof of his identity, of being someone defineable.

His clearly psychopathic ego inflation to some extent concealed or even neutralized his introversion. But neither his histrionics nor his endless monologues were object-related. He "needed" his partners not to communicate with them but merely to play in their presence the role of an ego.

Few details only about his childhood are mentioned in his case file. He had been the eldest of five children, all presenting problems of one kind or another. The father, a sailor, did not take an active part in the children's upbringing, since he was mostly abroad. The mother, a passive, pale woman without initiative, was unable to do more than cook their food and wash their clothes.

As a child, George had frequently appeared before juvenile courts, had been placed on probation or sent to reformatory schools, but all had been to no avail. His verbosity, his vanity and his lack of concern for others are mentioned several times and in different context as characteristics allowing for a clear distinction between him and other delinquents with whom he appeared together before the court. It was mentioned repeatedly that he was "different from his typically wayward pals", since he was much more interested in showing off than in naively enjoying the many happenings in an unstructured street-life.

At one time, it was thought that he suffered from a severe character-neurosis, and that psychotherapy should be tried. This, however, quickly proved to be a mistake : the boy, instead of reacting to the therapist in a person-to-person relationship, preferred to copy some of the latter's expressions of speech and behavior in a rather ridiculous manner.

CASE EIGHT (Unstable Psychopath)

Another case was that of FRANK, aged 25, a drug addict, indolent and apathetic like Jack (see Case Six) and ego-related like George. He, too, could always be found in the company of others, but not in order to show off but in order to imitate them, in their speech and behavior, in their expressed ideas and biases. His imitations were, however, devoid of all intentionality and did not prove any kind of personal attachment.

He had grown up in an orphanage, where he had not caused much trouble. His teachers described him as "a quiet boy who, although of normal intelligence, displayed little, if any, initiative". He did not learn a trade and left the orphanage at the age of 16 to work as a farm hand and later became an unskilled laborer on road constructions or similar public work projects.

His career as an addict started by chance, when he was 18 years old and someone introduced him to a gang of narcotic peddlers. This was a new role for him, which he played with the exact words and gestures of the one who had introduced him to cocain. When asked to describe his experiences he would answer in stereotypes borrowed from a lecture he had heard by chance.

But with the same ease he would repeat the words, and even the manner of speech of the social worker who tried to help him, or, alternatively, of the physician who had treated him. While being completely unaware of the discrepancies between the various roles he played in automatic reaction to changing environmental figures, he could convince those with whom he came in contact of being self-identical in his reactions, whatever they were.

When he was in need of money he would approach people known in the community for their religious or political or social ideology and orientation. He would present himself as a fellow of their ideas, sometimes on one and the same day. Usually he succeeded in convincing every one of them and managed to extract from them the money needed (though they represented perhaps the most extremely opposed trends of ideas). Although his imagination and intelligence operated only in reaction to some imitable stimulus, and never from within, as it were, these qualities were sufficiently well-developed in him to make his psychopathic "mirroring" effective.

(This, however, is not an essential condition of the presently discussed variety of drifting. Even a less intelligent and a less imaginative psychopath of this type would mirror the behavior of people in his environment, though he would, of course, be less successful. What characterizes this psychopath, irrespective of his level of functioning, is the fact that playing different roles in reaction to different chance stimulations from without does not only indicate instability—as it would in a non-psychopathic feebleminded person of the submissive type—but at the same time serves the purpose of proving his "egoity".)

CASE NINE (Neurotic Drifter)

The four "drifters" mentioned so far (Cases Five–Eight) have one characteristic in common in spite of the fundamental differences between the roots of their behavior disorders which lie in their feeblemindedness or in their psychopathic propensities. This characteristic is the absence of all unconscious conflicts, the absence of any "concealed level of meaning". The next case, on the other hand, clearly demonstrates patterns of neurotic unrest, of seeking something or someone unknown, undefined and undefineable, an unconscious intentionality.

SAM was a child born out of wedlock. His mother, an eighteen-year-old girl, physically much more developed than intellectually, immature and oversexed, with definitely hysterical traits, "decided" to bring up the boy alone, because she wished to prove her readiness for self-sacrifice, her goodness, her motherly feelings. The social worker, for whom it was not difficult to recognize the falsity of these professed motives, tried in vain to dissuade her and to obtain her consent to have the infant handed over to a pair of good and suitable adoptive parents.

The mother asked for help: she felt that she was entitled to public support since she had to work (as a servant in a small restaurant of doubtful repute) to support herself. A family was found who took care of the baby during day hours and the mother took it home in the afternoon, unless her "professional duties" prevented her from doing so. Thus, a strong element of instrumentalistic thinking determined her attitude, while the infant was exposed to an equally strong climate of uncertainty.

This lasted for one year. Then, the mother fell in love with a man who promised to marry her if she would give up the child. She agreed to having the child sent to a foster family but again opposed adoption. This was a kind of compromise between her wish to get her man and her tendency to maintain at least the illusion of being a mother.

From then on, the child grew up in an atmosphere of provisionality. He was sent from one foster family to another, according to the demands of the placement agency (which was not one of the best in the country). At first, the mother continued to visit him from time to time. But soon her visits became less frequent and less regular, until she ceased to see the boy when he was two years of age.

The child who was of good intelligence and took a vivid interest in all that happened around him, had already before shown many signs of unrest, feeding problems and sleep disorders. To the disappearance of his mother he reacted with a period of withdrawal into depressive moods accompanied by an intensification of his previous difficulties. After these moods subsided, he displayed strong fears, particularly at night. He woke up screaming and trembling, unable to account for his fears. This pathology persisted throughout his early years.

A second deviation that could be noted in these early years was his readiness to regress to earlier stages of his development, whenever he had to face a change, a transition to a new educational environment, a change in the composition of his foster family, a change in his physical condition (during or after an illness, for instance). This was all the more disquieting, as he seemed to pass smoothly and easily from one phase to the other, in motor functions, in bowel training, in speech, in general intelligence. And although he came out of temporary regressions with relative ease, it seemed that he lost part of his vitality and initiative after each of them.

During his kindergarten and school years (from 4 to 12) he lived with one foster family. His school records were satisfactory, though several of his teachers remarked that he tended to withdraw from time to time, and rather frequently, into states of day-dreaming. He had no friends but would passively follow any group of boys led by someone of authoritative character; and yet, he never showed much personal involvement in the group's activities. Once inside "the stream", he would do what he was told to do, almost automatically and certainly without any sign of emotional identification.

A significant change in his conduct and personality could be observed when he was transferred from his foster parents, to whom he had become attached, to a boarding school where he was supposed to remain until the completion of his secondary school program. According to the psychologists' reports, this change was due both to the somatic conditions of his age and to his separation from the foster family.

One of the first symptoms of his pathology was a fugue which lasted a fortnight. He was found in a forest, in a state of utter exhaustion and abandonment. He was unable to account for what he had done or to remember where he had been. His ability to concentrate on school studies decreased from week to week and his sleep became increasingly irregular. He liked to go on long excursions alone from which he returned exhausted. He would obstinately refuse to tell his teachers where he had been, as if it were one of the most precious secrets which he had to guard. From time to time, and without any intelligible cause, he seemed to recover his full intellectual capacities and in a few days reached the top of his class, particularly in the science subjects.

When he was 15 years of age, the withdrawal symptoms in his incomprehensible behavior irritated and worried his teachers to such an extent that it was decided to have him psychoanalyzed. During his early sessions he reported an ever-recurring dream in which he saw himself in a dark cave or cellar, in a mountain village or a forest, desperately searching for a way out, while he could not find it. A young girl would appear somehow; she had no eyes, no ears, no nose, only a mouth. He put his fingers into that mouth asking for guidance. She would laugh at him hysterically, reject him and then dance with some beastly looking man. He knew they were both naked but could not describe their forms. Together they would disappear and he woke up, sweating, screaming or whining. After awakening he was absentminded for a whole day.

The analysis was successful insofar as it helped the boy become more and more *aware* of the central problem in his life, that of searching for his unknown parents, his origin, his identity; but it did *not* help him overcome his obsessional preoccupation with that quest. He was unable to take upon himself full responsibility for being an individual in his own rights, as it were, being a beginning and not a continuation. He suffered, because he had been thrown into the world unlovingly, had been abandoned and rejected.

The older he grew, the more he cultivated a conscious and well articulated philosophy of nihilism and of denying the objective value of social or intellectual achievement. He *decided* to adopt a "drifting" life-style and succeeded extremely well indeed in this respect : though he passed his matriculation examinations with excellent marks and was accepted at a well reputed university department of physics, he preferred joining a group of addicts, because, as he said, it made him free of all moral bounds, allowed him to live in accordance with the conditions of his existence.

But behind his cynical proclamation of nihilism were hidden fears of annihilation. Although analysis had helped him become aware of these fears, he remained unable to overcome them. His defence was cruelty, particularly in his relationships with women, many of whom felt attached to him, only to discover that he was impotent and that he rejected them.

Already before he had reached the age of 18, he was once brought before the court on a charge of assault : during a drug session he had forced a young girl into sexual intercourse with a number of men, had then beaten her so severely that she remained unconscious. While all others left, he remained with her alone for the rest of the night and, in the morning, informed the police.

The case clearly called for psychiatric examinations, which were ordered by the court. The psychiatrist's report contains, in addition to the obvious psychoanalytic statement about compulsive tendencies to punish the unknown mother, another hypothesis, which seems to contradict the first one : it says that the young man "preferred" perceiving himself as being worthless and guilty of his fate to being maltreated by fate and abandoned. He was nonetheless sentenced to imprisonment.

Of his later life nothing more is mentioned than that he became a restless vagabond who spoke very little and avoided the company of everyone.

CASE TEN (Primary Aggressiveness)

GIL was born in the middle of World War Two. His sisters were already 18 and 15 years old, and his parents did not really want another child. But, when he arrived, they tried their best to revive their parental past and to satisfy the infant's needs.

The father was a quiet, simpleminded and hard-working man, rather withdrawn. He had to be in his little shop from very early hours in the morning and often came home only late in the evening. His presence in the family was therefore practically unfelt. He never took an active part in the children's upbringing. But when a son arrived, he was proud of his "achievement" and considered it his duty to advise his wife on how to deal with him. He also had more time, much to his regret, to absent himself from the shop, since business was slacking, owing to war conditions.

The mother, who had never been in steady health and was a basically insecure woman, was now increasingly beset by fears. It was not easy for her to return to her functions as a mother, but she nevertheless took good care of the infant. She resented being considered inadequate by her husband or being in need of his guidance.

The result was an atmosphere of tension, in which the child was doomed to grow up. The only stabilizing factor was the older of the two sisters, who loved the baby and helped her mother in every possible way (in contrast to the younger sister who was full of resentment and insecurity).

When Gil was two years old, three things happened which changed the course of his life. The oldest sister married and moved with her husband to another town. The child reacted with withdrawal and aggressiveness at the same time. Shortly afterwards, the father's shop was bombed out, and from one day to the other he remained penniless. He had to look for a new job, and, when he found it, felt degraded, since he no longer was his own boss. The mother suffered a nervous breakdown and withdrew from her maternal functions.

Gil, who from the beginning had been a very active and vivid child, reacted to these changes with loud and almost furious demandingness. Whatever wish he expressed, had to be satisfied immediately; otherwise he would not only shout but also smash up any object in reach, would beat his mother or his sister when they came near him, would soil his bed and his pants (after he had already been clean for many months). To the father's spankings he would show contempt; he would never cry or weep, even not when he hurt himself in the course of one of his frequent tantrums. It was a vicious circle: the more violently he demanded attention or attacked objects and persons in his environment, the more frequently he was punished, particularly by the father whose aggressiveness increased in direct proportion to his failure as the family's provider.

Already at the age of four, he was all day long on the streets, where he played among the ruins of bombed-out houses. One of his favorite games was: demolishing whatever the war had not completely destroyed. Though he was not alone in these games during the period following the war, he was the most ingenious, the most thorough in his operations. Already at this early age, he played leadership roles, although he was not looking for them, actually did not care.

When he reached school age he had become so much identified with those roles (of being a leader in destruction) that he could not find his place in any other activity, least of all in the learning situations of the classroom. And this in spite of the fact that he was highly intelligent. Neither the father (who had in the meantime succeeded in establishing himself again as a small shopkeeper) nor his mother (whose health did not improve) nor his teachers could cope with him. He was addicted to destruction and not simply "beyond control".

It was considered advisable to place him out, with a foster family or in an institution. But no suitable place could be found, since both the court and the placement agency were reluctant to make arrangements which might be unfavorable to his intellectual development. Meanwhile, he managed to pass from grade to grade, although he attended school sporadically only, and never came into open conflict with the law, or, at least, never could be arrested and charged with one of the numerous offenses he had committed, offenses of aggressiveness rather than of theft.

His court record started when he was 11 years of age. He was arrested together with four other youngsters who were thought to be responsible for a large number of housebreakings in the neighborhood. In each of these cases, severe damage was caused to property but little more than cash was stolen. It was this feature that drew attention to Gil, whose destructive tendencies were well known. Nothing, however, could be proven against him. Although all the others were found guilty, only one said in court that Gil "had told them what to do". But since this was a rather dull boy and he contradicted himself frequently, his evidence had to be discounted.

From this time on, Gil was suspected of being responsible for the organization of innumerable offenses of all kinds, from theft to arson, from molesting girls to wanton destruction of property. But for a long time he managed to remain in the background and was never found guilty, although his close contacts with delinquent groups were well known.

His behavior at home strangely differed from that on the street. He feared and hated his father and tried to avoid him as much as possible. He was quiet and almost considerate with his ailing mother, and the older he grew, the more signs of tenderness he showed her, though reluctantly, as it were. With his sisters he had no contact whatsoever.

This—second—period in his delinquent career lasted for about two years. He was between 13 and 14 when he was for the first time found guilty of a (minor) offense (of trespassing). The prosecutor tried to prove the boy's dangerous character by referring to all the cases in which he had been suspected but had not been found guilty. Although the court did not accept the prosecutor's arguments, it was decided to have the boy placed on probation.

This was the beginning of a new period: from now on, he was limited in his freedom and he had to maintain his aggressiveness and his hate in secrecy, had to conceal it not only from the police but also from his probation officer, a friendly elderly man. For a long time he rejected all attempts on the part of the latter to befriend him, and continued in his destructive activities. Rejection, for him, was not a weapon of defense, of protecting himself against the "danger" of a more positive world conception (as it would have been in oedipal behavior disorders). He simply hated the old man's friendliness as part of the social reality which he rejected, and he hated society even more violently because it included friendliness.

What, strangely enough, brought about a change in his outlook was the probation officer's passiveness: he never did anything to save the boy from trouble, such as an occasional commitment to a reformatory school or even to a prison; he never helped the police, either, to bring him back when he had escaped (which happened frequently). But whenever Gil felt a need for communication, he was available, day or night, told him of his own hopes and disappointments, doubts and beliefs, desires and weaknesses. He accepted the boy's philosophy of hate as justified; but at the same time he tried to make him understand that just because it was understandable and justifiable, there was no need to "translate" his philosophy into principles of behavior by way of imitating, as it were, society's aggressive trends.

Intellectually at least, the boy began to realize that his attempts to master a hostile world by cultivating his own system of destructiveness were as futile as they were ridiculous. Practically it took a long time until he dared, for the first time in his life, to admit his being dependent. It happened when, at the age of 16, after more than two years of contact with his probation officer, he fell in love with a girl a little older than he. She was very aggressive sexually and used him as ruthlessly as he had before used others, but at the same time became closely attached to him (although she continued to lead her promiscuous life).

For a couple of years, they lived together as husband and wife. He worked as a waiter in a shabby restaurant of the port area, but since he was unable to support the two of them, he did not object to her occasional escapades as a prostitute. His aggressiveness which had not subsided and found frequent expressions in the organization of hostile acts against authorities, was strangely contrasted by his irrationally blind dependence on the woman whom he adored. This split in his emotional structure reflected a very early lack of ambivalence, dating back, as it did, to the pre-oedipal period in his development.

One day, when the girl left him in a fit of temper, without any plausible reason Gil committed suicide, at the age of 20.

References

1. Abrahamsen, D. *Crime and the Human Mind*. New York, Columbia University Press, 1944.
2. Aichhorn, A. *Wayward Youth*. London, Putnam & Company, Ltd., 1944.
3. Alexander, F. and Staub, H. *The Criminal, the Judge and the Public*. Glencoe, Ill., Free Press, 1956 (revised ed.).
4. Alexander, F. The Neurotic Character. In: *Int. J. Psychoanal.*, **11:** 292–313, 1930.
5. Alexander, F. and Healy, W. *Roots of Crime*. New York, A. A. Knopf, 1935.
6. Bender, L. Psychopathic Behavior Disorders in Children. In: Linder, R. M. and Seliger, R. V.: *Handbook of Correctional Psychology*. New York, The Philosophical Library, 1947.
7. Bender, L. Organic Brain Conditions Producing Behavior Disturbances. In: Lewis, N. D. C. and Pacella, B. L.: *Modern Trends in Child Psychiatry*. New York, International Universities Press, 1950.
8. Birnbaum, K. *Die Psychopathischen Verbrecher*. Leipzig, G. Thieme, 1926.
9. Bowlby, J. *Forty-Four Juvenile Thieves*. London, Ballière, Tindall & Cox, 1947.
10. Bowlby, J. *Maternal Care and Mental Health*. Geneva, World Health Organization, 1951.
11. Broadwin, J. T. Juvenile Delinquency. In: *Psychoanalysis Today*, ed. S. Lorand. London, G. Allen & Unwin, 1948.
12. Buikhuisen, W. Research on Teenage Riots. In: *Sociologia Neerlandica* IV (1), 1966/67.
13. Burt, C. *The Young Delinquent*. London, University of London Press, 1938.
14. Camus, A. *The Stranger*. New York, A. A. Knopf, 1946.
15. Cannon, W. *The Wisdom of the Body*. New York, W. W. Norton & Company, 1932.
16. Cleckley, H. *The Mask of Sanity*. St. Louis, C. V. Mosby Company, 1950.

17. Clinard, M. B.　*Sociology of Deviant Behavior*. New York, Rinehard & Company, Inc., 1959.

18. Cloward, R. A. and Ohlin, L. E.　*Delinquency and Opportunity*. Glencoe, Ill., The Free Press, 1961.

19. Cohen, A. V.　*Delinquent Boys*. Glencoe, Ill., The Free Press, 1955.

20. Eissler, K. R.　Some Problems of Delinquency. In : *Searchlights on Delinquency*, edited by K. R. Eissler. London, Image Publishing Company, Ltd., 1949.

21. Erikson, E. H.　*Childhood and Society*. London, Imago Publishing Company, Ltd., 1950.

22. Erikson, E. H.　Growth and Crises of the Healthy Personality. In : Kluckhohn, C. K. and Murray, H. A. : *Personality in Nature, Society and Culture*. New York, A. A. Knopf, 1953.

23. Fenichel, O.　*Perversionen, Psychosen und Charakterstoerungen*. Wien, Internationaler Psycholanalytischer Verlag, 1931.

24. Fenichel, O.　*The Psychoanalytical Theory of Neurosis*. London, Routledge & Kegan Paul, Ltd., 1947.

25. Fine, B.　*1,000,000 Delinquents*. London, Victor Gollancz, 1956.

26. Frankenstein, C.　*Die Fehlentwicklung der Sozialen Funktionen*. (In Hebrew Translation.) Jerusalem, Szold Foundation, 1947.

27. Frankenstein, C.　Structural Factors in the Anxiety of Children. *Acta Psychol.*, **12:** 201–325, 1956.

28. Frankenstein, C.　The Psychodynamics of Social Behavior Disturbances. In : *Arch. Criminal Psychodynamics*, **2:** 82, 1957.

29. Frankenstein, C.　The Structural Meaning of Aggressiveness. *Acta Psychol.*, **14:** 253–280, 1958.

30. Frankenstein, C.　Das Unbewusste und die Tiefenzone des Seelischen. In : *Zeitschrift fuer Diagnostische Psychologie und Persoenlichkeitsforschung*, **6:** 185–210, 1958.

31. Frankenstein, C.　*Die Äusserlichkeit des Lebensstils*. Amsterdam, J. M. Neulenhoff, 1959. *Psychodynamics of Externalization*. Baltimore, Williams & Wilkins, 1968.

32. Frankenstein, C.　*Psychopathy*. New York, Grune & Stratton, Inc., 1959.

33. Frankenstein, C.　*Persönlichkeitswandel durch Fürsorge, Erziehung und Therapie*. München, Urban & Schwarzenberg, 1964.

34. Frankenstein, C. *The Roots of the Ego*. Baltimore, Williams & Wilkins Company, 1966.

35. Frankenstein, C. *Psychodynamics of Externalization*. Baltimore, more, Williams & Wilkins, 1968.

36. Frankenstein, C. *Impaired Intelligence*. In print. See also: *Israel Ann. Psychiat.*, **2:** 209–227, 1964. *Acta Psychol.*, **24:** 167–204, 283–313, 1964–1965.

37. Freud, A. *Das Ich und die Abwehrmechanismen*. London, Imago, 1946.

38. Friedlander, K. *Psychoanalytical Approach to Juvenile Delinquency*. London, Routledge & Kegan Paul, Inc., 1947.

39. Fromm, E. Individual and Social Origins of Neurosis. In: Kluckhon, C. K. and Murray, H. A.: *Personality in Nature, Society and Culture*. New York, A. A. Knopf, 1953.

40. Fyvel, T. K. *The Insecure Offenders*. London, Chatto and Windus, 1961.

41. Galbraith, J. K. *The Affluent Society*. London, Hamish Hamilton, 1958.

42. Glueck, Sh. and Glueck, E. *500 Criminal Careers*. New York, A. A. Knopf, 1930.

43. Glueck, Sh. and Glueck, E. *Juvenile Delinquents Grown-up*. New York, The Commonwealth Fund, 1940.

44. Glueck, Sh. and Glueck, E. *Unraveling Juvenile Delinquency*. New York, The Commonwealth Fund, 1950.

45. Goldstein, K. *The Organism*. Boston, Beacon Press, 1963.

46. Green, A. W. The Middle-class Male Child and Neurosis. In: Wilson, L. and Kolb, W. L.: *Sociological Analysis*. New York, Harcourt, Brace Co., 1949.

47. Gurvitz, M. Developments in the Concept of Psychopathic Personality. *Brit. J. Delinquency*, **2:** 88–102, 1951.

48. Hall, M. B. *Psychiatric Examination of the Schoolchild*. London, Arnold, E., 1947.

49. Hamilton, G. *Psychotherapy in Child Guidance*. New York, Columbia University Press, 1947.

50. Healy, W. *The Individual Delinquent*. Boston, Little, 1915.

51. Healy, W. and Bronner, A. *New Light on Delinquency and its Treatment*. New Haven, Yale University Press, 1936.

52. Henderson, D. K. *Psychopathic States*. New York, Norton, 1947.

53. Hinsie, L. E. Schizophrenias. In : *Psychoanalysis Today*, edited by S. Lorand. London, G. Allen & Unwin, 1948.

54. Hoch, P. G. and Knight, R. P. *Epilepsy*. New York, Grune & Stratton, 1947. (Hill, Foxe, Piotrowski, Mittelman.)

55. Hoop, J. H. van der *Conscious Orientation*. London, Kegan Paul, 1939.

56. *International Child Welfare Revue*, Vol. XV (4), 1961, 291–271.

57. Isaacs, S. *Social Development in Young Children*. London, Routledge & Kegan Paul, Ltd., 1933.

58. James, W. *Varieties of Religious Experience*. New York, Longmans, 1902.

59. Jung, C. G. *Psychologische Typen*. Zürich, Rascher, 1930.

60. Jung, C. G. *Ueber die Psychologie des Unbewussten*. Zürich, Rascher, 1943.

61. Kahn, E. *Psychopathic Personalities*. New Haven, Yale University Press, 1931.

62. Kanner, L. *Child Psychiatry*. Springfield, Ill., Thomas, 1955.

63. Kanner, L. Problems of Nosology and Psychodynamics of Early Autism. In : *Am. J. Orthopsychiat.*, **19:** 416–426, 1949.

64. Karpman, B. Milestones in the Advancement of the Psychopathy of Delinquency and Crime. In : Lowry, L. G. : *Orthopsychiatry: Retrospect and Prospect*. New York, Am. Orthopsychiatric Association, 1948.

65. Karpman, B. Symposium on : A Differential Study of Psychopathic Behavior in Infants and Children. In : *Am. J. Orthopsychiat.*, **22:** 223–267, 1952.

66. Koch, J. L. *Die Psychopathischen Minderwertigkeiten*. Ravensburg, Maier, 1893.

67. Kraepelin, E. *Psychiatrische Klinik*. Leipzig, Barth, J. A., 1921.

68. Leites, N. *Trends in Affectlessness*. In : Kluckhohn, C. K. and Murray, H. A. : *Personality in Nature, Society and Culture*. New York, A. A. Knopf, 1953.

69. Lennox, W. G.   Seizure States. In : Hunt, J. McV. : *Personality and the Behavior Disorders*. New York, The Ronald Press Company, 1944.

70. Levy, D.   *Maternal Overprotection*. New York, Columbia University Press, 1943.

71. Levy, D.   The Deprived and the Indulged Form of Psychopathic Personalities. In : *Am. J. Orthopsychiat.*, **21:** 250, 1951.

72. Lowrey, L. G.   Delinquent and Criminal Personalities. In : Hunt, J. McV. : *Personality and the Behavior Disorders*. New York, The Ronald Press Co., 1944.

73. Matza, D.   *Delinquency and Drift*. New York, Wiley & Co., 1964.

74. Morris, A.   *Criminology*. New York, Longmans, Green, 1938.

75. Muchow, H. A.   *Sexualreife und Sozialstruktur*. München, 1961.

76. Neumann, E.   *The Origins of Consciousness*. London, Routledge, Kegan Paul, 1951.

77. Ophuijsen, J. H. W. van   Primary Conduct Disturbances. In : *Modern Trends in Child Psychiatry*, edited by Lewis, N. D. C., and Pacella, B. New York, International Universities Press, 1950.

78. Partridge, G. E.   Current Conceptions of Psychopathic Personality. In : *Am. J. Psychiatry*, 1930.

79. Pearson, G. N. J.   *Emotional Disorders in Children*. New York, W. W. Norton & Company, 1949.

80. Piaget, J.   *The Moral Judgement of the Child*. Glencoe, Ill., The Free Press, 1948.

81. Preu, P. W.   The Concept of Psychopathic Personality. In : Hunt, J. McV. : *Personality and the Behavior Disorders*. New York, The Ronald Press Company, 1944.

82. Rabinowitz, R.   Symposium on : The Psychopathic Delinquent Child. In : *Am. J. Orthopsychiat.*, **20:** 232–236, 1950.

83. Redl, F.   *Children Who Hate*. Glencoe, Ill., The Free Press, 1952.

84. Reich, W.   *Der Triebhafte Character*. Wien, Internationaler Psychoanalyticher Verlag, 1925.

85. Riesman, D.   *The Lonely Crowd*. New Haven, Yale University Press, 1950.

86. Riesman, D.   *Some Continuities and Discontinuities in the Education of Women*. The Third John Dewey Memorial Lecture. Bennington, Vermont, 1956.

87. Rothschild, F. S. *Das Ich und die Regulationen des Erlebnis-vorgangs*. Basel, S. Karger, 1950.

88. Schneider, K. *Klinische Psychopathologie*. Stuttgart, G. Thieme, 1950.

89. Stott, D. H. *Delinquency and Human Nature*. Dunfermline, Fife. Carnegie Trust Fund, 1950.

90. Strauss, A. A. and Lehtinen, L. E. *Psychopathology and Education of the Brain-injured Child*. New York, Grune & Stratton, Ltd., 1947.

91. Thrasher, F. M. *The Gang*. Chicago, The University of Chicago Press, 1927.

92. Wells, F. L. Social Maladjustment. In: *Handbook of Social Psychology* (ed. C. Murchison), Worcester, Clark University Press, 1935.

93. Werner, H. *Comparative Development*. Chicago, Follett, 1948.

94. Wootton, B. *Social Science and Social Pathology*. London, G. Allen & Unwin, 1959.

Index